W9-AAZ-932

116
Ways to
Spoil Your Dog

116
Ways to
Spoil Your Dog

Margaret Svete

HYPERION

New York

Copyright © 2001 Margaret Svete

All rights reserved. No part of this book may be used or reproduced in any
manner whatsoever without the written permission of the Publisher.
Printed in the United States of America. For information address:
Hyperion, 77 W. 66th Street, New York, New York 10023-6298.

Book design by Lynne Amft

Library of Congress Cataloging-in-Publication Data

Svete, Margaret.
    116 ways to spoil your dog / by Margaret Svete.—1st ed.
       p. cm.
    ISBN 0-7868-8642-0
    1. Dogs. I. Title: One hundred sixteen ways to spoil your dog. II. Title.

SF426 .S88 2001
636.7'0887—dc21

                                                          00-054164

FIRST EDITION

10 9 8 7 6 5 4 3 2 1

This book is dedicated

to all of the homeless and abused dogs

in the world longing for

their opportunity to be loved

and spoiled.

Acknowledgments

My heartfelt thanks to all of the individuals, small businesses, and dog lovers who helped make this book possible. Their enthusiasm and support for the project truly made the preparation of this book a great experience. Many of them went out of their way to send information, samples, photographs, or information about other companies that they felt would be great additions to the book.

I want to thank my assistant and mother, Sharon Schurman, for all of her long hours of research and help in conducting interviews for the book; my editor, Alison Lowenstein, whose suggestions truly made this a better book; and my agent, Amye Dyer, who helped make this project a reality.

I couldn't have done it without my husband, David, with all of his support and understanding during this project. I know that he is happy to have his wife back.

And, of course, I can not forget my three dogs, Berry, Wanda, and Robin—not that they would let me. Their unconditional love and loyalty served as the inspiration for this book.

Table of Contents

Introduction 1

1. It's a Dog-Eat-Treat World 7

2. Table Settings: Dishware Is the Ultimate
    Accessory 29

3. Playtime for Fido 41

4. Doggie Style 58

5. Nouveau Leash 80

6. Looking Good—Feeling Grrreat! 94

7. Creature Comforts .119

8. Dog Care 140

9. Have Dog, Will Travel 166

10. The Grrreat Outdoors 191

11. A Picture's Worth a Thousand Words 210

12. Pawty Hounds 221

13. Happy Howlidays 236

14. Miracles of Modern Medicine 251

15. Leaving a Legacy .268

16. The Best Things in Life Are Free 274

17. Miscellaneous 280

18. Lend a Paw 295

19. Where the Goodies Are 299

116
Ways to
Spoil Your Dog

Introduction

*If you pick up a starving dog and make him
prosperous, he will not bite you. It is the principal
difference between a dog and a man.*

—MARK TWAIN

No matter what the situation—your boss yelled at you in
front of a room full of people, your significant other left
you for someone younger or richer, all of those bad things go
away when you finally get home, and your best friend greets
you at the door with a smiling face and his tail wagging. He is
so excited to see you; he doesn't care what anyone else thinks
about you. You are his hero. He loves you unconditionally.
What wouldn't you do for a friend like that?

The answer is that we are doing nearly everything for our
dogs. Our dogs have been promoted from "the family dog" to
a full family member. With their rise in social status our
dogs are enjoying a multitude of perks. We cook for them;
we buy them designer collars and outfits; we travel with them;
we put them into doggie daycare so they don't get lonely; and we
do whatever it takes to keep our dogs healthy.

*According to the American Animal Hospital
Association 84 percent of pet owners feel that their*

*dogs are a part of the family. (American Animal
Hospital Association's Ninth Annual Survey of pet
owners in the United States and Canada.)*

Let's face it. We have a certain need to make our dogs feel
special. With longer hours and more hectic schedules, we are
looking for ways to make up for time missed with our dogs. As
a result, many of us are putting our dogs' needs before our
own. Our dogs have standing appointments at the doggie
salon. They get regular checkups at the veterinarian. Some
dogs even get regular massages, while their owners only get
them as an occasional treat.

One city even changed their law books to reflect the rising
social status of canines. The Boulder, Colorado, city council
voted to change all references to "pet owners" in the city law
books to "pet guardians." Although the changes do not affect
any of the penalties for animal abuse, proponents of the
changes feel that the change in terminology evokes more compassion and responsibility for pets.

I am lucky to have three best friends—Berry, Wanda, and
Robin. Berry and Wanda are a beautifully matched set of
solid black German shepherds, and Robin is my beautiful
golden retriever. Like many people, I would do just about anything for my three angels. I have canceled holiday trips to stay
home when a member of the trio was sick. I have a "dog
nanny" that comes and stays with my dogs when I travel, so
they don't have to go to a kennel. And let's not forget to mention the small fortune in veterinary bills that I have each
month. (Mom is overprotective, so we go to the veterinarian
for any little problem.)

People ask why I wrote this book. That's easy: I love dogs.
I was lucky to grow up with one of the best dogs in the world,

my beloved cockapoo, Bingo. I remember when he died, my entire family grieved for him as they would for any person. It was then that I realized dogs are much more than pets—they are family.

Throughout college and graduate school my schedule did not permit me to have a dog. But soon after I got married, I talked my husband into getting a dog. I must have really done an excellent sales job, because David suggested that we get two dogs, so they could keep each other company. So Berry and Wanda entered our lives. They lived with us six months in Ohio before we all relocated to Florida. Several months later, Robin joined the family.

Self/Alan Wilco

Berry and Wanda served as inspiration for me when we relocated to Florida (this was before Robin's time). We lived in a community where there were very few young people, so it was difficult to make friends. David was traveling all of the time, our house was like the house from the movie *The Money Pit*, and I was lonely and depressed. I wondered if we had made a mistake moving to Florida. If it hadn't been for the fact that my dogs needed to be fed and walked, I probably wouldn't have gotten up in the morning. But I remembered that my great-grandmother always said, "When one door closes another one opens." Well, lots of doors had closed. One was bound to open.

One rainy morning I was lying in bed, and suddenly it hit me. I jumped up, startling the dogs, but they beat me downstairs as usual. I went to the yellow pages, looked up animal shelters, and gave one a call. The next day was my first as a volunteer. Eventually things rolled into place, and my life turned around. It was also through my volunteer work that I found Robin.

After all my dogs had done for me I wanted to find a way to repay them. I wanted more for my best friends than just their boring old nylon collars and stainless-steel bowls. I wanted them to have really cool collars, pretty bowls, and comfortable beds. So I started searching for unique items for my dogs. I was totally surprised to learn that other dog owners felt the same way I did. I discovered an entire world of upscale collars, custom-made dog beds, and hand-painted bowls. Intrigued, I started searching to see just what else was out there. I soon found a whole new world of products and services for dogs. I also realized that there were hundreds of things not easily found. I spent hours, even days tracking down items that I read or heard about. I thought to myself, *What a great idea for a book—helping people find unique ways to spoil their dogs.*

So here we are. This book rounds up some of the most innovative, unique, upscale, and fun ways to spoil your dog—from the simple to the outrageous. In this book you will find information about everything from giving your dog a really great name to locating someone to custom build a doghouse that looks just like your house (on a smaller scale, of course).

But it doesn't end there. In addition to this book, I have a Web site, SpoilYourDog.com, where you can find even more new and exciting suggestions for spoiling your dog, as well as service providers. You will even find more real-life stories about spoiled dogs.

1.

It's a Dog-Eat-Treat World

If a dog's prayers were answered, bones would rain from the sky.

—PROVERB

You pass by a bakery. You see biscotti, peanut-topped ice cream treats, and truffles. Getting hungry? Keep your paws off. These treats are for the dogs. That's right, the gourmet dog-treat business is booming. Dog bakeries are sniffing their way into major cities and even small towns. People are not only cooking dinner for their dogs, they are also throwing catered parties for their dogs. The days of feeding your doggie table scraps are over. Today's dog owners care as much about their dogs' nutrition as their own.

Our house is no different. We have a freezer stocked with dog bakery treats, home-baked biscuits, and doggie ice cream. In addition, we have several dog biscuit mixes sitting in the pantry. And Berry, Wanda, and Robin each have their very own personalized cookie jars full of, what else, canine cookies. My three dogs have learned to surround anyone that ventures near the cookie jars and have mastered the art of looking like they haven't been fed for days. The tactic usually works, however, and each dog gleefully trots off with a treat in mouth.

Today with the bone-anza of fun snacks for Fido flooding

the market, you no longer have to fear your dog will get bored of the same old treats. As I have discovered, dogs have nearly as many treats to choose from as we do.

Berry, Wanda, and Robin have the dream job of being gourmet treat testers. As part of their job they have sampled over a hundred treats. While many of the treats have been devoured immediately, those that didn't make the cut were left uneaten on the floor for Mom to clean up. The gang helped me pick out some of their favorites, guaranteed to have your dog drooling for more.

According to the American Pet Association, more than half of American dog owners are more attached to their dogs than to another person. (Statistics released by American Pet Association, March 1998.)

1. Recipes, Cookbooks, and Homemade Desserts

Look out Betty Crocker. Canine cookbooks are finding a home in a lot of dog lovers' kitchens. People who would never think of cooking for themselves or a spouse are getting out the pots and pans for their dogs. Even busy professionals who spend long hours at work have the attitude of "what's a few more minutes" to make sure that their dogs are eating well. Among the favorite menu items with dining doggies are liver, chicken, and hamburger.

With the cooking for canines trend growing by leaps and bounds, it is not surprising that there are recipes galore for Fido. In fact, a TV show devoted to cooking for dogs ran on the Food Network from 1998–1999. If you didn't happen to tune in, following are some cookbooks and recipes that your dog will be drooling over.

Dozens of canine cookbooks on the market make cooking for your doggie a treat. Here are two of our favorites. Three Dog Bakery offers the *Three Dog Bakery Cookbook* (Andrews McMeel Publishing). The book contains recipes for everything from Yappetizers to Sweets for the Sweet. Another great canine cookbook is *Bone Appetit!* (New Chapter Press) by Susan Anson. The book contains more than a hundred recipes including recipes for special stews.

Like surfing the Web? You will find that there are plenty of free Web sites with recipes for dog treats. Three of the Web sites, www.simplypets.com, www.dailydrool.com, and www.two dogpress.com, have enough canine recipes to keep your dogs drooling for a long time.

Even though I am not one to spend hours baking, on occasion I do venture into the kitchen to bake some homemade dog biscuits. My dogs can pick up the scent of baking biscuits from anywhere in the house. One whiff and they're stuck to me like glue, making sure that they do not miss out on any treats.

If you're looking to bake something absolutely "doggie-licious," these recipes received two paws up from my gang. Berry's personal favorite is the breath-freshening biscuit. He loves it for the taste; I love it because it really makes his breath smell good.

Recipes for Dogs

Berry's Favorite Breath-Mint Biscuits

2 cups whole wheat flour
1 tablespoon charcoal (available at your local
    health-food store)

2 egg whites, lightly beaten
3 tablespoons vegetable oil
½ cup chopped parsley
⅓ tablespoon chopped fresh mint
⅔ cup skim milk

Preheat oven to 400°F.

Combine flour and charcoal. In a medium bowl, combine egg whites, oil, parsley, and mint; mix well. Slowly stir in the flour mixture; then add enough milk to make a cookie-dough consistency. Drop heaping tablespoons of dough about one inch apart onto greased baking sheets. Bake fifteen minutes, or until firm and lightly browned.

Store cooled biscuits in a tightly covered container in the refrigerator.

Makes about twenty-four biscuits.

Carob Squares

4½ cups whole wheat flour
1 egg
¼ cup carob powder (available at health food stores)
1¼ cup water

FROSTING

1 package (8 oz.) low-fat cream cheese, softened
1 tablespoon real vanilla extract
2 tablespoons real honey

Preheat oven to 350°F.

In a large bowl mix ingredients. Knead dough on a lightly floured surface. Roll dough to quarter-inch thickness. Cut into four-inch by four-inch squares. Place on a cooking sheet. Bake for forty-five minutes or until a toothpick inserted and then removed from the center of a square comes out clean.

Frosting: Mix all ingredients. Apply to cooled bars.

In the Mix

If you are like me, your favorite words to see when cooking are "just add water." Then a premade mix is your best friend (after your dog, of course). Woofers and Melia Luxury Pet offer gourmet dog biscuit mixes complete with dog-bone shaped cookie cutters. Woofers also produces a Happy Birthday Cake mix made with real cheese. (Make sure you keep dog biscuit mixes out of the reach of your capable canine. While I was out one afternoon Wanda decided she did not want to wait for me to bake the biscuit mix I had left on the kitchen table. I returned home to find my once-black shepherd covered in white flour. She was quite a sight! Unfortunately so was the kitchen.)

To make your dog biscuits look just like those from the bakery, invest a couple of bucks in some dog-theme cookie cutters. The Two Dog Store at www.twodogpress.com sells cookie cutters shaped like dog bones, dogs, cats, cows, and even roosters.

Like to cook for your dog? You're not alone. The American Animal Hospital Association reports that 52 percent of pet owners have cooked at least one meal or treat for their pets. (American Animal Hospital Association's Ninth Annual Survey of pet owners in the United States and Canada.)

2. Low-fat Treats for Dieting Pooches

Pig ears are a hit with Berry, Wanda, and Robin. Each day at lunchtime Wanda comes to find and remind me that it is pig ear time. Unfortunately pig ears are high in fat. After several weeks of daily pig ears, I noticed my pooches were packing on the pounds. I was faced with telling the gang that they were doomed not only to a diet but to a life without their favorite treats.

Yip! Yip! Hooray! I am happy to report to pig ear lovers everywhere that low-fat pig ears are now available. My dogs love them just as much as regular pig ears.

Dogs getting sick of pig ears? Another popular and healthful alternative to pig ears is a low-fat, smoked trachea. Yummy.

 ## 3. High-end Biscuits

If your dog has gourmet tastes, and you have a few bucks to spend, this section is for you. Let's face it, giving treats is perhaps the most fun and simple way to spoil your dog. And even if you invest in gourmet treats, treats are still the one of the least expensive ways to show your dog you love him.

To dog owners like me, ordinary store-bought pet treats are simply not good enough for our "babies." So it should come as no surprise that the selection of gourmet dog treats has increased dramatically in the past few years. Five years ago if you and your dog asked for directions to the neighborhood dog bakery, people would have looked at you as though you were from another planet. Today you need not look very far for one. Dog bakeries are multiplying faster than rabbits. That's good news for our canine friends.

Make no bones about it: even to dogs with gourmet tastes, biscuits are best. Today a dog can choose just about any flavor he wants. In fact the dog bakery concept was born out of our dogs' love for biscuits. But dog bakeries serve up more than biscuits. They are like Starbucks for dogs. Scones, muffins, cookies, doggie doughnuts, and cakes are all on the menu for our hungry canines. Some bakeries have even reported that a number of passersby, enticed inside by the delectable treats in the window, are surprised to find out that the treats are for the dogs.

Wags to Riches: The World's Most Famous Dog Bakery

The Three Dog Bakery is the bakery that started the fresh-baked biscuit craze. It all began with a dog biscuit recipe and a dog-bone cookie cutter in a Christmas stocking. While exploring the dog treat sections in the local pet stores and supermarkets, Three Dog founders Dan Dye and Mark Beckloff realized that the treats were not only boring, they were also filled with ugly sounding chemical additives and preservatives. So the guys started baking using three dogs, Sarah, Dottie, and Gracie, as official tasters.

The beginning was rough. According to Dye, they literally had to scrape together the money to buy the ingredients. They also endured a lot of funny looks and wisecracks. In a bit of irony, Beckloff was bit by a dog on their first sale. But the pair never gave up, driven as they are by the desire to make *"high quality, all-natural biscuits that dogs would love."*

Dogs loved their biscuits. And once the bark got out, the guys never looked back. In fact the bakery literally grew 15,000 percent during its first five years. And the growth continues.

In mid-2000, Three Dog Bakery had grown to more than thirty-two stores across the U.S. and Canada. Their fresh baked products are also carried in major chains like PETsMART, Target, Neiman Marcus, and Hallmark.

One of the interesting things about the bakery is that their customers come from all walks of life. Their customers range from billionaires to those who save all week to purchase special treats for their dogs. It is truly amazing for one product to have such widespread appeal.

The immense popularity of the Three Dog Bakery has unleashed a whole new industry: gourmet pet treats. Now pet bakeries are located in every major city and in many small towns. In addition there are dozens of online pet bakeries that will send treats right to your door.

Dogs and their owners can still visit the original Three Dog Bakery in Kansas City, Missouri, or phone them at (800) 4TREATS, or visit them online at www.threedog.com.

Three Dog Bakery

The bakery that started it all, Three Dog Bakery (see above), carries a full line of bone-a-fide delicious dog treats that includes biscuits, bits, and cakes. All of their treats are

100 percent natural with no artificial flavors or colors. Biscuits and bits come in a wide number of flavors including peanut butter, carob chip, apple-oatmeal, and vegetable-chicken.

But biscuits and bits aren't all. Three Dog Bakery has tons of other treats with fun names such as Pup Cakes, Beagle Bagels, Scottie Biscotti and Snickerpoodles. Berry's favorites are the Itty Bitty Scary Kitties complete with spooky carob eyes.

But what's a bakery without cake? Three Dog's cakes are made from all-natural ingredients, with a touch of honey, and are topped with their famous creamy-dreamy frosting. The bakery has a cake for nearly every special (or not so special) occasion, including birthday, graduation, and wedding cakes. But I think their most creative cake is the annual "Yappy Mardi Paws" celebration cake for the Creole canine who loves to party.

Biscuits & Bones

The gang and I are lucky enough to live only five minutes away from a *grrreat* dog bakery. Biscuits & Bones in Aventura, Florida, is both a dog bakery and a pet boutique. Owners Diane Klotz and Jodi Greene opened the bakery in early 2000. Greene explains that while visiting her family her dog discovered that he loved fresh-baked biscuits from the local dog bakery. Unable to find a dog bakery nearby to where they live, Greene and Klotz decided to open their own bakery. It didn't take long for them to become the bark of the town.

Needless to say, Berry, Wanda, and Robin are thrilled with the opening of the bakery. Every week Mom makes her usual trip to the bakery to get the gang a new supply of treats. Among the gang's favorite treats are the Big Dippers, which are biscuits shaped like stars and fire hydrants dipped in carob on one side and yogurt on the other. They also love the bakery's Peanut Mutter Cups, which look like little peanut butter cups. Biscuits & Bones has also become locally famous

Biscuits & Bones Dog Bakery & Boutique/Alan Wilco

for their bone-shape special occasion cakes. I've even heard some women from my gym raving about the cakes in a spinning class. Greene and Klotz both attended cake-decorating classes so that they could give their cakes that true bakery cake look.

Howlin' Times at the Dog Bakery

Did you know that many dog bakeries offer more than just treats? Many bakeries have fun-filled activities for you and your dog. Most bakeries love to host canine birthday parties, weddings, and other celebrations.

Many bakeries arrange for visits from Santa Paws and the Easter Bunny. I even encountered a bakery that hosts a Yappy Hour complete with biscuits and water for the dogs and wine and cheese for the dog owners. Some even host singles' nights for dogs and owners looking for "puppy love."

Sweets for Your Sweetie

Mr. Biscuit in Blue Springs, Missouri, bakes some of the most unique and human-looking treats that I have found. Mr. Biscuit has been dishing out doggie delicacies since 1995. Their specialties include packages of Paw Dipped Truffles that come in gold foil or multicolor foil wrappers, "Bark"-lava, Pet E-4s, and boxes of Yippy Chippy Cookies. For breakfast, dogs can enjoy Mr. Biscuits Doggie Doughnuts, Doggie Madisons, and Beggin' Breakfast Buns along with their bowl of morning water. No word as to whether any K-9 cops visit for their daily fix of doughnuts.

For special occasions Mr. Biscuit has boxes of canine confections that look just like boxes of fine chocolates for humans. In fact, they look so much like the real thing that David mistakenly took a big bite out of one. Expecting the only surprise to be the type of filling in the candy, he was unpleasantly surprised to get a mouthful of carob. To this day he still thinks that I left the candy out for him to try on purpose. The canine "chocolates" are available in standard or assorted and are made with dog-friendly carob.

The Treat That Keeps on Giving

If you want to make sure that your dog receives a fresh supply of treats each month, enroll him in a dog-treat-of-the-month club. Most doggie bakeries offer treat-of-the-month clubs.

Doggie de Lites

Marie Marcoux started baking biscuits for her own and her friends' dogs as a hobby. Realizing there was a market for her biscuits, she rented bakery space in the country, and put her biscuits on the market under the name Doggie de Lites. When Marcoux and her staff started baking, it did not take long for the neighboring dogs to sniff them out. Often she and her staff would look out the window to find dogs sitting in the backyard of the bakery looking for some "freebies." As time went on, more and more dogs made the bakery backyard their second home. In fact, neighbors looking for their missing dogs learned to make Marcoux's bakery their first stop.

Doggie de Lites uses only all-natural ingredients in their biscuits. All of the flavors include skim products (except for the peanut butter since the flavor is lost in low-fat peanut butter) to provide nutritious treats that dogs dig. Doggie de Lites flavors include carob, peanut butter and wheat germ, parmesan cheese, and honey and oats, and come in resealable and bow-decorated bags. They are also available in holiday and dog-bone theme gift baskets.

In addition to providing nutritious treats for dogs, Marcoux believes that it is very important to provide employment opportunities for the handicapped. All of their baskets are handcrafted by the handicapped in the United States of America. They even use packaging materials that are easy for their employees to assemble.

> *Wondering if you should buy that box of biscuits? Here is a good rule of paw: If you can't pronounce all of the ingredients, you should probably put the treats back on the shelf.*

Treats to Help Dogs

Dixie Sisco was enjoying retirement from the corporate life at home with her three dogs. However, in 1999 Sisco thought of an idea that would allow her to help those she was passionate about—animals. Sisco was already cooking for her own dogs and realized that baking treats for other dogs would allow her to raise money for animal charities. As a result Dixie Pet Treats was born.

Sisco developed recipes that were tested by her expert taste testers, Ginger, Bandit, and Bear. All of Dixie Pet Treats's recipes are veterinarian approved. What sets Dixie Pet Treats apart from others on the market is that they have removed common allergens such as soy, wheat, corn, and yeast from the recipes, and all but the Cheesy Chips flavor are dairy free. In addition, they only use fruits and juices to sweeten their products, since fructose has a slower metabolization rate. Sisco also offers high-protein recipes for dogs battling cancer and makes softer treats for older dogs.

In addition to serving truly dog-friendly treats, Dixie Pet Treats also makes some of the most interesting flavors on the market. Their flavors include Banana-Apple Bites, Cheesy Chips, Luscious Liver, Peanut Butter–Carob Cookies, Salmon Surprises, and Sweet Tater–Punkin Pies. Berry, Wanda, and Robin have tried all the flavors and love them. I tried all the flavors, too. Although I didn't share the dogs' enthusiasm for the liver and salmon treats, the other flavors were actually quite good, particularly the pumpkin-flavored treats.

One of the things I found most appealing about Dixie Pet Treats is that a portion of all proceeds goes to animal charities. In fact when customers sign up for The Yummy Tummy Club, a portion of all the proceeds are donated to the Cherokee County Humane Society. Sisco also donates all leftovers to the same shelter.

Sisco not only donates her money, but she also donates her time. She is an active member of the Cherokee County Humane Society. She is also very active in animal rescue and has helped place countless dogs in good homes. *Pawsome!*

Best Kept Secret

Most of you probably aren't familiar with Honey Hound Gourmet Dog Biscuits. Let me tell you, dogs flip over them! They have fast become a favorite of Berry, Wanda, and Robin. The usually well-behaved trio has been known to jump up on Mom and run each other over to get their paws on these biscuits. Colleen Rumjue, owner of Honey Hound, started by baking biscuits for her own four dogs. What started as a hobby soon became a business. Rumjue notes that she experimented with the recipe for about a year before coming up with the perfect recipe. She proudly adds that she has never had a dog turn down one of her biscuits. She also cautions dog owners to take precautions while getting out the Honey Hound treat package to ensure that they are not injured by their excited dogs.

4. International Flavor for Pups

OK. So maybe a trip around the world with your dog is not in the biscuits. At least you can eat your way around the world. Just as we humans are able to sample flavors from places all over the world, so, too, can our dogs. Who needs to visit Rome when Rover can quench his taste for Italian with Pupperoni Pizza from Mr. Biscuit that is delivered in a real pizza delivery box. Or how about some biscotti for dessert? Barkers' Bakery carries several flavors of canine biscotti including Chicago Deep Dish Pizza and Honey Peanut Butter.

Is your pooch craving Chinese? Then he must try the Chow Mein Doggie Noodles To Go, which are packaged in a Chinese food takeout carton. And what Chinese meal is complete without a fortune cookie? Forechewin' Cookies are gourmet pasta cookies with real doggie fortunes on the inside. The cookies look authentic and also come in a Chinese food takeout carton. "Dog who chew shoe sleep in doghouse for sure" or "A treat in the paw is worth two in the jar," are some examples of some of the fortunes your dog may receive.

Forechewin' Cookies, CIGRRR's, Poochi Sushi/Alan Wilco

If your dog prefers the tastes of Japan, why not treat him to some hand-rolled Poochi Sushi from Creature Comforts? The Canine California Roll looks just like the human version. But don't expect the fish taste. The canine version's ingredients include peanut butter, rolled oats, and molasses.

5. Doggie Takeout

Wouldn't it be great if getting dog food and treats were as simple as picking up the phone and ordering? Now, in the time that it takes to phone in a pizza order, you can order a feast for Fido (of course, the delivery time may be a little longer than the thirty-minute pizza guarantee). The Pet Pantry, with several locations throughout the United States, is a natural pet-food franchise that delivers dog food and treats right to your door.

Smiley Dog Services in Seattle, Washington, not only delivers dog food, but also brings toys and other supplies right to your doorstep. One of the best features of the service is that you can sign up for an auto-delivery service, meaning that they will automatically deliver your dog's food based upon his usage. No more running out of food and making last-minute dashes to the pet store. Heard about a wonderful product your dog just has to have? They will also help track down those special order items your dog desires. And if you are new to the area, Smiley Dog will also refer you to local doggie daycares, sitters, and veterinarians.

6. Thirsty Dog

Is plain old water getting boring for your four-legged friend? A flavored mineral water may be the solution. Dogs across the country are lapping up Pawier Water, a vitamin-enriched, daily pet drink that comes in liter bottles.

Sometimes water just isn't enough. If your active canine is dog tired after a day of play, he can reenergize with a sports drink. Rebound, the world's first sports drink for dogs, is modeled after human sports drinks such as Gatorade.

Rebound rehydrates, replaces electrolytes, and adds vitamins and minerals after exercise. The drink contains less salt and sugar than the human versions and uses fruit sugar rather than refined sugar to provide a boost of energy without affecting the blood sugar level. The drink comes in two doggie-licious flavors, Lemon-Lime and Cool Ice.

7. Gift Baskets for Dogs

If you are looking for a great special-occasion gift for your dog, you might want to consider a gift basket. Most dog bakeries carry a selection of gift baskets for dogs. But if you do not feel like buying a premade gift basket, you will find that it is also very easy to put together your own great gift baskets. Some of the best gift baskets that my dogs have received have been homemade. Here are some easy suggestions for assembling unique gift baskets that your dog will love. It should be noted that the term "basket" is used loosely.

Is Max truly special to you? Win his heart with a wine-and-cheese basket. The "ingredients" include a wine bottle filled with dog treats surrounded by an assortment of cheese-flavored dog treats. Line the basket with different color bandannas and attach a bow on top to complete the presentation.

One of my good friends put this basket together for Wanda when she was recovering from surgery. Wanda loves to catch Frisbees. My friend filled the inside of a Frisbee full of treats. She wrapped it with clear plastic, and put a bandanna on top. You could also put a bow on top. While she was recovering, Wanda enjoyed the treats. After recovery, she enjoyed the Frisbee.

If you are trying to win the heart of a pet lover or her pet, consider the chocolate lovers' basket for two. Fill a basket or heart-shaped box with chocolates for your human sweetie and carob-coated treats for her sweet dog. Both owner and dog will love it. This basket has received rave reviews. A friend of mine even hid an engagement ring inside the basket. After asking for her dog's approval (as he was enjoying one of his treats), his girlfriend gave an enthusiastic "Yes!" They were married last September.

8. Howlin' for Ice Cream

Who doesn't love ice cream on those warm summer days? And anyone who has ever watched his ice cream scoop fall off the cone right into the mouth of a delighted doggie knows how much dogs love ice cream. So, why should we have all the fun? Behold doggie ice cream. Frosty Paws are frozen dog treats made primarily from whey, a dairy by-product. Because dogs have a hard time holding a cone between their paws, the frozen dog treats come in ice cream cups for easy serving.

Everyone knows homemade ice cream is the best. Making homemade doggie ice cream is simple. I have tried most of the recipes found on the Internet. However, through trial and error, I have come up with my own version of this frosty treat that's guaranteed to have your dogs' tails wagging. To make the treats look even more appealing to your canine, ice trays shaped like dog bones are available from Ice Dog. (Note: Because the recipe includes yogurt, which may cause your dog digestive upset, this treat should not be used as an everyday treat.)

Homemade Doggie Ice Cream

1 large container (32 oz.) plain or vanilla yogurt (My dogs prefer vanilla.)
2 bananas, mashed

1 tablespoon honey
1 cup water

Blend all together and freeze in small paper cups or ice cube trays. Microwave just a few seconds before serving.

9. Gummy Dogs

Unfortunately we can't be with our dog twenty-four hours a day to give them treats. Happily for our dog, there is now a way for them to treat themselves. The Yuppy Puppy Treat Machines are authentic gumball machines that dispense small dog treats. These machines have long dog bone–shaped dispensing handles that your dog presses down to give himself a treat. (Caution: Be sure to keep only a few treats in the machine, as some dogs will "over treat" themselves. I learned this lesson the hard way. Once Robin learned to use the machine, she treated herself to the entire thing. I returned home to an empty machine and a full dog.)

10. The Canine Connoisseur

Just as many of us love sipping on champagne, truly pampered dogs will enjoy sipping Champ-Pagne Spring Water. Bottled with natural spring water, these champagne bottles will add sparkle to any dog's life. If champagne goes right to your dog's head, as it does for many of us, he might prefer a fine bottle of Chateau Pooché. This elegant wine bottle is filled with dog treats; just uncork and serve.

The canine that enjoys a fine cigar has to have a box of CiGRRR's from Blonde With Beagle Productions, Inc. Each cigar box contains twelve all-natural dog biscuits shaped like cigars. President and CEO Josie Bell came up with the idea for the unique dog treat while assisting in the construction of the restaurant City Wine & Cigar Co. in New York City. Noting the number of dogs in the Tribeca neighborhood, Bell thought it would be a great idea to serve canine customers cigar-shaped treats that look just like their owners' cigars. Hence the treat, Ci-GRRR's, was born. It did not take long for the bark to get around and soon the treats went from being baked in Bell's kitchen to being baked in a commercial kitchen.

Other treats from Blonde With Beagle Productions, Inc. include CiGRRR Butts, which are smaller bits of the Ci-GRRR's doggie treats, and Tubos, which are individually packaged CiGRRR's in a tube. Tubos also come in theme tubes announcing "It's a Girl" and "It's a Boy."

Think Your Dog Is Spoiled?

Check out these spoiled dogs.

Lisa Ellis has a very spoiled rottweiler named Sadie. Sadie gets two home-cooked meals a day, drinks Evian water, has her very own custom-made bed, and has over twenty collars and matching leashes. Sadie turns her nose up at commercial biscuits, so each weekend Lisa bakes several batches of treats to last Sadie through the week. But Sadie lives for summer. Every Sunday, Lisa and Sadie have a cookout where each of them eat steak and ice cream (homemade doggie ice cream for Sadie) for dessert. And if you're wondering, Sadie always gets the largest steak.

Valerie has two shih tzus, Lucy and Charlie.

Lucy and Charlie refuse to eat their dinner unless there is fresh, warm gravy poured over the top. If that's not enough, Lucy whines until Valerie spoon-feeds her her dinner.

Every night a woman from my gym orders chicken with steamed rice from a nearby restaurant for her beloved pooch, BoBo. And forget regular tap water, she had a state-of-the-art water filtration system installed so her pooches can lap up only the purest water.

The Pet-Iculars

Dog biscuit and cake mixes: Woofers, select retail locations

Dog biscuit mix: Melia Luxury Pet, various retail locations, www.petfun.com

Cookie cutters: Two Dog Store, 888-310-2DOG, www.twodogpress.com

Low-fat pig ears: Doctors Foster & Smith, 800-826-7206, www.drsfostersmith.com

Low-fat smoked trachea: Doctors Foster & Smith, 800-826-7206, www.drsfostersmith.com

Three Dog Bakery, 800-4TREATS, www.threedog.com

Biscuits & Bones, 19017 Biscayne Blvd., Adventura, FL 33180, 305-466-9944

Mr. Biscuit, 118 Main St., Blue Springs, MO 64015, 816-220-3355

Doggie de Lites, 800-988-3596, www.doggiedelites.com

Dixie Pet Treats, www.dixiepettreats.com

Honey Hound Gourmet Dog Biscuits, www.honeyhound.com

Canine Biscotti, Barker's International Gourmet Bakery, Ltd., www.dogtreat.com

Chow Mein Doggie Noodles To Go: select retail locations

Forechewin' Cookies: Just Be Paws by Laid Back, select retail locations

Poochi Sushi: Creature Comforts, select retail locations

The Pet Pantry: various U.S. locations, www.thepetpantry.com

Pawier Water: select retail locations, www.pawier.com

Rebound: PETsMART and other retail locations

Frosty Paws: frozen foods department of most major grocery stores

Ice Dog ice trays: www.sitstay.com

Yuppy Puppy Treat Machines: select retail locations, www.Dog-toys.com

Champ-Pagne Spring Water: Sabre Enterprises, Inc., select retail locations

Chateau Pooché, 777-967-8222, www.chateaupooche.com

CiGRRR's: Blonde With Beagle Productions, Inc., 888-819-2477, select retail locations, www.blondewithbeagle.com

2.

Table Settings
Dishware Is the Ultimate Accessory

To his dog, every man is Napoleon, hence the
constant popularity of dogs.

—ALDOUS HUXLEY

If your dogs are like mine, their favorite time of day is dinnertime. Like most, my dogs know very well the meaning of the words "breakfast" and "dinner." Whenever anyone happens to say either one of those words, the dogs stop whatever they are doing and make a run for the kitchen with hopeful smiles on their faces.

Experts say that dogs have no concept of time. Well, Wanda certainly has a concept of when breakfast and dinner are to be served. At exactly the same time every morning and evening, Wanda comes to announce that it is time for her meal. In the mornings, as we head downstairs to the kitchen, we make the usual pit stop outside. Every morning Robin, whose mind is only on breakfast, has to be told at least twice to go to the bathroom. When I open the front door (our front yard is gated) Robin runs out with the other two, but quickly turns around and tries to sneak back in the house. I have learned that I have to guard the front door and point her back to the yard. Sulkily she returns to the yard to do her business, but as soon as she is done she bolts directly to the kitchen. As

I dish out their food, the gang's excitement builds. Berry gets so excited that he spins in circles, while Wanda and Robin sit eagerly with drooling mouths and wagging tails.

Because my dogs live for mealtime, I am always looking for ways to make their dinnertime more special. I found out that I am not alone. I discovered a woman whose dog, Mickey, has a different dog bowl for every day of the week and a man whose dog only eats from fine china. I also encountered lots of dog owners who, like myself, make sure that their dogs are fed before anyone else in the family. And I had several people tell me that they plan their meals so that they can eat at the same time as their dogs. I even met a couple that sets a place at the dinner table for their precious pooch.

According to pet boutique owners across the country, dog owners are no longer settling for plain old plastic or stainless steel bowls anymore. People want canine dinnerware that is attractive and complements their kitchen decor. In one of the more interesting examples, the boutique Wet Noses in Sarasota, Florida, can even arrange for someone to paint your doggie's dinner bowl to match your wallpaper among other things.

Rest assured, when it comes to canine dinnerware, there are hundreds of choices. Looking through the homes of dog owners you will find hand-painted bowls, whimsical dishes, fine canine china, and even doggie dining tables. No matter what your style, you are bound to find dinnerware that will keep your dog howlin' and happy.

11. The Dish on Bowls

It Started with a Dog Named George
Started in 1991, GEORGE, also known as the "Grand-daddy of the high-end pet lines," was the brainchild of Bobby

Wise and his late partner, Lyndon Lambert. The pair named their company for their wirehaired fox terrier named George. (What else?) Like many dog parents, Wise and Lambert wanted to spoil their dog, however, they could not find any dog products that seemed to fit George's personality. Nearly everything on the market at the time was either cheap looking or too precious for their pooch. Wise and Lambert figured they were not alone in their quest for hip, quality dog products. So, the pair hired manufacturers to create pet products that would be aesthetically pleasing to dogs and dog owners alike. The result was a line of products that has dogs across the country barking with delight.

It may be debatable whether dogs can actually read. But if they can, they will be thrilled with the dog bowls from GEORGE. The bowls are made from high-quality porcelain and feature tapered sides for stability and feature canine-friendly messages such as "Give your dog a bone" and "Good Dog." The larger Crown Bowl features the GEORGE crown logo on one side with the phrase "Every dog has its day" on the other side. And while your pup may not be able to read what is on the side of the bowls, as long as you fill them with his favorite food and drink you can rest assured that he will get the message.

Hand-painted

Hand-painted dishes are the dog's woof. There are dozens of companies designing artful and colorful canine dishes. Just take a look in your local pet boutique or on the Internet, and you will find all kinds of hand-painted doggie dinnerware. Wondering what's out there? Here's a look at what's on the table.

Art Itself. Joan Bolduc's Art Itself line of pet dishes has earned her plenty of recognition. Her line known as "the Sistine Chapel of pet dishes" has been featured in such movies as *As Good As It Gets* and *Indecent Proposal*, and in the television show *Mad About You*. The bowls have also been featured in numerous magazine and newspaper articles.

The bowls from Art Itself are a great way to pamper your pooch and enhance your decor at the same time. The handmade, hand-painted, stoneware ceramic designer dog dishes come in a variety of designs, colors, and sizes for every dog's needs. The designs are also available in their complement "yang" to make a coordinated food and water set. (For example if the design is white dog bones on black the "yang" is black dog bones on white.)

For a really unique bowl, Bolduc also offers combinations, and will even customize the bowls with your doggie's name.

Melia Luxury Pet. Melia Luxury Pet was founded in 1992 by David and Rebecca Volandt and was named for the couple's black labrador mix, Melia. The Volandts' first product was their Southern Style Corn Biscuit Mix. Best known for inventing the Flavored Tennis Ball (see "Playtime for Fido," page 41), Melia Luxury Pet now specializes in high-quality, hand-painted, personalized dog bowls with complementary wrought-iron raised feeders. All of the dishes are dishwasher safe and are signed by the individual artist. Their philosophy is "simplicity is the essence of good design."

Pawcasso. Pawcasso specializes in hand-painted ceramic bowls, treat jars, and matching floorcloths. Each of their pieces is lead-free, dishwasher safe, and is signed by the artist. Pawcasso offers several unique designs for your dog to drool over. Their Zebra Print Collection, an exotic black and white zebra print, was featured in *InStyle* magazine as a "Best Bet." Other popular styles include their Paw Print Collection, avail-

Pawcasso/Kris Hundt Photography

able in purple, green, black, and white; Floral Pet Collection with rosebuds and dog bones; and the Abstract Leopard Print. In their effort to help animals, Pawcasso donates a portion of their proceeds to local animal shelters.

Do It Yourself. Who says you have to let the professionals have all the fun? If you have time and artistic talent, you might want to take a stab at painting a bowl yourself. All you need is a plain dog bowl and some nontoxic ceramic or multipurpose acrylic paint, and you're ready to design a dish that's sure to fetch your dog's attention.

Bone-shaped Bowls

If you are looking for a bowl of a different shape, you will love the bone-shaped bowls from Creature Comforts. The bowls feature two separate compartments for food and water.

The bowls come in several different designs, but my favorite is the Green Plaid Bowl, which is painted mint green on the inside of the bowl with a dark and mint green and white plaid design on the outside. The Creature Comforts collection also includes a treat jar with a bone-shaped handle on the lid.

What a Dish!

Maybe you are looking for doggie dinnerware that doesn't look so, well, doggie. Even dogs with the most discriminating tastes will be proud lapping up their Pawier Water from these dishes.

For ultra-pampered pooches, only fine china and crystal will do. Hailing from London, Sheila Parness is world renowned for her collection of exquisite, high-end pet accessories. Her line of doggie dinnerware does not disappoint. The Bone China Dog Bowl is decorated with playful pooches around the outside of the bowl. The Parness Crest, granted by the Royal College of Arms, adorns the interior of the bowl. Or, if your canine is truly spoiled, serve his nightly filet mignon or Champ-Pagne Spring Water in the Sheila Parness Crystal Bowl. The clear lead-free crystal bowl is tapered so that dogs with long ears do not have to get them wet. The crystal bowl also has the Parness Crest engraved on the base.

There are even dog bowls that are silver. The limited edition solid silver dog bowl from Sheila Parness is decorated with the Parness Crest and comes in a suede box.

Caught with a Paw in the Cookie Jar

We all know that fire hydrants are a favorite among dogs. This fire hydrant will become one of your dog's favorite things, but not for the usual reason. This one holds treats. The bright red hydrant from Paw-licious looks like the real thing, just a lot smaller (and cleaner). Beware—it will probably be just as difficult to keep your doggie away from this hydrant as it is the outdoor variety. (Hopefully for different reasons.)

Another jar of note is a hand-painted porcelain cookie jar that is decorated with an artist's rendition of different dog breeds. Most American Kennel Club recognized breeds are available by special order. But here's the most adorable feature: The lid of each jar is painted with the message "Every tail should have a happy ending."

12. A Dinner Table for Your Pooch

Maybe a place setting at your dining-room table is not in your dog's future. But there is no reason he can't have his own table. Veterinarians agree that raised feeders are great for older doggies, arthritic doggies, and also larger breed dogs who must strain to reach bowls sitting on the floor. Not only is raised feeding easier on the joints but it also aids in their proper digestion.

If you think that it is time to give your dog an uplifting dining experience, you are in luck. The selection of raised feeders has increased over the last few years. In fact catalogs like *In the Company of Dogs* usually feature a wide selection of doggie diners to choose from. In fact, a recent copy featured wrought iron stands, Classic Harvest Tables, and even a Mod Marble Diner. Rest assured, from traditional to contemporary, you will have no problem finding the perfect set for doggie dining.

Status Symbol

Does your dog aspire to be a Gucci poochie? Check out the fabulous Gucci Dog double dog diner. Always on the cutting edge, Gucci's design consists of two bowls set within a Plexiglas brick. This doggie dinnerware comes in either clear or black while the bowls are made of stainless steel. If this set has your contemporary canine begging, be prepared to open up your wallet. This set sells for a cool $750.

Elegant and Traditional

The Pettables dining tables for dogs by Millicent (see photograph) has been featured in such swank stores as Bergdorf Goodman and in *Animal Fair* magazine. Long before veterinarians caught on, Millicent thought of the idea for her line of raised dog feeders after watching dogs eating from bowls on the floors. She thought that it just didn't seem right for them to be eating that way.

Myra Millicent Bograd designed her tables to be "pretty" so that people would be proud to have them in their homes. The tables from Pettables are little pieces of furniture that feature either crackled or distressed finishes in warm wood tones or antique white. Pettables are available with or without a painting of a dog on the top. The elegant tables are available

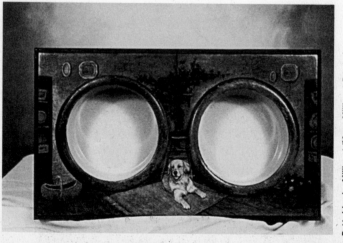

Pettables by Millicent/Myra Millicent Bograd

in four styles—Elegant Dining, Country Kitchen, On the Patio, and Checkerboard Square.

Think Your Dog Is Spoiled?

Meet Lincoln. Lincoln is a beagle that is treated like royalty at mealtimes. Each morning and evening a place is set for Lincoln at the dinner table next to his owners, Al and Donna Stewart. Just before each meal Donna lifts Lincoln into his custom-made chair, where his meal awaits him. And don't even suggest that Lincoln eat or drink from a dog bowl, this privileged pooch dines from the same fine dinnerware as his owners. Is your dog envious yet? There is more. All of Lincoln's meals are home-made (no Iams for this pampered pooch). While he usually eats chicken or hamburger and rice, on Thursdays, and special occasions, Lincoln dines on filet mignon (cooked medium rare).

Helpful Tips When Setting Your Dog's Table

Do you ever notice that your dog starts eating on one side of the room but finishes on the other? Sometimes the dog bowl even ends up under the table or cabinet with your dog trying desperately to get to his last bit of food. Then *you* end up hunting for missing dog bowls. As you may have learned dog bowls, particularly the stainless steel ones, and hard floors do not make for easy canine dining. The solution may be as simple as a place mat. Place mats are a great way to keep your dog's food in one place while he is eating. They are also a great way to keep floors dry around water bowls and to keep crumbs off the floor. (To tell you the truth, crumbs are not a problem at our house. Although Berry is quite the messy eater, Robin waits for him to finish and cleans up all the leftover crumbs. She is better than a vacuum cleaner!)

The Trixie & Peanut Catalog offers a white cotton terry-cloth feeding mat with a linen underside. The mat is embroidered with a small dog bone and the words "food" and "water" to indicate where each bowl goes. And, as it is inevitable for the mat to eventually get dirty, it is machine washable.

Melia Enterprises offers several hand-painted place mats to complement their dog bowls. The "floor cloth" mats are available oversized to catch all of your doggie's crumbs. The place mats have a white background. Styles include black paw prints and black border, red heart and black border, black bone and black border, and a funny dog face with black border.

Looking for a place mat that blends in with your home decor? Nobody said that all of your dog's accessories have to have a dog theme. I bought Berry, Wanda, and Robin place mats that match the place settings at our kitchen table. Home interior stores and even places like Wal-Mart usually have a great selection of place settings. However, when you are shopping for the perfect place mat for your dog, be sure to select one that is durable. Delicate, lacy place mats don't last very long at a canine's table.

13. Innovations in Dining

Are you one of those people always looking for products on the cutting edge? Are you always on the lookout for conversation pieces? Then you'll love the latest innovations in doggie dining.

Oh My Dog! You Won't Believe This!

Do you ever walk into the bathroom only to find your dog happily lapping up water from the toilet? You are not alone. Many dogs seem to find this bathroom fixture a more appealing water bowl than the one you have sitting in the very next room. Believe it or not, there is a safe way to let your dog enjoy his favorite pastime. How about a drinking bowl shaped just like a toilet. These fanciful drinking bowls are making a splash with dogs across the country. Like the real thing, the bowls are designed so that you can leave the seat either up or down. There is even a dog bone–shaped handle that "flushes" when pressed.

Automatic

Do you ever wonder if your dog is a camel? When Robin drinks water, she drinks water, often emptying the entire bowl. Of course, an empty bowl means having to refill it. If you ever get tired of refilling water bowls all day long, or if you are not going to be around to offer refills, you might want to consider an automatic water bowl. There are many on the market to choose from. However, many are not the most attractive things to have displayed in one's home. One of the nicest looking ones I found is Petmate's Le Bistro Waterer. Here's how it works: The automatic waterer has a clear water-cooler-style reservoir that fits into a base dish to ensure that your dog has a continuous supply of water. If you're looking for a matched set, Petmate also has Le Bistro Feeder. Similarly styled, the feeder serves your dog food on demand. It's a terrific way to make sure that your doggie is served his meal on time even when you're working late at the office.

The Pet-Iculars

WetNoses, 472 John Ringling Blvd, Sarasota, FL 34236, 941-388-3647, www.wetnoses.com

Dog bowls: GEORGE, 2411 California @ Fillmore, San Francisco, CA, or 1829 4th Street, Berkeley, CA, 877-344-5454

Art Itself, 888-600-9663, www.artitself.com

Melia Luxury Pet, select retail locations, www.petfun.com

Pawcasso, 817-277-2746, www.pawcasso.com

Bone-shaped dog bowl: Creature Comforts, select retail locations

Sheila Parness, London, UK, 011-44-207-338-4966

Fire hydrant cookie jar: Pawlicious Cookie Jars, 949-646-0445, www.paw-licious.com

Dog breed hand-painted porcelain cookie jars: select retail locations

Gucci Dog double dog diner: Gucci boutiques nationwide

Pettables: Millicent—Home and Dog, 201-444-6098, www.homendog.com

Terry-cloth feeding mat: Trixie & Peanut Catalog, 888-838-6780, trixieandpeanut.com

Toilet drinking bowl: select retail locations

Petmate's Le Bistro Waterer: select retail locations

3.

Playtime for Fido

*Money will buy you a pretty good dog, but it won't
buy the wag of his tail.*

—HENRY WHEELER SHAW

All work and no play makes Rover a dull dog. And if Rover had his way, he would play all day. For dogs, playtime ranks right up there with mealtime. Just take a look in the homes of dog lovers across the country and you are likely to see tennis balls, stuffed animals, and lots of other doggie toys scattered throughout the house. According to *The Making of a Blockbuster* by Gail Degeorge (Wiley, 1996) even billionaire Wayne Huizenga and his wife, Marti, have been known to have a stray plastic pork chop squeak toy decorating the floor of their south Florida mansion.

Between Berry, Wanda, and Robin, they probably have more than fifty toys. We have chew toys, chase toys, tug toys, and hug toys. All the things dogs love to do. Like most dog owners, I am always on the lookout for new and exciting toys and games for my canine kids. Because let's face it, just like human kids do, our canine kids can get bored with the same old toys.

The gang dug up some of their all-time favorite toys and games. Trying out all of these toys should keep your canine

41

companion happy and busy for a long time. And remember: A busy dog makes a happy dog, and a happy dog makes a happy owner.

14. King Kong

Probably most of you are familiar with Kong Toys. They are widely available at most pet boutiques and pet superstores. But I am always surprised at the number of people who aren't familiar with this great toy. Plus Wanda would never forgive me if I left the Kong Toy out of this book. I know that she will be thrilled to learn I am beginning this chapter with her favorite toy.

For those of you who don't know what all the fuss is about: The Kong Toy is a puncture-resistant, super-bouncy, conical-shaped rubber toy. The fun part about the toy is that you never know which way the toy is going to bounce once it hits the ground. But my favorite feature is that they are nearly indestructible. I have never heard of a dog destroying one. This is good news for those whose dogs feel their mission is to destroy all new dog toys.

I have never seen a dog love a toy as much as Wanda loves her Kong Toy. The toy provides her with hours of entertainment. She has a collection that she keeps stashed throughout the house. She even keeps a spare in her crate.

As soon as someone sits "in the Kong seat" on the couch, Wanda comes running over with her Kong for the person to throw for her. She will not go for a walk or a ride in the car without bringing a Kong along. She even brings it to the veterinarian's office as her "security blanket." One time Wanda dropped her Kong on one of our walks at her favorite park. A little while later she started crying, and I noticed that her toy was gone. We turned around and looked for it but could not find her beloved toy. On our walk the next day the park ranger, who knows Wanda well, sought us out to make sure Wanda got her Kong back.

The Kong toy comes in different styles and sizes. The best known Kong is the Red Kong. But the line includes so "mutts" more including the Dental Kongs and the Sport 'n Dog Training Dummies. But Wanda's all-time favorite is the Cool Kong, which is the Kong that floats in the water. Her favorite game is jumping in the pool after her Kong. In fact every time anyone goes near the pool, I think Wanda is saying to herself "Don't even think of getting in there without me or my Kong."

Did you know that dogs use body language to invite play? They bow and usually let out a "happy" bark or two. Sometimes people mistake this as an aggressive posture, but all that your dog is trying to say is "Let's play!"

15. A Bone Is Still a Bone

Anyone who says a bone is a bone is a bone has never seen Blue Ribbon Dog Company's Abstract Rubber Dog Bone. The cubist bone is made from a high-performance, injection molded, nontoxic, all-natural gum rubber that is suitable for chewing. And though my gang hasn't taken a shot at it, it's said that the bone will survive even the most persistent chewers. The brightly colored bones are available in orange, green, yellow, cobalt, red, and lilac—and in three sizes. Who said dogs don't appreciate art?

16. Tennis Anyone?

Here's a toy that's hard to go wrong with—the tennis ball. Tennis balls are not only high on the dog-appeal scale, but they are also high on the wallet appeal. And unless the game of tennis disappears off the face of the earth, these toys aren't going anywhere. That's good news in a world where dogs see their favorite toys come and go.

Dog toy makers are taking the tennis ball to new heights with some twists on the old classic. Here are some new ways to serve your dog's favorite toy.

A Ball That's Sweet

Play ball. Eliminate bad breath. What could be better than that? Mint-flavored tennis balls are a win-win gift. They give your dog long-lasting enjoyment, and they keep you from running every time your dog opens his mouth.

David and Rebecca Volandt, owners of Melia Luxury Pet, were the inventors of the Flavored Tennis Balls. The Volandts began by filling handheld pump spray bottles with spearmint extract and spraying tennis balls they had placed in a garbage bag. The concept of freshening dog breath with the flavored balls really worked. The extract was absorbed into the felt of the ball and the dogs' saliva would rinse the extract into their mouths.

Over seven years and many improvements later Melia still makes the Flavored Tennis Balls. In addition to the original Spearmint flavor, they now offer Vanilla, Orange, Brown Cow, Peanut Butter, and Black Jelly Bean. And to scent your own tennis balls or any other absorbent toys they now offer the Flavor Atomizer Bottle. Now your dog no longer has any excuse for bad breath.

Super Size It

Got a big dog? He'll roll over for the Jumball. The heavier construction of this oversized green-and-orange tennis ball makes it nearly impossible to pop, and it's large enough not to be a choking hazard. That's good news for owners of determined chewers. And although the ball is heavier than traditional tennis balls, it still floats. That's good news for swimmers.

TennisBone

The TennisBone is a dumbbell-shaped tennis ball toy that helps your dog have fun while learning to retrieve. Its shape makes it easy to throw and produces an unpredictable bounce. I tried it out on my gang and was pleasantly surprised with the toy's durability. Robin, in particular, loved the toy. As for safety, the toy is made from special nontoxic materials and contains no adhesives. And Wanda's favorite feature of the toy—it floats.

Balls of a Different Shape

Three Dogs & a Cat, Inc., has unleashed a new line of dog toys called Air Dog. The Air Dog Hybrid Tennis Toys combine all of the best attributes of plush, tennis, and rubber toys to make a super hybrid toy. The toys are the same color and style as traditional tennis balls. But these are not your average tennis balls. These toys have a Bone Ball–shape, a Square Ball–shape, and a Cigar shape. The "balls" are covered in plush felt to absorb impact, and because of their shapes they offer a fun, erratic bounce.

17. A New Wave of Fetch

If we could take a doggie opinion poll, we would probably find that nine out of ten dogs love to play fetch. Fetch is probably the all time favorite game between dogs and people. It certainly is a favorite at my house. There are not too many days that we don't get in a good game of fetch. And on those days we do not play, I am faced with a pouting Wanda.

Fetch never gets old for dogs. But just in case you and Rover are getting tired of the same old tennis ball, here are some new twists to America's favorite pastime.

Just Chuckit!

You throw a nice, new tennis ball. By the time it gets back to you it is covered in mud, drool, and things you probably don't want to know about. Your dog happily drops it at your feet, and you look at it thinking, "I really do not want to touch that thing?" Yet how can you let down your faithful friend?

Now there is a way for you to have your ball and throw it too, all without laying a finger on it. The Chuckit! dog toy not only allows you to not touch the slimy ball, but it throws the ball farther and faster than you can with just your throwing arm. The Chuckit! is kind of like a golf club with a scoop. You scoop up the ball and, for lack of a better description, "chuck it."

Wanda and I decided to take the Chuckit! out for a spin. It took a few tries to learn how to use the device properly. After a while we finally got it. It really worked. Much to Wanda's delight I was able to throw the ball fast and far. It really wore her out, and it's no small feat to wear out my energetic dog. But the part that I loved most was that I didn't get my hands slimy or sandy. *Yeah!*

A Handle on It

The Fling Thing toy is another great way to keep those hands slobber-free, while enjoying a game of fetch. The Fling Thing consists of a nylon rope handle attached to a tennis ball. The nylon handle not only keeps your hands clean, but also makes it easy to throw longer distances ensuring lots of exercise for your dog. Water-loving dogs will be particularly happy to hear that the Fling Thing floats.

How About a Game of Fetch?

You've seen the toys, now it's time to play the game. Fetch is a favorite at our house. The nice part about the game is that you can lie back in a lawn chair and relax while your dog does all the work. Provided that your dog is game.

Originally playing a game of fetch with Berry consisted of me throwing the ball and him catching it and running off with it. Not a very exciting game, huh? It also defeated the purpose of exercising him. I tried the advice of dog trainers, which called for 1) rewarding him for every step he took toward me with the ball; 2) showing no interest when he tried to play keep away; and 3) rewarding him when he would bring it back. However, this approach just did not work for Berry.

Frustrated, I finally devised a trick to help keep the game going beyond our usual one throw. I used two balls. I would keep one in my hand and throw the other one. Once Berry retrieved the first ball I would show him the second one. Of course, the second ball was the one he now wanted. He soon learned that in order to get the second ball he would have to return with the first one. Then, I would throw the second ball and so forth. Soon we finally got to play a real game of fetch. Now Berry loves the game as much as Wanda and Robin.

18. Things That Go Squeak

Berry is a ninety-pound German shepherd. He is a real alpha male—macho and on guard twenty-four hours a day. He has scared away more than a few people from our home. You would think that a dog like that would turn his nose up at a soft, plush squeak toy. Not my Berry. To the contrary, his favorite toy is a soft mallard duck toy with a squeaker on the inside. He carries that toy throughout the house and even sleeps with it.

Berry's love of that duck just goes to show you that dogs of all shapes, sizes, and temperaments love stuffed animals, particularly those with squeakers inside. Lucky for them there are hundreds of different stuffed toys to choose from. Berry helped me sniff out some of the most interesting stuffed dog toys on the market. Here's a look at what we found.

Doggie Revenge

We have voodoo dolls. Dogs have the Doggy Activation Toys. Let's face it. Even dogs would love the opportunity to get even with their archenemies. And since biting the real thing is frowned upon, these toys give dogs their opportunity. The toys are screen printed, firmly stuffed with a squeaker inside, and are fifteen inches tall. The toys come in several styles including a Doctor Doris the veterinarian, Big Mean Kitty, Postal Plaything, and Cat Burglar. A great way for your dog to vent his frustration.

Getting Squirrelly

Robin loves to chase squirrels. In fact if we let her, she would do it all day long. She loves chasing them up the tree and then barking at them as they jump from branch to branch. Since most of us prefer that our dogs not bring the real thing home as a present, there is the squirrel squeaky toy. The lifelike squeaky squirrel is covered in faux fur and is ruggedly constructed to withstand games of tug-of-war.

Plush Puppies

Plush Puppies offers some of the cutest and largest selections of soft plush toys for dogs. What sets Plush Puppies apart from traditional squeak toys is that they make lots of noise not only with squeakers but also with rattles. Custom-made for dogs, the toys are made with super-strong sewn seams, safe noisemakers, and no plastic eyes or noses for your dog to swallow. And the toys are parent friendly because they are machine washable. (We know that dogs love to get their toys dirty.)

And if you are looking for variety, Plush Puppies has it. You can choose from over one hundred different items in fourteen different categories with sizes ranging from junior, large, and jumbo toys. For added fun, all of the Plush Puppies characters are given names such as Oakley the Octopus (one of Berry's favorites), Wilbur the Weiner Dog, and Homer the Hedgehog. Additionally each toy tag includes fun facts and educational information about the real-life animal.

Plush Puppies also has some toys that are good for interactive play. For an indoor game of fetch, the Jingle Balls have a cute smiley face and have a tennis ball and a rattle inside. Dogs who love a good game of tug-of-war will love the Plush Puppies Bungees. Each Bungee comes with a squeaker, a rattle, and bungee cord stretch material.

A Toy That Laughs with Your Dog

Looking for a toy that does something more than squeak? The Wiggly Giggly Ball was introduced in June of 1999 and was selected as the Best New Dog Toy of 1999 by the American Pet Products Manufacturers Association. All your dog has to do is to nudge the Wiggly Giggly with his nose and it makes a hilarious noise. The toy is brightly colored and is suitable for both indoor and outdoor use. But the best part of the toy is that unlike many other talking toys, this toy does not require batteries.

19. All Day Fun

Trying to find a toy that will last for more than a couple of minutes in my home can be quite the challenge. It's nearly mission impossible finding a toy the dogs will like and that they won't be able to destroy in five minutes. Yappy news! These toys are meant to not only be long lasting, they are also meant to keep your dogs occupied for hours with little effort on your part.

Biscuit Ball

Looking for a way to keep your dog busy while you're away? Biscuit Ball to the rescue. The Biscuit Ball is a "stuff-able" dog toy designed to keep your dog busy and out of trouble. The Biscuit Ball is made from the same durable rubber as Wanda's beloved Kong Toy, so you can count on the toy being around for a while. Here's the scoop on the toy: The ball has biscuit-shaped holes that you can fill with biscuits or other treats. To keep your doggie occupied for hours, stuff the holes with pieces of biscuit or kibble mixed with peanut butter. Your dog will roll over for it.

The Unstuffed "Stuffed" Toys

Stuffed toys around our house do not remain intact for long. It usually takes Wanda less than five minutes to tear a hole in the toy. Within about thirty minutes, most of the stuffing is scattered around the house. While Berry is gentler with stuffed toys, he still has put holes in his share.

Enter Material Dog Toys. These toys are some of the most unique and highest quality soft squeak toys that I have come across. To the joy of dog owners across the country—myself included—toy designer Sharon Ritchey developed the "unstuffed" stuffed dog toy. It is the first stuffed toy designed with real-life dogs in mind. Ritchey designed the first Material Dog toy to help out a friend. Ritchey's friend has a black lab, BJ, who loves stuffed toys. However, when given a new toy, BJ feels it is his mission to tear the toy apart as fast as he can, leaving stuffing everywhere. Unfortunately for BJ, his play-time with his new toys never lasted long.

Hearing of BJ's dilemma, Ritchey set out to design a soft toy that would have the look and feel of a stuffed toy, but without the stuffing. Rather than being filled with stuffing Ritchey's toys have double fur layers giving the toys the same feel and fullness of a regular stuffed toy. And to make the toys more versatile, Ritchey designed the toy with a removable squeaker. Each toy has a velcro pouch that the squeaker fits into. The squeaker itself is sewn into a fur pouch so that dog-gie parents don't have to worry about their dog accidentally swallowing a squeaker.

I decided to put some of the Material Dog Toys through the Berry-Wanda-Robin test. If it could withstand the chew-ing and tearing from my gang, it could survive any dog. I started the guys with the Mallard Duck. Berry immediately ran off with it and started chewing and tearing. As soon as he turned his back, Wanda grabbed the toy and gave it her best shot. Even Robin, who usually does not like soft toys, took it for a chew. I was pleasantly surprised to see the toy hold up so well. It even survived a game of tug-of-war between Berry and

Wanda. We have since added the Rooster and Pheasant to the collection. As for the status of the original duck: six months and holding.

The Dog with All the Toys

Alex is a one-year-old, high energy Siberian husky. And Alex has more toys than any dog I have ever seen. Alex's human companions, Jim and Molly, spend more than fifty dollars a month just for dog toys for Alex. Alex accompanies the couple every time they go to PETsMART and is allowed to pick out two new toys each visit. In addition, Molly is always on the lookout for unique toys on the Internet. Molly laughs, "I think I single-handedly keep dogtoys.com in business." Jim adds, "Alex may have over five hundred toys. We lost count a while back."

20. Fly by Night

Do you hate the look your dog gives you when he happily brings his toy over to you at night and you tell him that it is too dark to play outside? Now you and your dog no longer have to call it quits when the sun goes down. In fact, you and your dog may find that with these toys the fun begins when the lights go on.

Light up your dog's life with a flashing dog toy. The Zap Ball lights up on impact and makes eight "wacky" sounds while its flashing. As your dog chases the ball some of the sound effects he'll hear include a ringing telephone, falling bombs, and chirping. The toy is made of a durable rubber for long lasting fun all day, all night.

You also might want to wow your dog with the Glo-Fetch ball. The ball is the "original" glow-in-the-dark ball for dogs. All you have to do is hold the ball close to a light source for a couple of seconds, and the ball glows. It really works. Its unique design allows for easier gripping and breathing while in your dog's mouth.

Buyer beware: With toys like these your dog will no longer allow you to be a nighttime couch potato.

21. A Not-so-bored Game

Move over Monopoly. There is a new board game in town. Believe it or not it is a board game that you play with your dog. No, your dog does not have to roll any dice, but he may have to roll over. My Dog Can Do That! is actually a unique training tool that helps strengthen the human-canine bond. The game uses positive-reinforcement techniques developed by dog-behavior experts. To play the game, you draw a card from the deck. Each card has a trick on it. The object of the game is to get your dog to do the trick in thirty seconds. When a trick is performed successfully, you can move your game piece around the board on your way to Hollywood. The first dog to get to Hollywood wins. The game has three categories of difficulty: beginning, intermediate, and advanced. It even comes with a training manual written by dog trainers, which teaches you how to teach your dog the tricks he may not know.

22. Better Than a Movie

You might not be able to find this video at Blockbuster, but it is sure to get two paws up from your canine companion. Doggie Adventure is the first video movie made just for dogs. The twenty-five-minute video is shot from a dog's-eye view—two feet above the ground.

Shot with a gyrocamera the video promises to mesmerize your dog as the camera races around the house, through a romp at the farm, and during a trip to the pet store—and the veterinary clinic. The video even offers a love interest. (It's OK. The video is rated G.) The film will leave Rover howling in his chair. It is a great way to keep your dog occupied on a rainy day or when you are out and about.

23. Treasure Chest

As do most dogs, Berry, Wanda, and Robin have a huge collection of toys. It is not uncommon to find Kong Toys hidden throughout the house or squeak toys on the stairs. With three dogs' collections of toys, our house sometimes looks like someone knocked over the toy shelf in the pet store. Luckily we can maintain some sense of order most of the time by storing unused and disliked toys in a toy box. I have to admit that I had never heard of a toy box for dogs until I came across one on the Internet, but it is a very practical idea.

Each day we pick up all the toys around the house and put them back in the toy box. Thirty seconds later, Wanda and then Berry and Robin rummage through the box to pull their favorite toys back out. But at least most of the toys remain in the box until Wanda decides to go back for more.

While you can really store your dog's toys in any kind of box or container, I came across some great dog toy boxes. They are kind of like the doggie version of a buffet—when your dog wants more, he can return for more goodies.

Here's a toy box that's not only fun for the dogs but is also a decorative item for the home. The honey pine toy box from

A Leg Up features a bone cutout on the front and the lid. The nice thing about the box is that the lid lifts off so there are no hinges or chains that can cause the lid to fall on a snooping dog.

Another unique toy box that I found is a bone-shaped toy box. As with the box above the lid lifts off with a bone-shaped handle for safety. The box comes in different sizes and colors. I also found that the box makes a good storage container for dry dog food.

There's no rule that says that you have to buy a *dog* toy box for your canine child. Children's toy boxes work just as well. My friend Janet Sanders bought a regular children's toy box for her beagle, Monique. But to make the toy box special, she hired two local women to hand paint the toy box for Monique. One of the most adorable I have ever seen, the toy box features a pair of puppies playing tug-of-war and is personalized with Monique's name.

What good is a toy box without toys in it? I am quite sure that most dogs prefer the full variety. Presenting your dog or a friend's dog with a box full of toys is like giving the dog his very own treasure chest. Fill it full of tennis balls, a stuffed toy or two, a Kong Toy, and even some treats. Your dog will be your best friend for life.

24. Games Dogs Play

Hide and Seek

When you were growing up, you probably loved playing hide and seek. The best part about playing the game with your dog is that he is always "it." If you have not played this game with your pet, it's definitely worth giving a try. The game is a favorite with Berry and Wanda (Robin cheats!). It is a great game to practice the "stay" command with your dog. It is also a great game to use if you are trying to teach your dog to perform a search of the house.

Here's how you play: Put your dog in the "stay" command. Then go hide somewhere in the house. Since your dog can not count to twenty and bark "Ready or not, here I come," you will have to call him when you are ready. If he seems to be having difficulty finding you, call to him again. When he finally finds you, he will be thrilled. Be sure to reward him with lots of praise and maybe even a treat.

Find the . . .

Find the treat is a game many dogs love. It's best to start off easy. Tell your dog to "stay" and then let him watch you hide the treat. Then come back to your dog and tell him to "find the treat." Each time make the treat a little more difficult to find until he can find the treat in even the most obscure places like the kitchen sink or your bedroom closet. Remember to give your dog lots of praise when he finds it. Eventually you can teach your dog to find other things like his toys or even your house keys. This is particularly helpful if you are one of those people who is always misplacing the house keys.

The Pet-Iculars

Kong Toys: most major pet stores, www.kongcompany.com

Abstract Rubber Dog Bone: Blue Ribbon Dog Company, select retail locations

Flavored tennis balls: Melia Luxury Pet, select retail locations, www.petfun.com

Happy Dog Toys, select retail locations, www.dogtoys.com

Jumball, TennisBone: Happy Dog Toys, select retail locations, www.dogtoys.com

Air Dog Hybrid Tennis Toys: Three Dogs & a Cat, Inc., select retail locations, www.dogtoys.com

Chuckit!: dog toy: select retail locations, www.petsmart.com

Fling Thing: PetsMart

Doggy Activation Toys: select retail locations, PetsMart

Squirrel squeak toy: select retail locations, www.dogtoys.com

Plush Puppies: The Kyjen Company, www.kyjen.com

Biscuit Ball, Kong/Milk-Bone: select retail locations

Wiggly Giggly: Multipet International, select retail locations

Material Dog Toys: select retail locations

Zap Ball: Ethical Products, select retail locations

Glo-Fetch ball: Rockywoods Inc., www.glo-fetch.com

My Dog Can Do That: select retail locations

Doggie Adventure video: Made-For-Dog Videos, Inc., select retail
    locations, www.dogvideo.com

Honey pine toy box: A Leg Up, select retail locations, www.tailsby
    thebay.com

Bone-shaped toy box: select retail locations, www.petsmart.com

4.

Doggie Style

The average dog is nicer than the average person.

—ANDREW ROONEY

Look out Cindy, Claudia, and Kate. Fashion has gone to the dogs—literally. For years it has been said that clothes make the man. Now it can be said that clothes make the dog. Canine couture is all the rage. Once limited to bandannas and polyester sweaters, canine clothing is now full of chic apparel including offerings from status-symbol designers such as Gucci, Burberry, and Donna Karan. In fact, a number of designers now offer dog-sized versions of the latest runway fashions. This new trend is seeing upscale pet boutiques popping up all over the country.

It is not uncommon for pets today to own several outfits. Teddy, my friend's Akita, owns designer collars and leashes, several sweaters and coats, two raincoats, a jogging suit, a custom-made bathrobe, doggie booties, and even a tuxedo for special occasions. Sally says that her Teddy is well worth it. He loves being dressed up and enjoys the attention he gets on the street, especially from the ladies.

The doggie-style phenomenon is not likely to go away soon. In fact, Fifi & Romeo partnered with a couple of well-known designers to show F&R designs on the fall 2000 run-way. Also "diffusion" lines (a fashion term for collections priced below top designer level) are just now coming out, guaranteeing a long life for canine couture.

This chapter features unique canine fashions that you are not likely to find in pet superstores. If you were to think of these fashions in terms of human stores, think of fashions ranging from Gap to Chanel. All of the apparel mentioned below is of high quality so that you will not have to worry about a piece falling apart as soon as you put it on your dog. After checking out all the fashions mentioned in this chapter, you might be left asking, "Who is better dressed? Me or my dog?"

25. Pet Styles of the Rich and Famous

Nearly everyone likes to know what the rich and famous are up to, and what they are spending their money on. The woof on the street is that they're spending it on their precious pooches. From ready to wear to couture, the sky is the limit when it comes to dressing dogs. In fact, designs by sought-after designers like Hugo Uys are reportedly fetching prices as high as four-thousand dollars.

Here is a look at some canine clothing lines that have caught the attention of celebrities and socialites. The secret's out. Now your canine can dress as fashionably as the Holly-wood and New York elite.

The Canine Couture collection from Fifi & Romeo has become a must-have for Hollywood stars. The collection was developed in the fall of 1998 by Hollywood costume designers Penelope Francis and Yana Syrkin. The inspiration for the collection came from their desire to keep their Chihuahuas warm. Francis was already making wool coats with faux fur trim for her Chihuahua, Claire, while Syrkin was making cashmere sweaters for her Chihuahua, Yoda.

The two women decided to combine their talents and form Fifi & Romeo to fill a niche in the doggie clothing market. Barney's New York was one of the first stores in the country to carry their line. Their canine clothing and accessories have since been found in the Neiman Marcus Catalog, Browns in London, Fred Segal, and numerous others.

Fifi & Romeo really took off when Oprah Winfrey proclaimed their pet fashions to be "the perfect present for the dog in your life" on her 1999 "Oprah's Favorite Things" episode. Since then, Fifi & Romeo has expanded its line to include luxury apparel and accessories for women, infants, and even home. Francis and Syrkin opened their first flagship store in West Hollywood late in the summer of 2000. In the chic boutique, Fifi & Romeo's canine cashmere sweaters hang on clothing racks next to those for the canine's human companions. In addition to the clothing line, the store carries dog-theme jewelry for people, pet carriers, and stuffed animals (dogs, of course).

The Fifi & Romeo line includes dozens of different styles of vintage cashmere sweaters, but their bestselling sweater is their signature beaded cash-mere sweater. The sweater is hand dyed and has hand-beaded trim at the neck and sequined flowers on the back for a unique, nostalgic look. Also popular is their bone-print sweater with a dog bone on the back and trim on the collar and sleeve. If your dog is whining to dress like Oprah's

Fifi & Romeo/©Trixie
& Peanut/Louis Irizarry

Solomon and Sophie, get ready to open up your wallet. The line starts at $150.

Paws for Style

To launch the new magazine Animal Fair, *a pet fashion show, "Paws for Fashion," was held in New York. The show featured one-of-a-kind creations from designers such as Tommy Hilfiger, Betsy Johnson, and Donna Karan. As Veronica Webb walked down the runway with her dachshund, Hercules, the crowd, including Gabriel Byrne and Hilary Swank, was howling for more. Featured outfits fetched $1,500 and up during the auction. Some of the models included a golden retriever in a leopard print outfit, a Maltese in a blue tutu, and a rottweiler in a Donna Karan sweater. Proceeds from the benefit went to local pet charities.*

Chic Dogs

What do you do when your dog's fur doesn't cut it? Get your pooch a fur coat, of course. Chic Doggie by Corey offers a line of leather and fur coats that is "to bark for." Former New York City investment banker Corey Gelman founded Chic Doggie in the fall of 1999. While shopping one day with her Chihuahua, Bear, who was wearing a leather and fur coat that Corey designed, the pair was approached by a fashion editor from *InStyle* magazine. The editor loved the coat so much that she asked if she could photograph the coat for the magazine. She subsequently encouraged Gelman to start a line of

Chic Doggie by Corey

coats for dogs. Hence to the delight of posh dogs everywhere, Chic Doggie by Corey was born.

The line became an instant hit among well-heeled dog owners in New York, Beverly Hills, Aspen, and Palm Beach. Corey's canine couture has been featured in *InStyle* magazine, *Vogue, BusinessWeek, Palm Beach Illustrated,* and numerous other major magazines, newspapers, and television shows.

The fur coats that started it all are handmade from soft leather and are trimmed with real Canadian beaver fur. The fur coat comes in several styles. Colors include black, chocolate brown, and red. The coats come in sizes tiny, six inches to extra large, fourteen inches. However, if those sizes do not suit your doggie, you can custom order additional sizes. If your princess wants a fur coat, she had better start saving her biscuits. The fur coat will set her back $450.

Since the original fur coat line was unleashed, Chic Doggie has added several canine clothing collections including python print coats, 100 percent cashmere coats with leather applique bones and hearts, and the Palm Beach Collection of reversible terry cloth and brightly printed scarves, coats, and blankets. The Palm Beach Collection is great for warm weather doggies that love to go to the beach or to be seen in hot beach fashions. In fact, the collection was so pupular that it sold out its first run even before it appeared in the Chic Doggie catalog.

26. Keep Warm—Look Grrreat!

A canine coat is a must-have for the fashionable cold weather canine. Seeing their doggies shiver during winter walks inspired several dog owners to design lines of canine over-coats to keep their furry friends warm. Canines now have a selection of coats as large as ours. In fact, many of the designs available for dogs are more appealing than some of the coats in our closets.

All Weather Leather

Leather and suede jackets are ever popular. In fact, I have several leather and suede jackets hanging in my closet. Now these popular jackets have gone canine. Wagwear's innovative line of canine outerwear includes a hooded leather jacket with a satin-quilted, reversible lining and a suede and shearling-lined jacket. Amy Kizer, founder of Wagwear, says of her line, "It's what I would wear if I were a dog." Kizer, who is a vet-eran of the fashion industry, studied at Parsons School of Design and modeled for more than ten years. Her two Shiba Inus, Lucy and Tonto, were the inspiration for the line. She launched Wagwear in 1998.

Corporate Canines

Everyone knows that the corporate world is "dog eat dog." Consequently the corporate canine needs to dress for success. For the dog on the fast track, Burberry offers a canine version of its signature trench coat. The coat is made from the same quality material as its human counterpart and is guaranteed to keep your dog looking like the top dog that he is.

Wild Things

To bring out your canine's wild side, try dressing her in a leopard fur coat from Maxx's Closet. The hooded leopard faux fur coat is lined in a black chenille that will have your dog sitting in the lap of leopard luxury. If your dog is ready for adventure, he'll want to dress the part in the Safari Jacket. For the full look of the jungle, the coat is lined in leopard print and includes a matching headband.

Social Dogs

Like many of us, some dogs like to have different coats for different occasions. Lucky Dog Co. carries a unique line of canine coats "For the dog with impeccable taste and busy social calendar." Designer Sandy Yu and husband/partner, Stephen Tong, (they were engaged at the time) started the Lucky Dog Co. when they bought a Yorkshire terrier puppy named Max. Yu couldn't find any clothes that she liked for Max, so she started hand knitting sweaters for him. The sweaters led to jackets and coats and eventually a full line of clothing for canines. Yu hails from the fashion industry and previously worked in product development for Donna Karan, Emanuel Ungaro, and Tong found that designing the canine lines were second nature. Yu explained Lucky Dog's philosophy: "It is everything you would want for yourself only translated into a dog."

The line includes luxurious Emperor and Opera Coats, Brunch Coats, Dress Coats, and Casual Coats. Coats of note include the Garnet Red Opera Coat, which is a shawl collar coat with a bow on the back and the Firehouse Coat with fire engine–red wool on one side and faux dalmatian fur on the other side. For those who are suckers for a dog in uniform there is the Army Coat, which is made with a denim-fatigue print, and the water-repellent Fireman Coat with black coated nylon and classic fireman clasps and reflective tape for safe night walking.

27. Rainy Day Dogs

Rain. Rain. Go away. You do not have to wait for a dry day to walk your dog. Canine raincoats keep your four-legged friend dry during those rainy days and help keep away that unappealing "wet dog" smell. For those pooches who love long walks in the rain or enjoy traipsing through puddles, a raincoat might be a good investment.

Waggin' Wear/Susan Fitzgerald

Waggin' Wear makes one of the bestselling doggie raincoats in the country. Susan Shaw started Waggin' Wear in early 1998. Shaw had previously designed hats for people. An avid dog lover, Shaw was encouraged by fellow dog lovers who asked, "Why don't you make a hat for dogs?" One night she dream up the name "Waggin' Wear," and a company was born. Her

Wagwear ® Trixie & Peanut Inc./Louis Irizarry

goal was to become the J. Crew or Eddie Bauer of the doggie fashion industry. She wanted to design clothes that were both "tasteful and affordable."

Her best-known design, and Robin's favorite, is the yellow raincoat with matching hat. The collar and outer shell are made from Waxwear, which is a water-resistant, wax-coated, cotton-based fabric. Since the coat has Velcro closures, the coat is reversible, and on sunny days the 100 percent cotton plaid lining can be the outside. The coat also features a treat pocket to carry treats for good dogs or house keys for doggie parents.

Though the coat also comes in red, brown, and black, the yellow raincoat is by far the most popular. Says Shaw: "Everyone wants the little yellow raincoat."

Wanda's favorite raincoat is Wagwear's hooded raincoat with removable quilted duck lining. The coat has a rubberized nylon shell and reflective trim. The coat also has a hood, although Wanda usually shakes it off so she doesn't miss out on any action on our walks. The coat comes in a selection of colors including black with silver stripe and in sizes up to twenty-eight inches.

28. No Sweat

No bones about it, sweaters have come a long way from the old one-look-fits-all days. Today's fashion-conscience canine can choose from casual to elegant, from classic to trendy. No matter what your canine's style, she is bound to find something to bark about.

I recently discovered just how practical a doggie sweater can be. My husband and I brought Berry, Wanda, and Robin on a ski trip. Berry and Wanda with their long, thick fur adapted quickly. Robin, however, took one step outside the lodge and ran right back inside. Even after lots of coaxing, she refused to go outside in the cold. Luckily we found a nearby pet boutique. Luckier yet I was able to find a couple of sweaters that fit Robin. She was very cooperative as I put her first sweater on her. I will have to say that she looked pretty cute in her new sweaters. But the most important part was that we could finally coax her outside so she could do her business.

Hand-Knit

What could be better to keep your dog out of the cold than his very own hand-knit sweater? Amy Goldman started making hand-knit sweaters for dogs several years ago quite unintentionally. Goldman had put up a sign in her building offering to teach people to knit. In response to the sign a woman called Goldman and asked if she could knit a sweater for a dog. Although Goldman had never made a dog sweater before, she gave it a whirl. The woman loved the sweater. After some prodding from her boyfriend, Goldman finally made another dog sweater and brought it to one of the New York boutiques for the owner's opinion. After several samples,

Goldman finally came up with just the right design, and the boutique ordered a dozen sweaters on the spot.

Eventually Goldman started CoverKnits. All of Cover-Knits's sweaters are hand knit from the finest 100 percent wool by skilled "old-world" craftspeople who work exclusively for CoverKnits. The fashionable turtleneck has plenty of give so that it goes over your dog's head easily and is comfortable for your dog. The sweater also features generous leg openings for comfort and mobility. The shape of the sweater provides maximum coverage for your dog's stomach while leaving plenty of clearance so that the sweater remains clean and unsoiled.

CoverKnits currently offers four styles of sweaters—single cable, double cable, broken rib, and two-tone. Their most popular colors are red, black, camel, medium gray, and snow, but they are happy to custom color a sweater for you. The sweaters are priced by size and Goldman adds that they will custom fit any size dog.

Hip to Be a Dog

GEORGE offers a line of wool sweaters that any dog would be proud to wear. Their line's sweaters are attractive but are not "frilly" or feminine. The line is popular with both the males and the females. Their Pink Wool Turtleneck Sweater is made of soft pink worsted wool, as is the Olive Ribbon Turtleneck Sweater that is accented with a brilliant orange stripe around the neck. Both styles are hand loomed in the United States. The Hand-Knit Alpaca Sweater with a traditional Peruvian design is hand loomed in Peru and is a smoother alternative to sheep's wool.

Move Over Chanel

Maxx's Closet by designer Barbara Hoch has a line of French designer-inspired canine sweaters, coats, and match-

ing bags that will have your dog looking like she just arriv
from a Paris shopping trip. The canine fashions have becon
the "must-have" apparel for fashion-forward canines. I
bones about it, the sweaters from the Paris Chic line are de
nitely *tres chic*. A favorite with the doggies is the Pink Pa
Chic sweater. The sweater has real pockets and is trimm
with black chenille and gold buttons. As the French say, *"O
la la!"*

Calling Martha Stewart

If you are an aspiring Martha Stewart, you might want
consider making a sweater for your dog. Several Web sit
offer instructions for knitting canine sweaters, includi
www.knitting.about.com, which lists a number of sites th
offer free patterns for doggie fashions.

29. Adventure Dogs

For the dogs that cringe at the thought of putting on a sweat
it's Wagwear to the rescue. The Prada-esque line caters to t
sporty dog. Founder, Amy Kizer, designed the line for acti
dogs who need something that is practical yet attractive. A
good news for the big guys: Unlike many of the canine fas
ions on the market this line caters to larger dogs.

Wagwear's most unique design is their canine scuba su
When asked how the scuba suit came to be, Kizer explain
that she is always trying to find unique materials for her fas
ions. She originally thought that neoprene would make a go
material for a doggie sweater since it was such a great mater
to keep dogs warm. The sweater eventually evolved into
scuba suit. The neoprene scuba suit is a pullover with silv
reflector trim. The suit is great for dogs that love to swim
the cold water.

Wagwear/Kevin Sweeney

Floating Down the River

More and more people are bringing their dogs along on water adventures such as yachting, fishing, and white-water rafting. In fact, last year my adventurous dog Wanda joined us on a rafting trip on the Youghiogheny River in Pennsylvania. But before Wanda could get in the raft, we had to put on her life jacket. Even if your dog is an avid swimmer like my Wanda, a life jacket is a very important necessity. Like people, dogs can panic if they fall overboard. Sometimes this can result in a tragic accident.

A good life jacket will fasten at multiple points and will have a grab handle to allow owners to lift dogs out of the water. You should also make sure that the jackets are reflective so that you can spot your doggie in all weather conditions. My dogs all own a Fido Float, which is bright orange and features a grab handle. The float is fitted with a special collar that keeps doggie heads and tails above the water. The float also features nylon mesh at the chest to keep your doggie cool while he is out of the water.

Fritzi the Marathon Swimmer

According to the Sarasota Herald-Tribune, *Fritzi, a fourteen-year-old dachshund, was aboard a yacht anchored at the Marker 4 Restaurant in Venice, Florida. While her owners were dining, she some-how let herself out of their room and must have fallen in the water while looking for her owners. When her owners came back, Fritzi was nowhere to be found. Many people joined in the search for poor Fritzi with no success. The next morning the search resumed. The search party looked all day, but could not find her. Fritzi was only a foot tall. Finally at 6:00 P.M., the search was called off, and her devas-tated owners went home thinking she was dead.*

Two hours later, Fritzi paddled over to a boat where the owner of the VIP Boat Club was working. He grabbed the dog, wrapped her in towels, and rushed to notify the owners. She had been in the water nearly twenty-four hours. It was speculated that Fritzi had somehow managed to rest in the water by leaning against pilings or climbing on clumped mangrove trees.

Fritzi and her owners were very lucky. Now Fritzi is the proud owner of a new doggie life jacket. Her

*owners say that they will never take her out in their
yacht again without it.*

30. These Boots Are Made for Walking

You are probably thinking, "Yeah right, my dog would not be
caught dead in booties." But booties are an important and
practical piece of clothing for dogs in extreme climates. In the
hot summer months blacktop can burn while in the winter
ice, snow, and snow-melting chemicals can irritate your
pooch's paws. Just think. Would you want to walk barefoot in
these conditions? Probably not. Yappily, there are many
styles of booties to keep your dog's paws in paw-sitively great
shape.

All Weather

Muttluks Booties come in two styles. The Yukon-fleece
booties keep your dog's feet toasty during cold winter walks
while the all-weather booties are breathable and waterproof.
Both booties feature leather toe protection and treated leather
bottoms to resist water and salt. The booties also have rib-knit
cuffs, Velcro fastening, and 3M reflective straps for night walking. Both styles are machine washable.

Seasonal

Cool Paws Production offers a complete line of booties to
protect your canine's paws in any condition. For the winter
months there are Polar Paws, which are made of Cordura
Nylon and thick fleece. For the hot summer there are Cool
Paws, which when soaked in cool water for forty minutes will
keep your pet cool all day. Finally the adventurous dog is not
left out. Tuff Paws, made from Ballistic Nylon and leather,

are designed to make those hikes over rugged terrain much more enjoyable for your canine hiking companion.

31. Sweet Dreams

Does your canine suffer from insomnia? Maybe he just needs some comfortable pajamas. Je T'aime Originals has been keeping doggies cozy at night for more than seven years. Owner Judith Buldoc was inspired to make the pajamas for her hairless dog. Today she offers more than twenty styles of doggie pajamas guaranteed to give your doggie sweet dreams. The fleece pajamas come in several sizes. They also carry velour pajamas for special occasions. And you will love this feature: The pajamas are fitted so that it is easy for your dog to make a midnight run to the bathroom when necessary.

32. Decking Out the Dogs

The dog that is always dressed to the K-nines surely needs a tuxedo. No gentledog's wardrobe is complete without one. Canine tuxedos are available from most of the major pet stores and pet boutiques. Many of these tuxedos even come with a top hat to complete the effect.

For the dog that prefers something a little more upscale, pet boutiques such as Zitomer Z Spot either carry or will order a tuxedo for that special occasion. At one boutique I even found a tuxedo complete with white French cuffs and gold cuff links.

The canine tuxedo by Lucky Dog Co. takes elegance a step farther with their Classic Black Tuxedo with tails. The tuxedo is made of 100 percent wool with satin lapels and matching cummerbund and sports a white tuxedo shirt with mini pleats. A black silk bow tie and either white bone or Scottish terrier–shape studs complete the look.

In tuxes like these, your canine will look as dashing as James Bond.

Tie One On

If your dog is like my Berry, he is not the tuxedo type. In fact, I think Berry holds the record for the fastest destruction of a piece of canine clothing. But I've discovered that he will wear a tie or bow tie. Ties and bow ties still provide that look of elegance and class but are less restrictive to a romping Rover than a full tuxedo. If your canine's a Casanova, he will want to check out the line of ties and bow ties from Dog's Day Out. The ties, guaranteed to make any dog the hit of the party, were made for dogs just like my Berry.

Denyse Binschus came up with the idea when she was looking for a way to dress up her dogs for Thanksgiving dinner at Grandma and Grandpa's house. Her dogs were not the hat and coat types. So she made ties and bow ties to dress them up.

The ties and bow ties from Dog's Day Out have safe and secure adjustable Velcro collars with full collar points. They are made from a cotton/polyester blend fabric. The collars are people friendly because they are machine washable, and they are very dog friendly because they are comfortable and light.

The ties and bows come in a large variety of fabric styles such as black satin, leopard, palm tree, and paw print. There is also a wide variety of seasonal fabrics including red satin, Christmas plaid, shamrocks, hearts, turkeys, and pumpkins. The ties come in sizes extra small to extra large and will fit neck sizes six inches to twenty-seven inches.

Party Girls

No, we haven't
forgotten the girls.
For the girl who
loves to party Chic
Doggie has
designed the
first-ever party
skirt for dogs.
The chiffon skirts
have three chiffon lay-
ers with a silk bellyband and
rhinestone beading on the belly. Pair the skirt with a strand
of pearls and Lady will certainly be the belle of the ball.

Chic Doggie by Corey © Trixie and Peanut/
Louis Irizarry

33. Bandannas & Scarves

If a closet full of canine clothing is not in your dog's future,
you might consider the ever-classic bandanna. A paws-down
favorite, even the toughest dog loves wearing a bandanna.
Even my Berry loves wearing bandannas, provided that they
are of a masculine print. When I put a bandanna on him, he
carries himself like a king.

Bandannas can be found in nearly every pet boutique.
Also many dog salons send groomed doggies home with a new
bandanna. Some places even offer personalized bandannas, so
that everyone can call your friendly canine by name. If you
are looking to start a bandanna collection, here are some good
places to start.

More unique than the typical bandanna, Pawkerchiefs by
Grande Paws are reversible with two distinctly different sides.
Lynda Harris started Pawkerchiefs in 1992 after Cayenne, a

shepherd–yellow lab puppy, came into her life. Because Cayenne was too small for regular bandannas, Harris began making her tiny scarves to wear. The "woof" about the scarves got around quickly and soon other dogs were begging for the scarves. And so Pawkerchiefs was born.

The unique scarves and bandannas are cut and sewn by hand and are available in nearly one hundred different prints—with new prints added every month. Among the prints are whimsical, bright primary-colored animal motifs, gentle floras, and holiday themes. What once began as a one-sided bandanna eventually evolved into Pawkerchief's reversible, double-sided style. It's great! You get two for the price of one.

How to Wear a Bandanna

Do you know how your dog should wear a bandanna? Most people make the mistake of tying them too tight. This can irritate your dog's neck. Erica Richter, owner of Salon Pooch-ini, offers these tips to ensure the perfect fit for your canine.

1. Hold bandanna on top of pet's back to determine the right length.

2. Fold the neck side (top) of the bandanna underneath until you achieve the correct length. The tip of the bandanna should fall one to two inches past your dog's shoulder blades.

3. Tie bandanna loose enough around the neck so that you can pull the bandanna over your pet's head without untying it. Make sure that it is not so loose that it can fall off all by itself.

4. Grab each side of the bandanna above the knot and pull away from knot. This tightens the knot and creates more slack around the neck.

Cashmere Scarves

For ultra pampered pooches only cashmere will do. Chic Doggie's hand-stitched 100 percent cashmere scarf should fit the bill. The Doggie Scarf fastens at the neck with a dog charm clasp and drapes over the back. The scarves also feature soft-leather bone or heart appliques. They can be custom monogrammed for an additional fee. The scarf is less restrictive than a coat but will still take the edge off chilly days. Sized just like a dog collar, the scarves come in sizes up to fourteen inches, but larger sizes can be custom ordered.

34. Spotlight on Dogs

Is your dog begging to be in the spotlight? GlowDog's reflective products will make sure that no one misses him. One night as GlowDog founder, Beth Marcus, was walking with Luke, the pair was almost hit by a car that did not see them. At the time, she was advising Reflective Technologies, Inc., who had just developed a reflective fabric called illumiNITE. A lightbulb came on in Marcus's head, and she and a friend designed prototype dog jackets with the material.

Marcus's surveys showed that dog owners were very enthusiastic about the product, so she bought the exclusive rights to use illumiNITE for pet products. She then formed GlowDog Inc. in 1997.

The GlowDog line has grown to include reflective jackets, bandanas, and collars. They have even added clothes and accessories for dog owners including coats, umbrellas, and totes.

Here is how GlowDog's products work. During the day, the products look bright and colorful. At night when an oncoming car headlight shines on the product, the driver sees bright white. I had the opportunity to try out GlowDog's bandana on my Wanda. I am happy to report that it worked great.

Lighten Up

Another way to make late night walks safer for your canine companion is by suiting him up with Protect-A-Pet's Flashing Collar. The collar was designed by Barbara Heyman to protect her cat that had a habit of bolting out the door every time someone opened it. Heyman worried that one day her precious pet would be hit by a car unable to see him. Unlike reflector collars that only light up once a car's headlights hit the collar, the flashing collar allows drivers to see your dog long before he is in front of the car—allowing more time to avoid an accident. All you have to do is press a button and the Flashing Collar emits a bright pattern of flashing lights, giving your dog maximum visibility in the dark. The collar operates on four button cell batteries, which are included, believe it or not. The collar will operate for up to one hundred hours of continuous operation and is water-resistant.

The Pet-Iculars

Fifi & Romeo, 7282 Beverly Blvd., Los Angeles, CA 90036, 323-857-7215, Trixie & Peanut Catalog, 888-838-6780

Lucky Dog Co. Coat Collection: select retail locations, www.luckyco.com

Chic Doggie by Corey, New York City, 212-752-WOOF, www.chicdog.com

Trench coat: select Burberry's and select pet boutiques

Hooded leather jacket: Wagwear, 888-924-9327, www.wagwear.com

Maxx's Closet: select retail locations, www.maxxscloset.com

Waggin' Wear raincoat: select retail locations, www.wagginwear.com

Reflector raincoat: Wagwear, 888-924-9327, www.wagwear.com

CoverKnits, 212-777-2401, www.coverknits.com

GEORGE, 2411 California @ Fillmore, San Francisco, CA, or 1829
    4th Street, Berkeley, CA, 877-344-5454

Neoprene scuba suit: Wagwear, 888-924-9327, www.wagwear.com

Fido Float: select retail locations

Muttluks Booties: Neopaws International, 800-DOGSHOE,
    www.dogshoes.com

Booties: Cool Paws Productions, select retail locations

Pajamas: Je T'aime Originals, www.pageweb.com/jetaime7/

Dog's Day Out, select retail locations, www.dogsdayout.com

Pawkerchiefs: Grande Paws, www.pawkerchiefs.com

Cashmere scarf: Chic Doggie by Corey, New York City 212-752-
    WOOF, www.chicdog.com

GlowDog Inc., 888-GLOWDOG, www.glowdog.com

Flashing Collar, Protect-A-Pet: select retail locations

5.

Nouveau Leash

*A dog is one of the remaining reasons why some
people can be persuaded to go for a walk.*

—O. A. BATTISTA

t used to be that the only accessories a dog needed were a
simple nylon collar and lead. Those days are over. Today a
g's accessories might include a designer collar, a leash with
rage compartments, Tiffany dog tags, or maybe even a gold
cklace. Styles run from elegant to whimsical; there is some-
ng for everyone. And as they say, "If the style fits, wear it."

As I researched this chapter, I was happy to learn that I
s not the only dog parent who showers her dogs with col-
s, tags, and now jewelry. Because the gang isn't really into
doggie clothing scene, I started looking for great collars as
ay to dress them up. What started as a simple quest for one
e collar for each of the dogs has turned into an entire col-
tion of collars, tags, and necklaces. Yes, even macho Berry
s been seen around town in a necklace, although we call it a
in—it just sounds more masculine.

The gang and I dug up some tail-wagging trendy acces-
ies to accessorize your canine. They are guaranteed to give
ir doggie a new "leash" on life.

35. Collaring All Dogs

Collars and leashes are an easy way to dress up any dog. Even the most macho dog seems to enjoy wearing a handsome collar. Berry and Robin love wearing dressy collars because of all the extra attention they get while wearing them. Even Wanda, who really doesn't care what anybody thinks about her, seems to smile a little more when she is wearing one of her stylish, hip collars.

In the market for a new collar? Here's a look at some styles rumored to be quite pupular with the pooches.

Collars: Amberhill, Fine Arf, Fine Arf, Fox & Hounds, Waggin Wear, Necklaces: Oh My Stars/Alan Wilco

How to Measure Your Dog's Neck for Collar Size

The manufacturer collar size for buckle-type collars indicates either the placement of the longest hole or the center hole. A safe way to determine your

*dog's collar size is to measure your dog's neck with a
cloth tape measure and add two inches.*

Label Conscious

Fashion designers are bark-raving mad for dogs. Chanel,
Louis Vuitton, and Gucci are among the elite designers wanting to leash well-heeled canines. Chanel's signature quilted
lambskin dog collar and matching leash come in three colors:
black, brown, and red. Louis Vuitton's Monogram Dog Collar
and matching leash sports a canvas front with a natural
leather backing and comes in sizes up to twenty-two inches.

And let's not forget the design house that started the
whole designer doggie trend: Gucci. Among Gucci's offerings
is a sleek, black leather collar and leash set that sports nickel
squares spelling out GUCCI DOG.

A Piece of Fine Arf

Lisa Greene got the idea for her Fine Arf Collection in the
early 1990s when she could not find a collar she liked for her
dog. Frustrated with the selections, she started making her own
collars for her dog. After receiving so many compliments on
her collars Greene decided to start her own company to make
dog collars. But before she started making dog collars, Greene
developed the Arf Tag. The tag was designed for dog owners
to wear on a chain around their necks like a charm. Once the
person tired of wearing the tag she could give it to her dog to
wear on his collar. Eventually her tags caught the attention of
Neiman Marcus, and Fine Arf Collection was off and running.

Greene unleashed her collar collection in the fall of 1998.
Her first collar offering was the Paw Print Collar. The two-
toned English leather collars are decorated with gold-tone
brass paw prints. The collars also feature jewelry quality brass

buckles and rings. Color schemes include black on red, red on black, and brown on green. A matching leash and personalized paw print I.D. tag are also available to complete the look. I liked the collar so much that I bought one for Berry. I also couldn't resist getting Berry another one of Fine Arf's stylish designs: the Breed Specific Collar. The Breed Specific Collar is styled like the paw print collar and is adorned with your favorite breed and matching breed I.D. tag. The elegant, two-toned leather collar is available in most dog breeds from Airedale to Yorkie.

Foxy Hounds

Fox & Hounds Ltd. has a line of collars and leashes that is to bark for. Owner Robin Kershner started the company in 1996 because of an unfulfilled niche in the market. When trying to find unique, quality, and handsome collars for her dalmatians, Zack and Lucy, for a Christmas party, she was disappointed to find that there were no such collars. Talking with other dog owners she realized that they, too, wished that they could find nice, upscale collars for special occasions. So she put together a business plan, and Fox & Hounds was born.

Kershner started small. She still recalls going to her first trade show and sitting at her booth with just four collars. But the collars really caught on, and the company has been growing ever since. "The new trend is to have a wardrobe of collars for your dog," Kershner explains. People are including their dogs in so many more social activities, and they want their dogs to look good. Kershner, who designs all their products, refers to the Fox & Hounds line as "high-quality fashion." Dog owners seem to agree. Her collars have been spotted on the dogs of Ving Rhames and Marilyn Manson.

Fox & Hounds's bestselling collars and leashes are from the Animal Print line. In fact, all three of my dogs have been spotted around town in their leopard print collars. These collars are made from imported Italian leather with stenciled animal print hair on haircalf. Fox & Hounds has even added matching women's belts to their collection because they received so many requests from women wanting to match their dogs. If you and your dog are begging to show off your wild side you can chose from cheetah, leopard, zebra, or dalmatian prints.

In the Mood

Now your dog can have his mood and wear it! The Moody Collar is an easy way to know whether Rover wants to kiss you or bite your head off. Just like the mood rings from the 70s, this collar lets you know just how your dog is feeling. The patent-pending leather collars are studded with stones that change color with body temperature to help you interpret your dog's moods. They also come in a sleek silver tin for a cool presentation. With your dog's collar comes a "your handy mood chart." For example when the stones turn dark blue your dog is in a "fun-loving, perky, frolicsome, sassy, tickled pink, ecstatic" mood. The chart is also quick to point out that every color, except black, also means "pet me, feed me, take me for a walk." I think that about covers it.

Do they really work? Well I tried the collar on Robin. After about an hour, I checked the stones and they were a blue-green. After consulting the chart I discovered that it meant Robin was "relaxed and cool." Well, if you know Robin, she is one relaxed and cool dog. It didn't hurt that the red crocodile leather finish looked really great against her golden coat.

Pretty in Pink

My Berry and Wanda are both solid black, and visitors sometimes get them confused. Much to my husband's amusement I like to dress my matching dogs in matching collars but in different colors. I look for pink for my little girl, Wanda, and masculine shades for my big boy, Berry. Unfortunately it is not easy to find upscale pink collars for larger dogs.

As you can imagine I was thrilled when I discovered The Cotton Candy Collection from Amberhill. The collection is a nice change from the traditional black-and-tan leather collars. The collars come in pink, baby blue, butter yellow, and minty green patent leather. (Of course I bought the pink for Wanda.) The collars and matching leads are adorned with silver-tone dog bones. While the set is feminine, it is not too "frilly."

Love the dog-bone theme, but would never think of putting pink on your dog (as I would never dare put a pink collar on Berry)? Amberhill's signature collection includes 100 percent Italian calfskin leather, Italian Crocodile, and English Bridle leather collars and matching leads in colors such as black, navy, and brown. And if you are tired of dog bones, you can choose from collars studded with fire hydrants, crowns, X's, or hearts. The collars are available in sizes eight inches to twenty-four inches, and the leads are all made to a standard four-foot length.

The Amberhill Collection grew out of Kristy Amber Dukelow's equestrian line of leather belts. Dukelow had been designing a collection of collars for her pug, Bear, as well as for her family's, friends', and clients' dogs. She finally launched the Paw Prints Collection in the fall of 1998. The collection has become a favorite among pet-boutique owners whose canine clientele love to sniff out the latest offerings.

Puppy Per-suede-sion

Maybe all you need is a little per-suede-ing to get Fido that new collar he's been howling for. A twist on the leather collar— suede collars have grown in popularity. In fact, Wagwear's bestselling items are their suede shearling collars with matching leashes. The suede collars are lined with a plush, soft shearling for the dog's comfort, while the leash handles are also lined for your comfort. The collars have a brushed-nickel roller buckle and the leashes have a brushed-nickel swivel clasp. The collars come in yellow, orange, olive green, and dark blue.

All for One

All for one and one in all. Those who are always looking for innovative products will love Blue Ribbon Dog Company's Woven Wool All-In-One Collar and Leash. The All-In-One is made from reinforced woven wool webbing, which loops through an "O" ring to form the one piece collar and leash. The All-In-One's high-tension weave and weather resistance ensures long life. For your comfort, the unique leash and collar has leather tabs and leather-padded handle. The All-In-One is available in blue stripe, green stripe, and khaki stripe.

The Blue Ribbon Dog Company was founded by Matthew Morris in 1994. The product line is currently designed and manufactured by the BRDC Group Inc., which was cofounded by Michael Lowry and Jee Hyun Song. The BRDC Group designs and manufactures products for dogs under three labels: Blue Ribbon Dog Co., K-9 Sport, and Red Rover Brand. The company's products target all levels of the market and are sold at stores including DKNY, Paul Smith, The Conran Shop, Eddie Bauer, and Resoration Hardware among others.

Playful and Whimsical

Who says that Rover always has to be elegant and dressy? We don't always run around in our cocktail dresses and suits. If you are like me, you probably prefer to kick off your shoes and wear something comfortable. For weekend fun or casual get-togethers with his doggie buddies, your dog will be the top dog donning these trendy, whimsical collars.

GEORGE has several hip collars made from colorfast cotton webbing. The Good Dog, Daisy, and Stick collars feature GEORGE's trademarked designs. The Good Dog collars lets your dog know how you feel by featuring GEORGE's "Good Dog" design embroidered several times around the collar. The matching leash has "Good Dog" embroidered once on the handle. The Daisy and Stick collars are fashioned similarly.

Berry, Wanda, and Robin love to kick back in their playful collars from Waggin' Wear. Their collars and leashes are constructed from 100 percent color cotton trims that are handwoven in Guatemala. The collars are backed with durable nylon webbing so that your dog can romp at the dog park without worrying about tearing or breaking his collar. They also are made with a state-of-the-art quick release buckle with a locking feature that enhances both strength and convenience. The collars and leashes are adjustable and hand washable and come in several fun designs including the Red Dog and the Black Dog, which feature colorful doggies on parade.

Waggin' Wear's latest line of collars and leads are designed specifically to coordinate with Waggin' Rainwear and Winterwear. The collars and leads are made from plaid ribbons woven in France. As with the Guatemalan line, they are backed with rugged nylon webbing and feature only top of the line hardware. The collars are adjustable and are available in five different sizes to ensure the perfect fit for your doggie.

Lead Time

Love walking your dog, but hate trying to carry along all of the walking necessities? There is a leash that can help free up your hands. The black leather leash from Wagwear comes with a removable nylon reverse pouch. The pouch gives you the convenience of bringing along baggies, treats, and keys without having to carry them. The leash is especially helpful when walking multiple dogs.

36. Jeweled Doggies

You've got the collar. You've got the leash. But Rover's neck still looks bare. "What's missing?" you ask. A necklace or chain maybe? That's right. One of the hottest trends in doggie world is doggie jewelry. Dogs across America are sporting beads, pearls, silver, and gold. Doggie necklaces are a great way to add some sparkle or pizzazz to your dog's life. Want to put the woof back into your dog's bark? Check out these sure-fire attention-getters.

New York Posh

Based in New York City, Chic Doggie by Corey's line of dog jewelry has been become a must-have for the well-heeled pooches of New York, Palm Beach, Beverly Hills, and Aspen. In fact Chic Doggie's jewelry was even worn by Sigourney Weaver's Italian greyhound, Petals, at her doggie wedding.

Chic Doggie's bestselling pieces are the faux pearl necklaces. Among the collection are white or black pearl necklaces with a rhinestone ball and a white pearl necklace with a gold bone charm. The necklaces come in sizes up to fourteen inches, but additional sizes can be custom ordered. When ordering one of Chic Doggie's necklaces, be sure to add two inches to your dog's neck size for the proper fit.

Have a few more bones in the bank? Chic Doggie also has several pieces made from sterling silver. The bestselling of the silver necklaces is the Bone Necklace. The necklace is a strand of dog bones with a larger dog bone that fits through the toggle. The necklace is also very popular among doggie mommies, myself included. The nice thing about the necklace is that one

side is flat so that the
necklace lies nicely
against the skin.

The sterling silver
necklace with a large
heart pendant is the
favorite of designer
Corey Gelman's dog,
Bear. The front of
the heart can be en-
graved with your dog-
gie's name on the
front and "If lost,

Chic Doggie by Corey

please call my mommy/daddy at ———." The necklace also
makes an adorable charm bracelet for doggie moms.

Charmed Life What does a dog living a charmed life need?
Charms, of course. To complement many of their pieces,
Chic Doggie offers over fifteen different charm styles including teddy bears, hearts, and paw prints. Their charms fit on
most necklaces or small dog collars and are available in sterling silver or 14k gold.

California Chic

On the West Coast the doggie jewelry line by Oh My Stars!
is making a splash. The line was started in early 1998 by sisters Marcy Esparaza and Mikan Gosuico. Marcy and Mikan
came up with the idea for the canine jewelry while out shopping for themselves. It did not take long before their canine
kids, a schnauzer named Pepper and a black labrador named
Rogue, had a collection of necklaces for every occasion.
Gosuico explained, "Everywhere we went, people commented
on the necklaces." So, the two sisters launched a doggie jew-

elry company. The name for their company "came to them" while on a walk with their dogs. As a woman approached them she saw the necklaces on the dogs and exclaimed, "Oh my stars!" The woman then went on to ask where they got the necklaces. She was their first customer. The necklaces have since become hot sellers.

Oh My Stars! uses only high quality glass and ceramic beads in their jewelry. While the jewelry is not meant as a collar replacement, the jewelry is durable. Each piece must pass the Rogue test. Rogue wears the jewelry when he goes to the dog park, swimming, and even on rafting trips.

To see if the jewelry would withstand the everyday rigors of one of my active dogs, I tried out a couple of the necklaces on Wanda. Wanda tried out some of Oh My Stars! more whimsical designs. Wanda sported the To The Moon necklace, which features turquoise beads decorated with little stars and moons, and the Rainbow, which features an array of brightly colored beads. (It looks great with Waggin' Wear's Black Dog Collar.) The necklaces withstood Wanda's wrestling matches and wild chases with Berry, her daily swims, games of fetch, and her daily walks.

Oh My Stars! necklaces range from elegant pearls to whimsically colored beads. Their more popular designs include the Amore, which is a rhinestone necklace featuring silver-plated beads, a decorative clasp, and a pewter logo tag. For the feminine set, Oh My Stars! recently introduced the Monique. The pink necklace was named for the company's best customer, a beagle named Monique.

On the more playful side the Carib (Berry's favorite) gives your dog the look of the islands with turquoise, yellow, and black beads. Finally the Santa Fe (Robin's favorite) is made of turquoise and silver beads and is a great complement piece for leather collars.

Tag the Dog

Even pampered pooches need dog tags. High-end doggies looking for high-end tags need look no farther than Tiffany & Co. The famous jewelry store has sterling-silver tags for your golden dog. The Paw Print, Bell, and Dog Bowl shape tags can be engraved with all of your dog's important information.

For every breed there is a tag. At least that is true of Fine Arf Collections' brass name tags. The polished brass tags are available in forty-seven breeds or K-9 icons. They can be engraved on the back with your dog's name and your telephone number or can be worn just as a collar charm. Owner Lisa Greene pointed out that the tags aren't just for dogs. Dog lovers have used them as luggage tags and zipper pulls.

Diamonds Are a Dog's Best Friend

We all know that diamonds are a girl's best friend (after her dog, of course). Well, for some lucky pooches, diamonds are a dog's best friend (after their owners, of course). Because of the cost involved, diamond dog collars are not items that collar makers or jewelers readily keep in inventory. But for those lucky dogs whose owners can afford it, there are diamonds to be worn!

If you are wondering just how many bones a diamond dog collar will set you back, here are some figures. London's luxury department store, Harrod's Department Store once sold an $11,510 diamond-studded collar. And a Dallas man made the news when he presented his rottweiler with a $35,000 diamond and gold collar for Christmas. Up the road from me, a man dropped by the Chanel Boutique looking for a diamond dog collar for his girlfriend's dog. When they explained that a diamond dog collar was not the type of item they had readily available, the gentleman settled for a $5,000 necklace that could be used as a collar. Even Elizabeth Taylor has gotten in on the act, presenting her Maltese, Sugar, with a $4,000 diamond and sapphire collar.

At a slightly lower price you can give your precious pooch a one-of-a-kind diamond dog collar. The collar consists of two carats of diamonds bezel set into thirty-five grams of 14k white gold and secured into a half-inch wide nylon strap. The nine diamonds are white in color and eye clean. Virtually every part of the collar is solid gold including the buckle. As an option, you can add a hand-engraved 14k white gold dog tag with your dog's name and phone number to ensure that, if lost, your doggie will be returned safely.

Sheila Parness's offering in the diamond department is the Ruby and Diamond Acorn Dog Collar. The Burgundy crocodile collar has an acorn-shaped ruby and diamond pendant and gold buckle. The collar is available in sizes to fit necks eight inches to eighteen inches.

The Next Best Thing

While most of us would love to drape our dogs in diamonds, most of us do not have thousands of dollars to spend on diamond dog collars. Luckily rhinestone and crystal collars are just as attractive and make just as much of a statement.

The Crystal Collar and the Swarovski Heart & Bone Collar from Fox & Hounds Ltd. are great ways to add a little sparkle to your dog's life. The Heart & Bone Collar is made from high-quality black leather and is adorned with silver Swarovski bones and hearts with red crystals. The collar also comes with a Swarovski red heart crystal charm attached to the D ring. The Crystal Collar consists of two to four (depending on size) sparkling rows of European crystal rhinestones that are hand-sewn onto high-gloss black leather with sturdy metal fittings. I liked it so much that I bought one for myself.

Matching leads are also available. (Note: Neither collar is recommended for dogs that tend to scratch their necks a lot.)

Crown Dog

Show your dog that she is queen of the house by giving her
a Pet Tiara from Fox & Hounds Ltd. The rhinestone tiaras look
just like those of human royalty. Designer Robin Kershner
explained that the tiaras are perfect for weddings or other formal occasions. Styles range from the dainty, The Silver Princess
and The Pearl Princess, to the all out ornate, The Queen.

The Pet-iculars

Designer label collars: Chanel, Louis Vuitton, Gucci, boutiques

Fine Arf Collection: select retail locations

Fox & Hounds Ltd.: select retail locations, www.foxandhounds.com

Mood Collar: www.moodypet.com

The Amberhill Collection: select retail locations

Wagwear, 888-924-9327, www.wagwear.com

All-in-one Collar: Blue Ribbon Dog Company, select retail
    locations

GEORGE, 2411 California @ Fillmore, San Francisco, CA, or
    1829 4th Street, Berkeley, CA 94710, 877-344-5454

Waggin' Wear, select retail locations, www.wagginwear.com

Necklaces and charms: Chic Doggie by Corey, 212-752-WOOF,
    www.chicdog.com

Necklaces: Oh My Stars, select retail locations, www.ohmystars.com

Tiffany dog tags: Tiffany's boutiques

Brass tags: Fine Arf Collection, select retail locations

Diamond Dog Collar: www.PetVogue.com

Ruby and Diamond Acorn Dog Collar: Sheila Parness, London,
    United Kingdom, 011 44 207 338 4966

6.

Looking Good—Feeling Grrreat!

*A dog is the only thing on earth that loves you
more than he loves himself.*

—JOSH BILLINGS

Tara starts her day with a session with her personal trainer. From there she is off to have her hair done. Then it's manicure time. And to complete the day she has a massage. Sounds like a great day. But it's a dog's day. You see Tara is a standard poodle.

Canine pampering has come a long way baby. Gone are the days of washing the dog with the garden hose. Today's dogs have standing appointments with their groomers, massage therapists, and personal trainers. And did you know that grooming facilities now refer to themselves as beauty salons or spas, likewise groomers as stylists? Treating dogs as people is big business. Increasingly doggie spas and salons offer services that mirror those available in our high-end day spas and salons. Dog parents want their dogs to look their best. They also feel better knowing that their canine companions are being pampered with extra amenities such as massages, pedicures, and therapeutic baths. As a result the doggie spa industry has become more than a billion dollar a year industry.

But the quest to make our dogs look and feel good goes

beyond spas and salons. Spa products for home use have become a booming business. Take a look on the shelves of any pet boutique and you will find a large selection of premium shampoos, conditioners, and doggie colognes. And we are not talking cheap sprays to cover dog smell. We're talking high-end doggie colognes that are priced as high as many exclusive human colognes.

And dog parents not only want their dogs to look good; they also want them to feel good. People are concerned like never before with their dogs' overall well-being. They call massage therapists for their stressed or injured doggies and take the time to educate themselves on alternative remedies like aromatherapy.

Basically most of the products or services that we use to make ourselves look and feel better are now available for our dogs. And if something is not available now, it probably will be in the near future.

Is Lady due for a makeover? Want to make her feel better? Here are some suggestions to help your dog put her best paw forward.

37. Canine Coiffure

When it comes to posh dog spas and salons, New York has the market cornered. New York boasts some of the most exclusive doggie salons in the United States. But upscale doggie salons are digging a niche in other communities as well. Here are some salons that are getting "bark-tacular" reviews from their canine clientele.

Did you know that the standard poodle is the most challenging breed to groom because of the scissors work required to maintain their appearance?

Karen's For People + Pets

Karen's For People + Pets has been grooming the pooches of New York's elite for over twenty-five years. Owner Karen Thompson is recognized as a leader in the pet care business. Others in the industry rate her high-tech beauty salon and retail store as the ultimate pet salon. In fact, her reputation is so great that hotel concierges across the city recommend her salon to visiting guests traveling with their dogs.

Karen's is widely known for its state-of-the-art grooming equipment and beautiful scissors grooming. In fact, the salon reminded me more of a modern human beauty salon than a grooming facility. Karen's uses only top-of-the-line equipment, including hydraulic tables, clippers that hang from the ceiling, stainless-steel molding, and a ceiling-rigged dryer system. One of the salon's highlights is its cream-colored tile Kohler Tea-for-Two bathtub, which is as elegant as bathtubs found in many luxury homes.

In addition to the salon, Karen's For People + Pets has one of the nicest boutiques in New York City. The boutique carries everything the posh dog needs including collars studded with Swarovski crystals, Karen's own line of treats and shampoos, and exquisite custom-order European dog beds. I also noted a wide selection of carrying bags, coats, and sweaters, many of which are from the Karen's line.

Doggie Do and Pussycats Too!

Doggie Do and Pussycats Too! has been keeping New York's chic dogs well coiffed for more than ten years. The salon, created by Howard Binder and Larry Roth, boasts one of the largest and most professionally accomplished staffs in New York City. Binder and Roth proudly noted that some of their groomers have won medals at international grooming competitions and are heavily immersed in the "show world."

The salon is truly one of a kind with respect to its staff, grooming services, and the way they treat pets. New York's posh dogs enjoy hot-oil treatments, shampoos, haircuts, blow-drys, and even French manicures. Binder and Roth are also quick to point out that they will go to great lengths to ensure the comfort and happiness of their four-legged (as well as two-legged) clientele. As an example, they refer to an experience with renowned author Barbara Taylor Bradford. It seems that her two bichons frises developed a skin condition that was perplexing Binder and Roth for a time. They then discovered the culprit—New York City's water supply was too harsh for the dogs' delicate skin and coat. The solution: The two dogs are now bathed in Evian water.

Now *that's* pampering!

While your dog is being groomed you can enjoy Doggie Do's designer boutique, which features custom collections from around the world (England, France, Italy, Spain, Canada, and, of course, the United States). Owners can choose from leather collars and leads, handcrafted and painted feeding servers, ultra-chic bedding, and exquisite jewelry for both pets and people. Or you can pick up some of Doggie Do's own signature line of all-natural gourmet doggie biscuits. They come in an array of flavors and contain no preservatives.

Salon Pooch-ini

Berry, Wanda, and Robin all have standing appointments at Salon Pooch-ini. Owner Erica Richter started the salon because of her immense love of animals. Using Karen's For People + Pets as a model, Richter's goal was to establish a salon that would be both pleasing to people and animals.

The salon's interior is fashioned after an upscale beauty salon with rustic Spanish-tiled floors, faux painted walls and glass blocks, plants, and paintings hanging on the walls. All of the cages are stainless steel and are cleaned with bleach after its occupant goes home. Prior to her opening, Richter faced opposition from neighboring businesses fearing they would be inundated with "dog odor," but she has since won them over by working diligently to keep the salon spotless.

While at Salon Pooch-ini, dogs enjoy massages during their baths, personalized attention and playtime, "paw"-dicures, and teeth cleaning. Classical music can also be heard playing in the background. Richter explains that the music not only calms her, but it also seems to have a calming effect on her doggie clients.

Richter also tries to accommodate clients' special requests. The only request that she can recall turning down was a client's request to dye her poodle "Lucille Ball–red." She just couldn't bring herself to do that.

From personal experience, I know that Richter has all the patience in the world. While Robin is very cooperative, Wanda and Berry can be quite the challenge. Berry insists on jumping into the tub all by himself, while Wanda loves to jump out of the tub mid-bath.

Berry has also become known as the salon enforcer, barking at dogs that get a little too rambunctious. Amazingly most dogs seem to heed his warnings. He just has that way with other dogs. Rumor has it Berry once aspired to serve in the military. That is, until Mom came along, but that's another story.

Brickell Pet Grooming

Miami dogs are lucky to have another great beauty salon in the area. Stretch limousines are commonly seen pulling up in front of Brickell Pet Grooming. Limousine transportation is one of the many upscale perks offered to VIPs—very important pets. The salon offers hot oil shampoos, manicures, pedicures, massages, and skin treatments. The salon is constructed like a house complete with kitchen, living room, and even a backyard and patio. This is also one of the few cageless grooming facilities in the United States. Instead of being placed in cages, the freshly cleaned canines are put in doggie rooms and allowed to play with other dogs.

Madeline's Pet Grooming Salon

Madeline's Pet Grooming Salon has been in operation since 1961. The salon is one of the largest and most modern equipped in the country. According to the *San Francisco Chronicle* the salon serves nearly five thousand clients from nearby Silicon Valley and other nearby San Francisco Bay areas. Madeline's has earned a fantastic reputation for the salon's "Humane Bath Procedure," which includes protection for eyes, ears, and sensitive body parts and for the special attention given to older or disabled dogs. The salon is also very people friendly offering transportation for your dog and extended hours for pickup and drop off.

In addition to the traditional services, the salon is also widely known for its groomers' scissors work and aesthetic styling. And a feature that sets Madeline's apart from most other salons is that all dogs are fluff-dryed by hand; they are never cage dryed. As a service to dog owners, Madeline's will also give you the Madeline's Pet Groomer Report and Health Alert Form, which summarizes their observations about the general health condition of your dog and recommendations for veterinarian care.

Finding the Right Stylist

When looking for a new salon for your precious pooch, you might want to take the time to check them out in person first. And here's why.

I took a trip to New York to check out several of the places that I wanted to mention in this book. I was shocked when I toured a popular facility. As soon as I entered the place, I smelled dog. Then, as I was brought past the grooming room, I was surprised to see a layer of hair clippings on the floor that was at least an inch thick. It was obvious that the room had not been swept all day. It would probably be a safe guess that if they couldn't even take a few minutes to sweep the floor, they probably weren't giving the doggie clients the attention they deserve.

Erica Richter has some handy tips to follow when looking for a trustworthy stylist.

1. **Cleanliness**. Does the facility smell clean? Are there dog-hair trimmings all over the floor?

2. **Cages**. Are the cages large enough for your dog? Cages should also be made from a material such as stainless steel that can be cleaned with bleach. Are there enough cages for all dogs, or must dogs share with others?

3. **Training**. Are the groomers formally trained?

4. **Time**. What is their length of time for grooming? According to Richter, "Four hours is the standard." She adds, "Be suspect of one-hour in-and-out service. Your dog is not being handled the way you want."

5. **Products**. Do they use good quality products? Cheap shampoos can irritate dogs' skin.

38. Launder-Mutts

Self-serve dog washes across the country are really cleaning up. Dog owners really seem to like them since they offer a happy medium between washing the dog at home and taking them to the groomer. Let's face it, weekly visits to the groomer can get expensive. As for bathing at home—well, let's not go there.

Most dog washes have everything that you need on the premises so that you do not need to haul all of your grooming supplies with you. My favorite features are the tub restraints to keep dogs like my Wanda from jumping out during the bath. But most people like the fact that when they are done, they can just leave without having to deal with the "after-bath" mess—particularly drains clogged with dog hair.

Doggie Bags & Baths is a gourmet dog bakery and self-service dog wash, near Atlanta. Owner Christine Wyman wanted to open a dog bakery but was looking for "a way to take it one step farther." Having three shelties at home, Wyman knew the challenges of trying to bathe a dog at home, but it was her husband who suggested adding the dog wash.

The 1,450-square-foot shop includes an open kitchen with an island and a full retail section. Behind the kitchen are four self-serve bathing stations. The upscale bathing stations are elevated so that you do not have to bend over to clean your dog. A variety of shampoos, dryers, and brushes are also available.

Wyman notes that many customers bring both their human and animal children to the store. "They make an adventure out of it. The kids really enjoy helping give their dogs baths."

Saturdays are the store's busiest days. A typical Saturday may see twenty-five to thirty dogs come in for their baths. But you don't have to worry about your doggie getting bored while you wait. Dogs have the opportunity to play together while waiting for their turn in the tub.

39. Elements of Bathing

OK. You have decided to tackle the task of bathing your dog. Before you begin, you will need to gather a few things to make the bathing process go as smoothly as possible. Once your dog gets a look at some of these grooming products, you might find her waiting in the tub and ready to go. (Well, we can wish, can't we?)

Tips for Washing Your Dog

Erica Richter, owner of Salon Pooch-ini, offers some tips that will help make the process more pleasurable for you and your dog:

1. Prepare to get wet. In other words: Don't wear your good suit.

2. Have patience. Don't think that you are going to be done in thirty seconds. To do a good job takes time.

3. Always brush and comb coat prior to bathing to remove excess and matted hair.

4. Place cotton balls in your dog's ears to keep water out.

5. Use warm water rather than hot or cold. Although we like hot showers, hot water can cause a dog to overheat. As for cold water: How would you like to be given an ice-cold bath?

6. Use a good quality DOG shampoo. People shampoos are harsh on a dog's skin and coat. Don't forget or ignore the feet, "armpits," or the rear end. Also, use a tearless shampoo on the head, neck, and ears. Try to avoid getting shampoo in your dog's eyes.

7. Rinse well. Shampoo residue can leave a dog's skin itchy and red.

8. Try to remove as much water as possible by towel drying.

9. Do not use the high setting on your hair dryer. The high heat may cause your dog to overheat. Many dogs don't like the dryer anyway.

10. Celebrate. You have a clean dog. At least until he goes outside and rolls in the mud.

Sham-pooch

If you are adventurous, patient, or, depending on the dog, crazy, you sometimes bathe your dog yourself. In my case, this is only a last resort. Surprisingly Berry loves baths. He jumps right in the tub and patiently waits for me to finish. On the other hand, Wanda is, to put it nicely, a challenge. Although she will spend an entire day swimming in the pool, she runs in the other direction when I try to get her into the tub. Once in the tub, she waits until she is entirely covered in soapsuds to decide that is the time to jump out of the tub and make a mad dash around the house—leaving Mom and house soaked and soapy. After several soakings I decided that when it comes to my dogs, dog bathing is best left to the professionals.

Luckily for dog owners not all dogs are as uncooperative as my Wanda. And if your dog is game, giving her a bath is really not that bad. In fact some people really enjoy giving their dogs a bath. There are several shampoos available that are the same quality of those used in upscale doggie salons. So, even if you do it yourself, your dog will smell just like he walked out of the salon. The best part is that your wallet will be a little thicker.

For dogs who are tops, Origins has the Top Dog gift set. The set includes Silky Coat Dog Shampoo, Comb Improvement Detangler, a tasty treat, and a stainless-steel bowl. The Silky Coat Dog Shampoo is a gentle shampoo that washes out easily. It also contains Citronella oils to keep away nasty bugs and has a lavender scent to keep your dog smelling sweet. The Comb Improvement Detangler contains conditioning wheat protein as well as aromatic oils such as lavender to make coats silky and smooth. Both the Silky Coat Dog Shampoo and the Comb Improvement Detangler smell terrific and are available individually.

Does your dog deserve to be treated like royalty? Of course he does. After all we know who sits on the throne and acts as if we are there to serve. Bathe your regal beagle in the line of shampoos and conditioners from Sheila Parness. It is the same line used on Queen Elizabeth's eight pampered pooches. Imported from London, Parness shampoos and conditioners contain walnut extract and soothing and calming chamomile for doggies with delicate skin. Parness recognizes that, just as people do, dogs have different types of fur. Included in the product line are puppy shampoo and conditioner, medicated shampoo, dry hair shampoo and rich conditioner, and regular shampoo and conditioner. For after and in between shampoos, Parness has a Gloss Coat Spray that contains glycerin and jojoba to keep doggie's coat looking healthy and shiny.

Don't Forget to Dry

Now you're done with the bath, and it's time to dry off. Believe it or not there are actually towels made just for dogs.

And with towels like these who could blame a dog parent for wanting one for their doggie or even themselves. Unlike ordinary, everyday towels these canine towels are adorned with dog-theme motifs to ensure that dog owners don't mistake them for their own.

I have to admit that I purchased a set of dog-theme towels for Robin. Although she loves to swim, her favorite part of swimming is the part where she is toweled off afterward. In fact, she loves being toweled off so much that when it is Berry and Wanda's turn, she tries to sneak in for more.

Robin's first set of towels were the "Good Dog" towels from GEORGE. The cotton towels are plenty soft and have held up well through many cycles in the washing machine. The towels measure 22" × 38". If you happen to work out, you will happen to find that the towels are the perfect size for the gym. On several occasions Robin has caught me with her towels in my gym bag.

Need something more along the size of a full bath towel? I discovered the plush white cotton terry-cloth towels available through the Trixie & Peanut catalog. The towels feature an embroidered bone outlined in black. The towels come in two sizes, bath towel (23" × 52") and bath sheet (27" × 59"). If you happen to have a bathroom with a dog motif, these towels make great accessories.

If your precious pooch chills easily or soaks up water like a sponge (like my Robin), she might like to snuggle up in a warm robe after a bath or swim. Catalogs like In the Company of Dogs and most pet boutiques carry terry robes that give your dog a place to tuck his wet, furry body after bathing or swimming. They also help eliminate that drenching water shake-off.

The Brush-Off

Did you know that you should brush your dog daily? Professional groomer Erica Richter is a big fan of brushing everyday because nearly all breeds, short hair to long hair, shed and oftentimes there is an undercoat. In addition, medium-long to long curly coats, such as those on poodles, mat easily.

Brushing your dog's coat untangles matted fur, stimulates the skin to produce oil, keeps your dog's coat shiny, and helps you find any ticks or fleas that may have taken up residence on your dog. But brushing your dog is also beneficial in other ways. Daily brushing removes hair before it ends up in the corners of your house. Because most dogs love being brushed (my Wanda being a notable exception), it strengthens the bond between you and your dog.

Your dog will be happy to be given the brush off with these brushes by GEORGE. The GEORGE dog brush is made with natural tampico bristles and the handles are made of 100 percent oak with the GEORGE logo stamped in the top. The GEORGE leather handle dog brush is imported and is made with natural pig bristles. The handle is white cedar with a GEORGE branded leather strap.

Got a few bones to spare? Then the Pure Finest Bristle Pet Brush from Sheila Parness is the brush for your dog. Handcrafted in England, the brushes are adorned with the Parness crest. The bristles are designed to stimulate natural oils and promote a healthy, shiny coat.

The Gift of Grooming

A grooming set is a great gift for a friend whose dog looks like he hasn't seen the bathtub in a while or for the dog lover who loves to groom her furry friend. While places like Deca-

dent Dogs offer prepackaged grooming sets, you can easily
assemble your own customized grooming set. Simply fill a
basket full of all those things that keep Rover looking good
like a high-quality shampoo and conditioner, pet brush and
comb, a dog-theme towel, and some cologne for in-between
bath freshening.

40. Chanel K-9

Everyone loves the way their dogs smell when they come
home from the dog salon. Unfortunately, as most of us know,
that wonderful, fresh, clean dog smell doesn't last as long as
we would like. Within a few days your sweet dog starts to
develop that not-so-sweet doggie odor. Thank goodness for
doggie colognes and deodorants.

Want your doggie to smell like your favorite cologne? Well
he might not smell exactly like you do when you are wearing
yours but the colognes from Nature Labs come awfully close.
The colognes are imitations of such popular human colognes
as Polo Sport and Tommy Hilfiger. But these canine colognes
sport more interesting names such as Bono Sports, CK-9,
Tommy Holedigger, and White Dalmatians.

The cologne sprays from Sheila Parness are some of the
finest doggie colognes on the market. The colognes are packaged (and priced) just as those for humans. Belgravia is the
Parness signature fragrance and can be used for either male or
female dogs. If you are looking for something a little more
gender specific, Henry is a more masculine fragrance designed
for your beloved male, and Henrietta is a feminine fragrance
designed for your precious pooch.

The Natural Approach

Aromaleigh's Canine Aromatherapy Deodorizing Spritz Sprays are a natural alternative to synthetically fragranced dog colognes. The sprays are not overpowering as some colognes tend to be. The sprays contain essential oils to naturally deodorize, repel insects, and soothe your dog's coat. The sprays come in six scents: Citrus, Spicy, Floral, Woody, Herbal, and Minty. Additionally Aromaleigh's sprays can be used on a pet's bedding, as a home fragrance, and in the car. People can even use them, too. I guess even people can smell a little doggie at times.

Why Do Dogs Love to Roll in Smelly Things?

Ever wonder why your dog runs right from his bath to roll in something with an unpleasant odor. Animal behaviorists believe that dogs roll in "smelly" things to mask their scent. Wolves roll in dead carcasses or the feces of their prey to mask their scent so that they can sneak up on their prey when hunting. Unfortunately this is a trait that dogs have not lost through domestication.

The Nose Knows

Sometimes you walk into the room where your dog has been, and you realize that dogs do not always smell like a rose. Luckily there are ways to combat those unappealing odors that doggies can leave behind. Now you might be wondering just how keeping your home smelling fresh is a way to pamper your dog. Here's the way it works: The better we feel about our canine companions, the better we treat them. The better we treat them, the happier they are. And so forth. Additionally you have probably discovered that dogs are very sensitive beings. They know when you find something offensive about them. Your doggie does not want to be the source of displeasure in your life. That being said, here are some ways to keep your house smelling fresh as a daisy.

Deodorizing candles are a great way to fill a room with pleasant aromas. Unlike sprays, candles last for hours. Just be sure to keep them out of reach of curious canines.

For years beeswax candles were burned in hospitals to sanitize and deodorize the air. Burt's Bees has a room deodorizing beeswax candle that also contains essential oils of lavender and cedar to increase its effectiveness. I decided to try out the candle for myself.

Berry, Wanda, and Robin often spend their days with me in my office. As you can imagine an office with three dog inhabitants can start to smell pretty "doggie." I burned the candle for about thirty minutes and noticed a big difference. But knowing that I am often oblivious to doggie odors, I asked my husband to come in and be the judge. He could not detect any doggie odors. Now I always keep the candle in my office for those times when the office smells more like a kennel than an office.

We recently found out that David is highly allergic to dogs. His doctor recommended that we not allow the dogs to sleep in the bedroom anymore. As you can imagine, this did not go over well with me or the gang. So rather than banishing the dogs out of the bedroom at night, we invested in several air filters around the house. They really made a big difference. David noted that his breathing is much improved, and the bedroom does smell a lot fresher. I also noticed that the filters really cut down on the dust around the house. But perhaps the most pleasant side effect is that the humming noise of the filters help drown out the sounds of snoring from my husband and Robin allowing me to get a good night's sleep.

41. Canine Aromatherapy

While most people think of aromatherapy as scented candles and bath products, it is "mutts" more than that. The true purpose of aromatherapy is the therapeutic use of essential oils to promote healing and wellness. In recent years, people have turned to this form of alternative medicine to help them with their ailments. Now aromatherapy has sniffed its way into the canine world.

Aromaleigh was started in 1993 by a certified aromatherapist. Aromaleigh's canine grooming products and botanical remedies are 100 percent natural. They are hand blended and are specially formulated for dogs. The line uses high-quality, therapeutic-grade essential oils in dilutions that are safe for your dog.

For those who are new to aromatherapy or those who are unsure what to buy for their dogs Aromaleigh has assembled the Pampered Pooch Holistic Aromatherapy Kit. The kit contains five of their most popular canine products. The Canine Itchy Skin Spritz can be applied anywhere your doggie has a little itch or scratch. Canine Breath Spritz contains essential oils to freshen breath while reducing "stinky-breath" bacteria in the mouth. The Clean Ears essential oil blend aids in fighting off infections and also helps to loosen earwax to aid in cleaning. Canine Healing Ointment helps prevent infection and speed up the healing process. And a few drops of the Canine Calm Down massaged on your dog's neck and chest promises to calm Rover down on trips to the vet, during thunderstorms, or in other stress causing situations.

Scratch a dog, and you'll find a permanent job.

—FRANKLIN P. JONES

42. Rub It In

A few years ago, if someone had suggested a massage for my dogs, I would have looked at them and said something like, "You've got to be kidding!" That all changed when my Wanda sprained a muscle in her leg while playing fetch. The veterinarian prescribed rest and aspirin for the pain. But if you know my Wanda, you know that she is not one for rest. Luckily a friend of mine is a massage therapist. Teresa always did a great job for my husband and me, so I called and asked her if she could work on Wanda's leg. Wanda was a little reluctant at first, but then she loved it. Teresa showed me how to massage Wanda's leg myself. In no time Wanda was out chasing her Kong Toy around the front yard. I was a convert.

Massage can benefit dogs as much as humans. Massage speeds the healing process from surgery, alleviates arthritic pain, and relieves stress. So it is not surprising that most dog spas offer canine massages. There are also a growing number of massage therapists across the country that prefer four-legged clients to the two-legged variety.

Based in Boca Raton, Florida, Michael Holloway is a nationally certified massage therapist who founded Pet Massage Services, Inc., in 1996. His successful practice includes several long-term clients—many of whom have been seeing him regularly for more than three years. Holloway has little need to advertise as the majority of his clients are referred to him through veterinarians and word of mouth.

Through therapy that includes deep-tissue massage, Holloway is able to help dogs suffering from hip dysplasia, arthritis, nerve damage, back and disc problems, and fears or phobias. His method of therapy combines massage, stretching, and an exercise regimen. The therapy is intended to complement whatever the dog's veterinarian prescribes. The advantages of canine massage are reduced pain levels, tissue swelling, and stiffness in the joints while increasing flexibility, mobility, and improving the quality of life.

Holloway cites many examples of the amazing results that massage therapy can have. One of the most dramatic involved a golden retriever named Mac. Mac was suffering from hip dysplasia. He had become crippled when he was less than a year old. Mac's parents had several options: 1) do nothing and leave poor Mac in pain, 2) put Mac through hip replacement surgery, or 3) try a physical rehabilitation program including massage therapy. Mac's parents decided to try physical rehabilitation and called Holloway. Holloway started with deep-tissue massage and trigger-point work to help reduce muscle swelling, tightness, and pain. Because Mac was so young and energetic they began swim therapy. Mac started with fifteen minutes every other day and worked up to thirty minutes every other day. All the while Mac continued with massage to work out the sore muscles from all of his new exercise. After three months a walking regimen was added to Mac's activities. Now Mac leads a normal, active life. He looks forward to his swims and walks. Before therapy Mac was barely able to move. Now Mac jumps up on the couch for his afternoon naps and jumps up on the bed to sleep at night. Much to Mac's parents' joy, his veterinarian recently reported that Mac is in the best shape that she has ever seen him.

A session with Holloway starts at fifty dollars per half hour. He also offers reduced rate multi-visit packages. He prefers to come to the client's home because dogs are usually more relaxed in familiar surroundings.

Want to try some massage techniques on your canine companion? Michael Holloway offers some practical tips and some Do's and Don'ts:

1. Lay the pet on its side and rock to calm and relax them.
2. For trouble areas in a dog's body use a squeeze and release method of the skin and muscle tissue to relieve pain and tension.
3. For injured areas, apply ice for ten minutes every two hours to relieve swelling and pain.
4. When beginning massages with your pet, be patient with yourself and with your pet, it may be the first time for the both of you.
5. Always check with your vet if you have any doubts.
6. Massage will bring you and your pet even closer together.

Do's

1. Do make a special time for massage.
2. Do enjoy your time with your pet.
3. Do be consistent. Consistency brings about change.
4. Do exercise together—swim, walk, and play.
5. Do check with your vet if you have any questions or doubts.

Don'ts

1. Don't be afraid to use strong pressure, your pet will tell you if he doesn't like it.

2. Don't make sudden changes in your pet's lifestyle.

3. Don't massage deeply on a pet with cancer.

If you would like to learn more about how to give your dog a massage, here are several resources that you can turn to. Two videos, *Effective Pet Massage for Dogs* and *Effective Pet Massage for Older Dogs*, hosted by Jonathan Rudinger, will teach you the basic methods of massage for your dog. In addition there are several books available that address canine massage: *Canine Massage: A Practical Guide*, by Jean-Pierre Hourdebaight and Shari L. Seymour and *The Tellington Touch: A Revolutionary Natural Method to Train and Care for Your Favorite Animal* by Linda Tellington-Jones and Sybil Taylor are both highly acclaimed books demonstrating techniques for massaging your doggie.

43. Doggie Etiquette

Do you look longingly at other people's well-behaved dogs as your dog is pulling you down the street? Does your dog bark at everything that goes by your house? Does your dog turn around and walk the other way or pretend he doesn't hear you when you call him? Your dog could probably use a few sessions with a dog trainer.

As dogs are welcomed in more and more establishments, dog parents want to make sure that their dogs know how to behave. Unruly dogs often ruin things for all of the other well-behaved dogs. Unfortunately, as many of us have discovered, dogs are not born trained. I would bet that nearly every one of us has experienced times when we've just wanted to pull out our hair over our dog's behavior. Teaching a dog to be well behaved requires time and patience from his owner. Remember, sometimes even the best-mannered dogs require a refresher course.

On those days when your dog is pulling you down the street, it may make you feel better to know that you are not alone. Even the dogs of the rich and famous sometimes require doggie intervention. When they need help, here's who they call.

Mathew Margolis

When you think of dog trainers, one of the first names that comes to mind is Mathew Margolis, a.k.a. "Uncle Matty." Margolis has coauthored numerous books on dog training and behavior and has appeared on several television shows as a dog behavioral expert. He is the pioneer of "love, praise, and affection" training. In addition, Margolis established The National Institute of Dog Training, which is one of the largest and most respected dog training facilities in the United States. Dogs are sent from all over the world to the Southern California Institute, which conducts training and problem-solving programs.

Shelby Marlo

Shelby Marlo is a canine behavioral specialist and trainer based in Los Angeles. She has trained the dogs of some of the hottest names in Hollywood and has been a guest expert on several television programs and magazines. She teaches her philosophy of training in her book, *Shelby Marlo's New Art of Dog Training: Balancing Love and Discipline* (Contemporary Books). According to the book, Marlo advocates positive reinforcement rather than the old style of military training. It also teaches dog owners to try to see things from a dog's point of view.

Bashkim Dibra

Bashkim Dibra's unique method of training has made him one of the best-known dog trainers on the East Coast. He is often cited for his work with animal-related causes, including Paws Across America, a campaign to promote responsible pet ownership and to help pet owners learn proper care and training techniques for their pets.

Where to Find a Trainer?

Don't have a movie star budget? Looking for a trainer a little closer to home? The Association of Pet Dog Trainers (APDT) Web site (www.apdt.com) offers a trainer-search option that allows you to search for dog trainers by state. The organization encourages the use of positive reinforcement in dog training.

44. It's Graduation!

A Kansas State University study found that families with pets produce children with higher IQs. Children with pets also develop greater empathy and understanding for other people's feelings. It's not known, however, whether we have the same effect on our canine companions.

What's graduation without the cap and gown? Yes, on your dog's graduation from obedience school he can proudly accept his diploma in his very own canine cap and gown. Mary Goehring made the first canine cap and gown for her golden retriever, Raleigh, for his obedience class graduation. Needless to say Raleigh was the hit of the ceremony. Since then

Goehring has made graduation attire for a number of obedient canines. The gowns come in several sizes to fit dogs up to one hundred pounds and come in black, red, and royal blue. And to make sure the cap doesn't fall off before it's time to turn the tassel, it is fitted with an elastic band.

Think your dog is smart? 57 percent of pet owners think their pet is smart, while 18 percent think that their pet is a genius. (Source: American Animal Hospital Association's Ninth annual survey of 1,200 pet owners in the United States and Canada.)

The Pet-Iculars

Karen's For People + Pets, 1195 Lexington Ave., New York, NY 10028, 212-472-9440, www.karensforpets.com

Doggie Do and Pussycats Too!, 567 Third Ave., New York, NY 10016, 212-661-9111, www.doggiedo.com

Salon Pooch-ini, 1019 Kane Concourse, Bay Harbor Islands, FL 33154, 305-864-1944

Brickell Pet Grooming, 21 SW 11th Street, Miami, FL 33130

Madeline's Pet Grooming Salon, 820 Kiely Blvd., Santa Clara, CA 408-243-1333

Doggie Bags & Baths, 1480 Buford Drive, Suite A, Lawrenceville, GA 30043

Origins Top Dog Gift set: www.origins.com, most Origins stores

Sheila Parness Shampoo, Brush, Cologne: London, UK, 011-44-207-838-4966

GEORGE Shampoo, Good Dog Towel, Brushes: 2411 California at Fillmore, San Francisco, CA, or 1829 Fourth Street, Berkeley, CA 877-344-5454

Bone-motif towels: Trixie & Peanut, 888-838-6780, www.trixieandpeanut.com

Maxx's Closet, select retail locations, www.maxxscloset.com

Canine Clothing Company, www.canineclothing.com

Grooming gift set: Decadent Dogs, www.decadentdogs.com

Nature lab colognes: select retail locations

Aromaleigh deodorizing spritz: www.aromaleigh.com

Burt's Bees, www.burtsbees.com

Michael Holloway, Pet Massage Rehabilitation: Boca Raton, FL

Jonathan Rudinger massage video: www.petmassage.com

Mathew Margolis, 11275 National Blvd., Los Angeles, CA 90064,
    800-670-9663, www.unclematty.com

Shelby Marlo, Los Angeles, CA, www.shelbymarlo.com

Caps & gowns: www.SmartDogg.com

7.

Creature Comforts

Let Sleeping Dogs Lie.

—ANONYMOUS

Canine furnishings have come a long way in the last few years. Gone are the days when dogs slept on old blankets or on dog beds flat as a pancake. Since dogs have moved from the doghouse to the family house, dog parents want to make sure that Fido's furniture is as comfortable and attractive as their own. And one of the latest trends is for dog parents to buy or custom order doggie furnishings that match their home decor. As a result, the business of canine furnishings is booming. And we're not just talking about typical dog beds; there are designer beds, cushy couches, and even loungers. Who would have guessed that we would see a dog bed with the Gucci label?

And if a bed is simply not enough for your precious pooch, consider giving him his own room. Couples like Kelly and John Klosterman are turning spare bedrooms into "dog" rooms. Others take their dogs into consideration when purchasing a new home—making sure that there are enough bedrooms for Rover to have his very own room. And a number of interior decorators have reported being asked to decorate a room or two just for the family dog. Woof!

Berry, Wanda, Robin, and I asked some of our friends across the country to bark back with their favorite dog furnishings. You'll be surprised at the number of offerings. Bedtime and lounge time will never be the same.

A good dog deserves a good home.

—ROGER CARAS

45. Fabulous Furnishings

If your dog is like my Wanda, keeping her off the couch is no easy task. One of Wanda's favorite pastimes is lying on the couch with the TV tuned to *Frasier*. (She just loves that dog, Eddie.) Trying to get her to relinquish her seat is like trying to move an elephant. To the relief of many unseated dog lovers, Beastly Furnishings has come up with the solution for dogs like my Wanda. Give them their own couch.

In 1999, interior designer Carol Copple "unleashed" a furniture line that includes doggie sofas, chaise longues, and daybeds perfectly proportioned for dogs. Copple originally conceived the line of pet furniture as custom originals for her clients' furry friends. However, the demand for the stylish furniture grew so much that Copple formed the company Beastly Furnishings. Labeled "Stylish Furniture for Your Cherished Little Beast," the line has been selling like hot dogs at a baseball game. The line has also caught the attention of the media and many celebrities. The doggie furniture has been featured on several shows including *Donny & Marie* and *Later Today* and in magazines such as *Star Style* and *The Robb Report*.

One of the great things about the furniture line is that the pieces sit low so small doggies do not have to struggle to hop on. Beastly Furnishings come in three sizes so that you can choose the dimensions that best suit your favorite friend.

The furniture line comes in a variety of fabrics and a sample swatch guide is available as well. Each piece comes with a removable slipcover and two matching designer throw cushions. All of the fabric coverings feature stain protection and are dry-cleanable so that you never have to live with doggie odor. The furniture forms are made of a lightweight polyurethane foam while the cushions are filled with synthetic downlike fiber that retains its shape and fluffiness. And if none of Beastly Furnishings's fabrics suit your decor, all you have to do is send them your fabric to be made into a totally custom slipcover.

Copple has found that dogs prefer their own furniture to the human variety. I had the opportunity to see if this was true using Wanda as my test dog. As I mentioned, Wanda loves sprawling out on our couch rather than on her own dog

Beastly Furnishings/Paul Otero

bed. A friend of ours had just purchased one of Beastly's animal print chaises for her bulldog Max. She allowed us to come over and give the chaise a test drive. I had no problem coaxing Wanda up on the chaise. Once there she plopped down and made herself at home. She really did seem to enjoy it, but more importantly she stayed there rather than jumping up on my friend's furniture. The only problem was that Max wasn't too thrilled. He looked downright disgusted. Wanda just smiled that devious smile of hers as she glanced at Max lying on the floor. There is no female who takes the phrase "ladies first" to heart more than my Wanda.

Responding to requests for even more offerings, Copple has recently added some new products to the Beastly Furnishings line. The sleeping bags are great for more contemporary interiors and are perfect for canines that love to snuggle under the covers. And, of course, every sleeping dog needs a pillow for comfortable sleeping. The pillows feature fine stitching and overstuffing. Both the sleeping bag and pillows are made with the same upholstery-quality fabrics used for Beastly's furniture line.

46. Dog Dreams

According to an American Animal Hospital Association survey, 46 percent of pet owners let their furry companions sleep on the bed with them.

Many people share the bed with their dogs. Sometimes a dog or two will decide to sleep in my bed, but for the most part the gang prefers their own beds. While there is a bed for each of our dogs, at bedtime the first dog into the bedroom gets the first choice of beds. Often Wanda, who is the straggler when coming to bed, checks out the two occupied beds before deciding to sleep in either the remaining bed, on the floor, or in my bed.

Doggie in the market for new bed? He is one lucky dog. Designer and custom-made dog beds are all the rage. No matter what your or your dog's taste, you are bound to find a bed to suit both of you.

A Bed Fit for a King

Karen's For People + Pets in New York City carries luxurious European-made dog beds. These handcrafted wooden beds are the ultimate in canine luxury. Beds like the special-order Louis XVI bed feature hand-carved mahogany frames, gold trim, velvet upholstery, and embroidered throw cushions. All upholstery is removable for dry cleaning. As you may have already guessed the ultimate in canine luxury does not come cheap. Treating your dog like Louis XVI will set you back a royal $3,900.

Beastly Beds

While living in Great Britain, designer Diana King observed many beautifully designed dog beds in people's homes. After returning to the United States, she could not find any beds that looked as beautiful or were made with the same quality. And since King lives in the country, it is not practical for her dogs to sleep on her own furniture after romping around outside all day. King realized her dogs both needed and deserved a bed of their own. Consequently she started designing her own line of dog beds called Beastly Beds (not to be confused with Beastly Furnishings).

Beastly Beds is a collection of traditionally made, "real furniture" dog beds that are hand finished and painted and complement a variety of interior design styles. The wood beds come with a coordinating cushion to enhance the look of the bed while making it comfortable for Rover. King also does custom work, making special cushions or working with special fabrics.

Some of Beastly Beds' designs include the Country Cottage, which is an old-fashioned, hand-painted wooden bed. The bed has a relaxed feeling and is great for a home with country accents. The cushion is deep filled to keep dogs warm and snuggly. The bed comes in antique white with a black-and-cream checked cushion or in Maine blue with a red-and-blue floral cushion. The Country Cottage bed is suitable for dogs weighing up to fifty pounds. For a more regal style, the Regency is a solid mahogany four-poster bed with ebonized uprights and gold finials. The bed has a rich antique finish and will go with a variety of room decors. The bed comes with a tailored green velvet cushion cover that easily slips off the foam base and is machine washable. The Regency is best for small and medium dogs like pugs, Jack Russell terriers, and Italian greyhounds.

Beastly's latest style is the Zelda. The Zelda is a contemporized "Recamier" and is made from mahogany. Like the Regency, the bed comes with a machine washable green velvet cushion. The bed is best suited for dogs under thirty-five pounds.

Beastly's Big Dog Bed is one of my favorites. Nearly all of the upscale dog beds are made for dogs weighing less than sixty pounds. So dogs like my Berry and Wanda are often left out. The Big Dog Bed, which is available by custom order only, is suitable for dogs weighing up to 125 pounds. The rectangular bed is hand painted with subtle tones. A dark plaid cushion sits inside the wooden frame making it perfect for the library, living room, or bedroom. The cushion cover zips off and is machine washable. The bed is large, however, measur-

Beastly Beds/Pig Farm Photo

ing 37" × 26". Consequently the bed is not suitable for homes with very limited space.

A Dog Named Wally

The WallyBed was named for a beloved dog named Wally. Out of frustration from using other pet beds, Wally's owners came up with the idea for a practical and durable dog bed. Wally, of course, was the original bed tester, and he loved it. To see if other dogs would love the beds as well, Wally enlisted some of his canine friends. They loved their WallyBeds, too, preferring the WallyBed to their regular beds. Hence, the first WallyBed was born. Since then, the WallyBed line has expanded to make sure that there is a WallyBed to suit all dogs.

The Standard WallyBed is best suited for home use and has a square shape with rounded corners. The design and assorted sizes give dogs room to curl up while leaving plenty of space on all sides for their full body to be on the bed. To blend with different dog colors and home decors, the beds come in Cream Shearling, Brown Bear, or faux Cheetah, Leopard, Gray Lynx, and Cow fur prints. Dogs love the beds because they are so comfortable; people love them because they're machine washable and dryable. And traveling dogs will be yapping with delight to learn that they never have to be without their WallyBed. Wally also has carrier/crate beds to fit in a variety of standard crates and carriers for dogs.

Wally has something extra special for the small short-haired guys. Small- to medium-size dogs will love cuddling up in the Hooded WallyBed. The opening of this unique bed is supported enough for the pet to be able to get in the pouch, but is soft enough to rest as a cover over your little doggie. The versatile bed is reversible. It can also be turned over and used as a regular bed or cushion.

A Bed That's the Bow Wow

If you and your dog love animal prints and fur, then you'll both lie down for the beds from Bow Wow Meow. Bow Wow Meow's beds are made with 100 percent acrylic faux fur and are as soft as the real thing. And to make the beds even better, the covers are 100 percent machine washable.

Owner Lisa Love started the company in 1997. She got the idea for the beds after buying some faux fur that looked so much like pelted mink that "she just had to buy it." Not knowing exactly what she was going to do with the fur, she spread it out on the floor of her home. Her two dogs—Buddy, a miniature Yorkie, and Katie, a Jack Russell—came right over and plopped down on the fur. Since the pair liked the fur so much, Love decided to cover their existing dog beds in the fur. The dogs loved them.

Love believes that the fur-covered beds are a natural for dogs, particularly when the fur is the same color as the dog's fur. As Love explains, "Young puppies never sleep alone. They sleep in piles with their siblings and mother. Consequently it is instinctive for dogs to want to lie against soft fur." Love also believes that it is instinctive for dogs to want to camouflage themselves in fur similar to their own color.

Originally Love only made beds for small dogs. Although she had received many requests to make larger beds, she preferred to stick with the small beds. Love changed her mind, however, when she was sent a photo of Lizzie, an eighty-pound doberman pinscher sheepishly curled up in the tiny bed. Lizzie inspired Love to introduce a second, larger line of beds.

Bow Wow Meow's original beds are oval-shaped, measure 16" × 20", and are six inches tall at their highest point. The base of the beds features various fur animal prints, while the top rims of the beds are trimmed in extra "lux-furry-ous" faux fur. The bed rims are lower in the front to allow your dog easy access to the bed. The small beds are available in several fabulous fur styles including The Hollywood Pet Bed, The Parisian Pet Bed, and the Sable Mink Pet Bed.

The larger beds are rectangular shaped and measure 35" × 45". The beds have refillable interior pillows with shredded foam. The beds come in two styles: The Cappuccino Dog Bed and the Ocelot & Mink Dog Bed.

Affordable Comfort

Here is proof that a great dog bed doesn't have to cost you a paw and a leg. The Bowser Donut Bed is a favorite among many pet boutique owners. As the name implies the bed looks like a donut. The outer ring provides comfort and security and the removable inner cushion can double as either a crate or travel mat. The Donut Bed is made with heavyweight upholstery fabrics for great durability. Fabrics include 100 percent brushed cotton or sueded microvelvet in many colors and patterns. All fabrics are color safe and are 100 percent machine washable. The bed is overstuffed with high-memory polyester fiberfill to ensure long-lasting spring and form.

Sleeping Dogs

This is a bed bound to be a conversation piece. Snugga Luvs has designed a whimsical dog bed with canvas dog detail portraying a sleeping dog. The bedcover is made of a durable soft fleece and is filled with 100 percent Poly fiber. The bedcover is removable and machine washable. The Snugga Luvs bed is cream and comes with either cream or black dog features.

Call of the Wild

Lions and tigers and bears. Oh my! Everyone's wild about the Wild Animal Plush Toy Pet Beds, which are designer pet beds that are shaped in the form of wild animals. They are some of the most adorable beds I have ever seen. These original beds are made from a range of plush fabrics with airbrushed details. Each bed is hand stuffed and is fabricated with a special quilting technique. One of the bed's unique features is a sculptured, nestlike cavity to cradle and shelter your dog. Each design has lifelike soft contours for ultimate comfort.

The beds feature various wild animals lying on their backs. Your dog lies in a cavity on top of the animal's stomach and is cuddled by the animal's head and four paws. Among the original wild animal designs available are Jasmine the Giant Panda, Shelley the Harp Seal, Savanna the Lion Cub, Rexxy the Lion, Eugene the NW Brown Bear, and Moonshadow the Sea Otter. The beds measure from twenty-nine inches to thirty-five inches long. There is also a larger bed, Bronte the South African Leopard Cub. Bronte is thirty-six inches long and features a twenty-four-inch cradle area.

Fairy Tail Ending

Every fairy tale has a happy ending. For the dog living the fairy tale life, designer Sheila Parness has created a line of beds that will ensure your dog has a happy ending each day.

Perhaps Parness's most magnificent bed is a plumed bed that is a replica of one manufactured in eighteenth-century France for the canines of royalty. The four-poster mahogany bed is three feet by four feet and is made of imported silk with four hand-carved pineapples painted in goldleaf. The bed is accented with hand-curled ostrich feathers and silk pompoms. The bed shown (see photograph) is similar to one that Madame Pompador had for her own dog at Versailles. Ms. Parness presented the bed as a gift to France for the Versailles palace.

Sheila Parness/Sheila Parness

There's More

Still haven't found a bed that's just right? In addition to the beds already mentioned, catalogs like *In the Company of Dogs, L.L.Bean, Doctors Foster and Smith,* and *Frontgate* carry selections of high quality dog beds in a variety of price ranges.

47. Cover Up

For some dogs no bed can replace the feel of cuddling up in their very own blanket. A fellow doggie parent, Ann, shared with me that she had spent a fortune in dog beds and furniture trying to find something that her Phoebe would use. Ann hated the old blanket that Phoebe loved, but Ann did not have the heart to take it away until she could find something else that her precious pooch would use. Ann lamented, "It would be like taking away Linus's blanket." Finally, hundreds of dollars later, Ann came across a doggie quilt in a catalog. Phoebe loved it, and Ann finally tossed out that old blanket. Dogs like Phoebe who prefer the feel of a blanket to a bed or just love to cover up, will love these attractive options.

Cashmere Comforts

Chic Doggie by Corey has a hand-stiched, ultra-soft 100 percent cashmere blanket that will have your dog basking in the lap of luxury. The blankets come in a variety of colors and are trimmed with doggie print ribbon. They are adorned with either heart- or bone-shaped soft leather appliqués. Or if you prefer the blankets can be custom-monogrammed with your doggie's name or favorite saying. The blankets are also an elegant way to keep your precious pooch from shedding on your furniture. To match the blanket, Chic Doggie also makes cashmere pillows with bone-shaped appliqués. But beware, I have been told that once a canine goes cashmere, she never goes back.

Is Spike looking for something a little less feminine? The canine quilts from GEORGE will give him something to lie down for. Their quilts come in a variety of designs from neutral to trendy. One of my favorites is the Brown Corduroy Quilt, which features the GEORGE stick logo with soft creme sherpa on the underside. Or for your perfect little angel the Holy Dog Quilt displays a dog with a halo over his head.

Of course, you can also find beautiful quilts or comforters at most home-interior stores. If you're good with a needle and thread, you can always make your own doggie quilt. You can find quilt patterns at local craft shops as well as free quilt patterns on the Internet. And if sewing is not your thing, a local craft store can likely recommend someone who makes quilts.

Think Your Dog Is Spoiled?

Just how far will you go to keep your canine comfortable at night? For a long time I thought that I was the only dog parent who practiced "contortion sleeping." That is, sleeping in uncomfortable positions to accommodate the dogs sleeping on the bed. However, I was surprised to learn just how far dog parents will go to keep their "children" comfortable at night.

Beth Miller puts her Beagle, Howie, under the covers with her at night. She also shares her pillow with him even though his snoring keeps her up half the night.

Kelly and John Klosterman's Great Danes each have their own bedrooms and queen-size beds. Every night the dogs are tucked in and read a bedtime story.

Jane sends her husband to the bedroom down the hall every time he snores, while her rottweiler, Duke, is free to snore as loud as he likes.

Dina Morris had a custom bed, complete with satin sheets, designed for her Yorkie, Candy.

Helen and David Sherman leave the TV on at night because it is the only way that their lab/shepherd mix will sleep.

Angel is a 150-pound mastiff who insists that his human companion, Leslie, hug him while they sleep. If Leslie removes her hand, Angel takes her hand in his mouth and puts it back. If she moves her hand again, Angel starts whining and pawing at her arm to put it back.

48. Bedtime for Bowser

What dog wouldn't have sweet dreams after being read a bedtime story by his human mom or dad? Inspired by her dachshunds, Cooper, Slate, and Maddy Lou, Leigh Ann Jasheway wrote *Bedtime Stories for Dogs* (Andrews McMeel Publishing). The book is a collection of canine versions of fairy tales and nursery rhymes. Your dog will love to curl up to hear the tales of "The Three Little Pugs" or the nursery rhyme "Three Small Dogs." Reading the stories to your dog is not only a great way to send your dog off to sleep, it is also a great way for you to wind down after a stressful day.

49. Go to Your Room

Toby has his very own bedroom, TV/playroom, and a spa room. You are probably thinking that Toby is one lucky child. Lucky? Yes. Child? Well, a child with four legs. Toby is a German shepherd. When it comes to interior decorating, many people are keeping their doggies in mind. Builders and interior designers report that dog rooms are becoming increasingly popular. And believe it or not, it is not uncommon for dog lovers to request that builders install such dog amenities as designated doggie showers, private stairways, and terraces.

Usually spare bedrooms, dog rooms may look like any other kid's bedroom with the exception of the dog motif. With the wide variety of dog-sized furniture now available, the possibilities for decorating are endless. Some lucky dogs have their very own TV, VCR, and stereo. One couple even installed a door so that their dog could enjoy some afternoon rays on an outdoor terrace.

Monique, a beagle, has a bedroom (see photo) complete with a custom-built Victorian doghouse with a stained-glass window. The room is decorated with canine-theme artwork and accessories including a custom-painted toy box for all of her toys. Like any other little girl she even has her own jewelry box for her collection of necklaces.

How's this for canine comfort? One California couple took the concept of canine comfort to a new height. Several years ago the couple made the news when they put a four-room addition on their home for their beloved pooches. The addition consisted of a TV room decorated with artwork, a grooming room, and an art gallery with portraits of dogs. There is also a "repose" room for peace and quiet.

Janet Sanders

🦴 50. In the Doghouse

Normally I feel that dogs should share our homes with us and
should not be banished to an outdoor doghouse. But if your
dog is lucky enough to have one of the following houses, you
might never be able to coax him back into yours.

There is a company that will custom design and build the
doghouse of Rover's dreams. La Petite Maison, known for
their custom children's playhouses, arose from interior
designer Michelle Pollak's desire to design for children. Looking through a design magazine she noticed several playhouses
that she thought were fabulous. She immediately picked up
the phone and called the builder. At the time, Alan Mowrer
was only building the playhouses as a part-time hobby, but it
didn't take long before building playhouses became a full-

time job for him. After several requests from customers the company started offering custom doghouses.

All of La Petite Maison's houses are places that your dog can be proud to call home. While the homes can be completely customized to your specifications features in previous houses have included a copper roof and a bay window so that your dog can keep an eye on outdoor activities. The home exteriors are highlighted by elegant entranceways with swinging doors. The home is constructed with "human home" quality materials and is extremely durable. Homes can be customized with finished drywall interior, crown molding, Plexiglas French windows, exterior synthetic stucco, and wood shutters. There is even a covered rear dog entrance in case your dog needs to make a quick getaway.

La Petite Maison's houses boast spacious interiors and hardwood or stone floors. Various wallcoverings are available.

La Petite Maison/Dale Swenarton

One home included hand-painted dog-theme wallpaper featuring bones and paw prints. Most dog parents choose to adorn the walls with dog-theme artwork. The homes can also be equipped with air-conditioning and interior low-voltage recessed cam lighting so your doggie is never left in the dark.

As a final touch you can add flower boxes to match the house. But it is up to you to plant the flowers. (Be sure not to plant flowers that are toxic to your precious pooch). All of their homes can be customized to fit your dog's size or your space requirements. La Petite Maison will even build a doghouse that is a replica of your own house. As you may have already guessed, custom homes do not come cheap. Houses start at $5,000 and, according to Michelle Pollak, "The sky is the limit!" Because the homes are too large to be shipped, they are built on site, anywhere in the country.

Maybe being in the doghouse really isn't so bad.

When a Dog's Home Is a Castle

You may never live in the mansion of your dreams, but there is no reason that your dog can't. The Neoclassical Pet Mansion is the perfect gift for the dog that is the king or queen of the manor. Hand designed in Great Britain for the Parness Collection, the mansion is made of hard wood and is hand painted in pure gold. Like a true castle the indoor mansion has a domed top with ball finial, three circular windows, curved breakfront façade, and a rear hinged door for dogs that like to sneak out the back. On the inside there is a down-filled green velvet cushion for doggie comfort.

While the mansion is much cheaper than the human version, it still boasts a royal price of nearly $14,000.

Sheila Parness

Make It Yourself

If you are like me, the prospect of building a castle for your dog does not exactly have you running for the hammer and nails. I'm afraid that any doghouse that I would build would soon have a condemned sign hanging on the front door. Thank goodness not everyone possesses my less than great handyman skills. Those of you handy with a hammer might want to build Rover his very own palace. *Making Pet Palaces: Princely Homes and Furnishing to Pamper Your Pets* by Leslie Dierks (Lark Books) offers more than thirty-five projects including outdoor palaces, indoor mansions, imaginative play spaces, and even retro-fifties feeding stations. Designs run from whimsical to elegant and rustic to contemporary. The designs are inexpensive, easy to make, and very impressive.

Fine Barkitecture

Want to check out some of the greatest doghouses ever made? For the ultimate in canine architecture check out the book *Barkitecture* by Fred Albert (Abbeville Press). The book assembles a collection of the most fantastic doggie homes ever built. The book includes doghouses of all shapes and sizes including ones modeled after the stealth bomber, a Chanel handbag, and even an accordion player. Commentary including the creator's inspiration and even the dog's reaction accompany each house.

Petchitecture

Petchitecture is an annual event put on by Pets Are Wonderful Support (PAWS), a nonprofit organization that helps those with AIDS keep their pets. The event showcases architectural and artistic designs built for some of the nation's most prominent pets. For the event, prominent architects and interior designers are partnered with celebrity pet owners. Past dog owners and dogs have included Elizabeth Taylor and her Maltese, Sugar, and Magic from the Old Navy commercials. Designs have sold for as high as $1,500. Petchitecture has become an annual tradition in San Francisco held each year in early spring.

The Pet-Iculars

Beastly Furnishings, 402–392–1976, www.beastlyfurnishings.com

Karen's For People + Pets, 1195 Lexington Ave, New York, NY 10028, 212–472–9440

Beastly Beds, 518–398–6617, www.beastlybeds.com

Gucci Dog Bed: select Gucci boutiques

WallyBed: Max Enterprises, select retail locations, www.wallybed.com

Bow Wow Meow Store for Pets: select retail locations, www.barkavenue.net

Donut Bed, Bowsers Beds: select retail locations

Snugga Luvs: select retail locations

Wild Animal Plush Toy Pet Beds: www.epetbeds.com

Chic Doggie blanket: Chic Doggie by Corey, 212-752-WOOF, www.chicdog.com

GEORGE dog blanket: 2411 California at Fillmore, San Francisco, CA, or 1829 4th Street, Berkeley, CA, 877-344-5454

La Petite Maison, Denver, CO, 877-404-1184, www.lapetitemaison.com

Sheila Parness: London, UK, 011 44 207 338 4966

8.

Dog Care

*There's just something about dogs that makes you
feel good. You come home, they're thrilled to see
you. They're good for the ego.*

—JANET SCHNELLMAN

*According to the American Animal Hospital
Association more than 75 percent of pet owners feel
pangs of guilt when they leave their pets behind.*

You know the feeling. You are leaving for work or a trip.
Your doggie comes to the door with you thinking that he
is coming, too. When you tell him he has to stay, he probably
gives that sorrowful look that leaves you feeling like the worst
dog parent in the world. Some dogs don't stop with a look.
Wanda whines. Berry cries. Some dogs even resort to destruction to convey their displeasure at being left behind.

Luckily for you and your dog there are alternatives to leaving him home alone all day long. Doggie daycare centers are
springing up all over the country. Pet sitters and dog walkers
are now commonplace. And luxury dog resorts welcome the
dogs of vacationing parents. There are even ways to make
your stay-at-home dog feel less alone.

So, if you are tired of feeling guilty every time you leave
the house, look no farther. The gang and I sniffed out some

grrrreat doggie daycares, resorts, pet sitters, and easy tricks to keep your doggie happy while you are away. You may find that your dog has a better time than you do.

If you are lucky, there are several doggie daycare facilities or kennels in your area. Choosing the best one for your pet can be difficult. Elizabeth Gabriel from The Dog House offers these tips for choosing a good doggie daycare or kennel.

1. Owner participation. A good owner is onsite the majority of the time. "I don't care how much people are paid. If it is not your business, you will not take care of it like you would if you owned it."

2. Are there enough people on staff to handle all of the dogs? Is the facility large enough to accommodate all of the dogs?

3. Does the center have an outdoor play area?

4. Are large and small dogs separated from each other?

5. How much do the people owning/running the daycare know about dogs and behavior? If they offer agility equipment, do they know how to use it safely?

6. Is the facility clean? "We pride ourselves on being so clean you could eat off the floor." (Gabriel concedes that she has not tried this personally.)

7. Does the facility have good ventilation? Good ventilation curbs smells and airborne diseases.

8. Is the place dog proofed? Meaning: Are there any exposed wires begging to be chewed? Are there any nails sticking out? Are outlets covered when not in use?

9. Door access. What separates the front door from the area where the dogs are playing? Distance? Barriers? At The Dog House they use a double gate system so that there is

not direct access to the lobby. A dog or person must open one gate and close it behind them before opening the next gate, thus creating a "holding pen." In addition anyone entering the facility must be "buzzed in." This helps reduce the chances of a dog slipping out the front door.

10. What are the facility's health policies? Which vaccinations are required by the daycare? Does the facility keep track of vaccination due dates or do they rely on the owner?

11. Does the facility allow surprise inspections? You should be suspicious of daycares or kennels that require appointments for visits.

12. Do not choose a facility based upon how "cute" or "high-tech" it may be. Gabriel adds, "Internet cameras may let you see your dog playing, but they do not let you know how the facility smells."

51. Every Dog Has His Daycare

Nap time, playtime, movie time, and treat time. No roughhousing or you are sent to the corner. Sounds like the good old days of kindergarten. Except in this class the kids wear collars and eat off the floor. Daycare has gone to the dogs.

Doggie daycare is a growing trend. These facilities are sniffing their way into most major cities across the country. Doggie daycare has become so pupular that many doggie daycare centers can not keep up with the demand from busy owners wanting care, entertainment, and exercise for their furry friends. In fact prior to San Francisco's extremely pupular K9 to 5's move to a larger space, anxious doggies were placed on a waiting list of up to a year.

Most dog owners think of their dogs as their children. To

many of us leaving a dog home alone all day is like leaving a child home alone all day. Just as we do, dogs need companionship and interaction. At doggie daycare dogs play, go for walks, and make friends with other dogs and people. Best of all for many tired, overworked parents is the fact the dogs come home tired and ready for bed.

As I toured doggie daycares across the country I found that the West Coast has the best selection of high-quality doggie daycare. In fact the Los Angeles area has some of the best in the country. Not to say that the East Coast doesn't have its share of doggie daycares. But when it comes to cleanliness, size, amenities, staff friendliness, and owner accessibility, it's hard to beat the West Coast daycares.

So, just what goes on at doggie daycare? Here's a look inside of some tail-wagging, trendy doggie daycares.

The Dog House

The Dog House in Los Angeles hosts approximately thirty dogs a day. The doggie daycare is designed to be appealing to dogs and people alike with murals and artwork covering the walls and plenty of light inside. During their daily visits, dogs participate in paw painting, ceramics, swimming, sunbathing, story time, and movie time. And in case you're wondering, the ceramics consists of making paw-print impressions to bring home to Mom and Dad. Dogs are also surrounded by lots of toys and make use of the very popular wading pool.

Open since 1994, the doggie daycare was one of the first doggie daycares in the country. Owner Elizabeth Gabriel originally operated a very successful dog-walking business. She thought it would be great if there was a place where doggies could play all day while their parents where away at work. There were already daycares for children, why not for dogs? Soon after, dogs started to love being sent to The Dog House.

Holidays are extra special days at The Dog House. For instance on Valentine's Day all the female dogs pose for pictures dressed in boas and pearls. And although the males do not get dressed up, they do pose for pictures in front of festive red foil background.

The Dog House is also home to the Hollywoof Spa where doggies are treated to a day of luxury. Among the services at the spa are massages, manicures and pedicures, medicated baths, and even an herbal wrap. There is also a retail section that carries unique doggie products. An added bonus is that your dog may be able to rub paws with some celebrity pets. Past and present clients have included the pooches of Kevin Costner, Courtney Thorne-Smith, Carrie-Anne Moss, Marilyn Manson, Elisabeth Shue, and Geena Davis.

Elizabeth noted that The Dog House is willing to go the extra mile for their clients. She believes in spoiling the owner as well as the dog adding that regular clients (canine clients, that is) receive free baths. She has also escorted dogs to weddings, picked up boneless, skinless chicken breasts for an owner short on time, and has even shuttled pooches back and forth between divorced parents so that the parents would not have to see one another.

Hollywood Hounds

Across from the Chateau Marmont Hotel, Hollywood Hounds has been called the dog equivalent of La Costa or Canyon Ranch. The quaint cottage is decorated with colorful murals and boasts a palm-shaded patio with a gazebo for celebrations. Previous clients have included the dogs of Julia Roberts, Paula Abdul, and Ozzy Osborne.

Inside, the facility doggies have a view of the garden and a hundred-foot run. Outdoors, the daycare has lots of exercise equipment, including a tennis ball machine for those dogs who love to fetch and fetch and fetch. Dogs also participate in friendly games of floor hockey. As I envisioned dogs running around with hockey sticks in their mouths, I learned from owner Susan Marfleet that in the game of dog hockey the handlers hit the balls around and the dogs chase them.

Hollywood Hounds is known for its "Grrroom Rrroom" where dogs enjoy makeovers by Oscar Casabelo (the Jose Eber of canine coiffure). Dogs wishing to be pampered can enjoy shiatsu massage, "pawdicures," or maybe even some highlights for their fur. Later dogs can also catch up on the latest fashions in the boutique. Dog have an upcoming special event? Hollywood Hounds loves to host doggie birthday parties, bark mitzvahs, and weddings in the gazebo.

According to a PETsMART Survey 27 percent of pet owners arrange for daycare for pets.

Hounds Lounge

Hounds Lounge offers dogs a full day of fun and social activities. Sisters Ann Marie Spinelli and Karen Spinelli-Madigan own and operate the daycare and grooming facility. The pupular doggie daycare has a large indoor play area that has lots of slides, tunnels, and toys to keep dogs occupied during the day. Dogs who prefer a more relaxed day can lounge on one of several couches to watch doggie videos or take a little nap, while sun worshipping dogs can catch a few rays on the back patio.

Along with daycare Hounds Lounge has a state of the art grooming salon where your dog can enjoy a relaxing bath in a deep-cleansing Jacuzzi bathing system. The salon only uses organic products. Doggies with dry skin or other skin problems can be treated to a hot oil treatment. Or, if you really want to pamper your pooch, treat her to a half-hour massage from Ann Marie, a certified masseuse (certified human masseuse, that is) who has plenty of experience kneading away canine aches and pains.

In addition to daycare and grooming services Hound's Lounge also offers shuttle services to the veterinarian or to and from your home. Hound's Lounge will happily organize and host a dog event complete with music, games, party hats, ice cream, and a piñata full of treats. Realizing that not all dogs are daycare material, they also offer pet sitting and dog walking services.

K9 to 5

K9 to 5 is one of the most popular doggie daycares in the country. Each day the daycare hosts up to seventy canines, sixty adults and ten puppies. The secret to the daycare's success is their constant effort to provide doggies with plenty of one-on-one attention throughout the day. Owner Laura Smith explains that the attention includes petting, praise, and extra

K9 to 5 / Amanda Jones

loving. Dogs are given plenty of exercise at the daycare. To ensure this, each dog is walked daily and is able to play all day with other dogs in the supervised play area. K9 to 5 also has lots of toys for dogs to play with and even a jungle gym for dogs to practice their agility exercises. The daycare also has several dens for dogs wanting a little peace and quiet.

K9 to 5 also offers a puppy program, which was one of the first in the Bay area. According to Smith one of the goals of the program is to teach puppies important social skills. A trainer works with the pups teaching them beginning obedience commands and teaching them proper behavior such as what to chew and what not to chew. The program also helps you with the all-important crate and house training by teaching your dog the appropriate places to eliminate.

Something that sets K9 to 5 apart from other doggie daycares is their use of aromatherapy. K9 to 5 actually has an in-house aromatherapist who selects essential oils that create a relaxing atmosphere for the dogs. Smith explains that in the mornings a soothing and calming scent such as lavender is diffused through the air in the dogs' play area. As a result the dogs become noticeably calmer. The scents are used to neutralize doggie tensions and encourage the canines to play nice.

Fuzzy Buddys Daycare

Before Barb Sanderson opened Fuzzy Buddys, she lived the corporate life. Faced with putting together "the look" every morning before going to work, she decided that enough was enough. Knowing that Seattle was a very dog friendly city and realizing that there was a need for such a place, she opened the city's first doggie daycare.

Fuzzy Buddy has a large indoor play area and an outdoor exercise yard that is double fenced for security. Each staff member is certified in animal CPR and first aid. They are also experienced in both handling and training.

Inside, there are plenty of dog beds, toys, and even couches for dogs wanting to chill out during the day. Outside there are kiddy pools and agility equipment. Dogs also participate in activities such as blowing bubbles and soccer. Although I have never witnessed one myself, I have been told that doggie soccer matches are quite the sight.

Doggie Do and Pussycats Too!

Doggie Do and Pussycats Too! is not only a first-class grooming salon, it is also one of the best doggie daycares in the city. The daycare facility is completely cageless and has succeeded in effectively and gently socializing dogs of many different breeds. Owners Howard Binder and Larry Roth note that many of the dogs who come on a daily basis have formed little doggie "cliques." They are enthusiastic when they see their other doggie buddies and can't wait to get to daycare in the morning.

The attendants (also known as *fun counselors*) instigate doggie play periods, playing games that promote aerobic exercise. At other times the fun counselors read children's storybooks to the eager doggies. After a midday nap, lunch is served. Doggie Do and Pussycats Too! only serves high quality food and springwater as well as organic biscuits for mid-morning and mid-afternoon snacks.

The facility has an outdoor courtyard where doggies are taken to frolic (weather permitting) and to enjoy sunshine and fresh air. And because the courtyard is completely enclosed by tall brick walls, doggies can safely romp and play off leash.

Binder and Roth have plans to open a truly five-star doggie hotel in early 2001. The Ritz-Canine Hotel will boast suitelike accommodations and a magnificent sky-top play solarium for the canine guests. In the entranceway of the chic hotel hangs a crystal chandelier while a spiral staircase leads to private suites. The hotel will also have a twenty-four hour attending staff as well as one of New York's renowned veterinarians and his staff on the premises every day.

Dog-ma

Dog-ma is a seven thousand square foot indoor/outdoor daycare and cageless boarding facility located less than a mile from the United States Capitol and the Supreme Court. It has the distinction of being the first facility of its kind in the D.C. area.

According to an article in *Roll Call*, owner Rebecca Bisgyer gave up a long-hours corporate job realizing that it was getting in the way of caring for her own dogs. After coming home after twelve hours of work she felt guilty looking into the eyes of her dogs. Now her daycare caters to the people living the life she once lived.

A day at Dog-ma includes group and individual play, toys snacks, naptime, and general obedience. If dogs prefer they can lounge in the TV room on plush dog beds or a sink in a cushy sofa. Dog-ma is not for every dog. They only accept well socialized, non-aggressive dogs that have been spayed or neutered.

In addition to daycare, the facility offers bathing and grooming. They also have an HMO (Health Maintenance On-Site) in which the staff monitors vaccination, heartworm, and flea control and lets you know when it is time for updates. They have a veterinarian who visits weekly for checkups and shots. And for busy clients Dog-ma offers a doggie shuttle.

Canine Recreation

You might be surprised to find that nearly 40 percent of our canines are overweight. Like many Americans, dogs eat too many treats and get too little exercise. Many of you are probably thinking it's hard enough to keep yourself in shape let alone your dog. What's a dog parent to do? Enter canine recreation centers. Canine recreation centers are becoming the bark of the town. These centers offer the same services as traditional doggie daycare facilities. However they place a large emphasis on doggie exercise. It should come as no surprise that the craze started in health-and-beauty-conscious Los Angeles. But these health-conscious clubs are sniffing their way into other parts of the country. Here is one canine recreation center that received two paws up from their four-legged members.

The Loved Dog Co.

The Loved Dog Co. is a doggie daycare/cage-free kennel that was proclaimed "Best of the Best . . . a Disneyland for dogs" by *Good Morning America*. The unique facility has also been featured in *Marie Claire* and *Travel Weekly*, and on CNN. Owner Tamar Geller opened the facility out of her love for dogs. After serving as an Israeli intelligence officer, Geller had the opportunity to observe wolves in their natural habitat. Her observation of wolves transformed into diligent study and fueled her mission to improve the quality of life for both dogs and their owners.

Geller's philosophy is apparent at The Loved Dog. The doggie daycare goes above and beyond traditional daycares by providing its daytime residents with not only interaction with other dogs but also lots of physical activity. The emphasis at The Loved Dog Co. is on fitness. But not people-type fitness.

You won't find aerobic equipment or classes at this canine recreation center. Instead doggies play all day in an indoor park that is equipped with tunnels and slides. Additionally dogs engage in fun activities such as tug of war, chasing, and fetching. On request, The Loved Dog Co. will also provide swimming lessons at a nearby lake for doggies that love the water.

The Loved Dog Co. also has the distinction of being Southern California's first totally cage-free boarding kennel. Dog owners need not feel guilty leaving their dogs behind at this kennel. After doggie guests play all day at the indoor park, overnight guests retire upstairs to pine-covered (no chain-link fences here) hotel-like mini suites with music. Each suite has a child's bed, and as an added touch a cookie is left on the pillow. Dogs can either sleep alone in their own room or enjoy a slumber party with one of their newfound doggie friends.

52. Playgroups

Want your dog to get his exercise in the great outdoors? Here are some alternatives to the indoors canine recreation scene.

Puppy Pals

At Puppy Pals, dog fitness instructors start picking up their canine clients first thing in the morning. Dogs are divided into playgroups according to size. The big guys meet in one shift while the small guys meet during a second shift. While at the ranch, dogs play ball, Frisbee, run through creeks, and take long walks up and down the hills of the canyons. During the brisk on-leash hikes, dogs enjoy the scenic sights, sounds, and smells of local canyons and mountains. A few of the favorite spots include Will Rogers State

Park, the Michael Lane Fire Road above the Highlands, and Temescal Gateway Park. Sometimes the doggies go for a field trip to the beach for sun, surfing, and sand digging. Before returning the exhausted dogs home, trainers hose down all paws and send doggies home with notes telling canine parents what their dogs did that day.

Eastside Puppy Pals

Eastside Puppy Pals is a playgroup for canines in Bellevue, Washington. According to *Dog Fancy* magazine, Nora Lenz started for dog owners who work all day and have no choice but to leave their dogs home alone all day. Each day dogs are picked up and taken to a designated off-leash area in a local park. The dogs then romp and play together for a couple of hours returning home tired and ready for bed.

53. They're No Last Resort

If you are like me, you hate the idea of putting your dog in a kennel. I can not tell you how many vacations I have skipped because I could not bear putting Berry, Wanda, and Robin in a dreary cement kennel. I have also noted that many kennels have caught on to the fact that dog owners feel the same way I do and now refer to themselves as canine Hyatt Regencies or Hiltons. However upon visiting many of these "luxury" facilities I have been disappointed with some of the kennels' ideas of what luxury means.

However you will be happy to know that there are several pet resorts across the country that are the very definition of canine luxury. These resorts cater to dog owners who truly want their dogs to be pampered while they are away. In contrast to traditional kennels, pet resorts offer many of the canine comforts from home. While a stay in a pet resort may cost you more, you will have the peace of mind knowing that your dog is being pampered with soft bedding, rooms with windows, TVs, and VCRs. Plus many resorts offer much, much more.

The Kennel Club LAX

Several resorts are receiving two paws up from dogs across the country. One of the nicest and largest in the country is The Kennel Club LAX. Situated near the Los Angeles International Airport, The Kennel Club LAX has counted among its guests the pooches of Christina Ricci, Charlize Theron, and Bond-girl Denise Richards.

The kennel offers large indoor suites ranging from standard to luxury accommodations. However the kennel's most popular accommodations are the fourteen individual theme cottages. The cute cottages are decorated as a small child's room and are furnished with a lounge bed, TV, and VCR. I

The Kennel Club, LAX/Clark Prestridge

also noted that the cottages are large enough to hold several canines if your family happens to have more than one four-legged member. And if you want your dog to have the ultimate in pampering, you can check your dog into the VIP suite that comes with all of the cottage amenities with the addition of your doggie's very own twenty-four-hour personal attendant.

The Kennel Club assures dog owners that they can check their worries at the door. They use the most advanced air-purification system available to ensure that doggies remain in a temperature-controlled and virtually viral-free environment. All of the staff members are trained for animal emergencies, and there is a veterinarian on call twenty-four-hours a day.

To keep doggies occupied during their stay, The Kennel Club offers a wide variety of services. There is dog massage, yappy hour (complete with doggie ice cream), doggie daycare, kindercare, a geriatric program, pool time, personalized exercise programs (including a weight reduction program with a treadmill), agility, aerobics, and even a picnic in the park. And to make the getaway complete, pampered pooches are picked up and dropped off in a limousine.

Owner Sharon Graner stresses that the staff of The Kennel Club will go the extra mile to accommodate their clients' requests. And owners have made some unique requests over the years. One owner whose dog stayed in one of the cottages wanted to make sure that it came with cable TV. It seems that his dog loved to watch the stock prices throughout the day. Another client wanted his dog to be taken to McDonald's every day for a Big Mac. Other clients have requested that their dogs be fed filet mignon for dinner, while others make tape recordings of their voices to be played for their dogs at bedtime. Sharon can only remember turning down one request. An owner lamented that his dog was lonely and wanted him to be fixed up with a female dog. Sharon politely told him, "That's not the type of hotel we are running here."

The Cottages at Kennelwood Village/Kennelwood Pet Hotel

The Kennelwood Pet Hotel is recognized as one of the best in the country. Kennelwood offers a variety of accommodations, activities, and locations in the St. Louis area. The hotel provides twenty-four-hour supervision for your dog and has an Electrified Pure Air System that ensures your dog is breathing clean and bacteria-free air.

At Kennelwood, accommodations start with the Standard, which includes an indoor room with adjoining patio, air-conditioning, ceiling-mounted infrared heat, and piped-in music. Of course, pampered dogs preferring something a little more luxurious may choose to spend their vacation in The Cottages at Kennelwood Village. During my visit I noted that all of the rooms are large enough to accommodate roommates and are whimsically decorated.

There are three levels of accommodations within The Cottages at Kennelwood Village. They begin with the KennelClub Suites, which come with TV, VCR, toddler beds, and full housekeeping. The lodges are the next class up and are over seventy-square feet with all the amenities of the suites plus a personal valet. And for the ultimate, your dog can stay in one of the Grand Lodges. The Grand Lodges have all of the amenities of the Lodges but the rooms come with a view. Picture windows allow dogs to enjoy a view of the grounds.

All suites, lodges, or grand lodges receive satellite TV tuned to the Animal Planet Channel. Guests are treated to bedtime stories after their nightly treats. Dogs also enjoy aromas such as vanilla in their suites or lodges. Canine cottage guests are taken out a remarkable five times a day for play and exercise, and the rooms are monitored twenty-four hours a day for cleanliness. And if you wish your dog can enjoy the services of a certified massage therapist. Kennelwood also offers a roomies option. If your dog would like to room with another dog, Kennelwood will arrange for an appropriate roommate for your lonely canine.

The Kennelwood Pet Hotel, the sister hotel to The Cottages at Kennelwood Village, was opened in 1995. The facility offers all the amenities you would expect a fine hotel including Standard to Luxury accommodations, doggie PlaySchool, DayCamp, Bizzy Bones, and Yappy Hour. In addition, guests are taken out five times per day.

The Kennelwood Pet Hotel offers luxury accommodations in the Cabanas and KennelClub Suites. The suites give your dog the opportunity to vacation in such hot spots like the Caribbean, Hawaii, Alaska, and even Fisherman's Wharf. During your dog's stay in the suites, he will have a toddler bed, VCR and satellite TV, and the services of a personal valet.

Paradise Pet Lodge

Paradise Pet Lodge is a five star pet resort that truly resembles paradise. Situated on thirteen acres in Woodinville, Washington, all of the kennel buildings have zone-controlled radiant heat in the floors, multiple skylights, ceiling fans, plants, ventilation systems, and twenty-four-hour music. Accommodations range from standard to luxury.

One of the buildings on the property has an indoor atrium complete with a waterfall. Also located in this building are nine luxury, special theme suites such as the Tropical Suite, Jungle Room, Mountain Lodge, and Oriental Suite. All suites are furnished with beds, televisions or radios, and rugs. The suites are designed for the dog who enjoys "the finer things in life."

While visiting the lodge dogs can participate in a number of activities. Dogs can go for a nature walk through the thirteen-acre complex. They can also take part in individual or group play sessions.

Paradise Pet Lodge is one of the few boarding facilities that offers a canine cuisine menu. All menu items are made on the premises and with human grade ingredients. Menu items include garlic chicken, teriyaki pork, oyster sauce beef, and turkey stew.

Paradise Ranch

Considered the crème de la crème of pet resorts or the non-kennel alternative, Paradise Ranch offers cageless boarding for dogs in a country club setting. Paradise Ranch has two homes on the property for doggie lodging. Both the main house and the Bed and Biscuit Inn are reminiscent of a couple of Spanish-style haciendas.

During their stay, doggies have all the comforts of home. In the daylight hours each guest is given hours of daily access to the outdoor playgrounds and playtime with the other canine guests. Each playground has either a cabana or covered veranda for shade and shelter. One of the most spectacular features of the grounds is the lush tropical landscaping. Vacationing doggies are surrounded with lots of palm trees, plants, flowers, waterfalls, and an in-ground pool shaped like a dog bone. There are even several parrots (in large cages) on the property to give to feeling of a true tropical setting.

The interior decor is as nice as that found in a luxury home. And because people actually live on the property dogs are able to enjoy a true homey atmosphere. Just as they would at home each evening, doggies gather in the family room to watch TV with the nighttime staff. When it is bedtime, the dogs go to sleep in various theme suites. Each suite is actually a full-size bedroom that is tastefully furnished and whimsically decorated. There is a child-size bed in every room. And at night the staff puts down plenty of dog bedding so that the canine guests may have their choice of places to sleep. Each suite also has a daily maid service that changes and makes the bed, fluffs the pillows, and cleans the room. During their stay canines can also opt to sleep with a human bed buddy on a full-size human bed for a nominal fee.

Paradise Ranch owner Kristyn Goddard originally owned a kennel in Texas. After seeing how unhappy the dogs were in the kennel, barking and pacing back and forth, she suggested to her husband, William Davis, that they offer in-home boarding in their own home as an option. Though they were unsure whether or not people would pay the additional fee for in-home boarding, they began offering the service. Soon after, they had a home full of dogs and an empty kennel. They realized that they were on to something. Since Davis was a dog trainer, they could also offer training classes for those dogs not quite ready for in-home boarding. Wanting to move back to their home state of California, Goddard and Davis decided to relocate to the Los Angeles area, which is a natural for their country club-style boarding facility.

Paradise Ranch has been in operation since 1997. The facility is almost always filled to capacity. The SUV that delivers canines to and from their home is almost always in use. One of the most impressive things that I noticed as I toured the facility during a surprise visit was the lack of barking. If you have ever toured a boarding kennel, one of the first things you notice is the deafening sound of barking dogs. During my tour I only noted a stray bark here or there as the dogs were romping around the one and a half acre property. All the dogs appeared to be having a fantastic time.

Unfortunately not all dogs are welcome at Paradise. All

dogs must be spayed or neutered. Dogs must additionally pass a thorough evaluation that ensures they have good social skills and proper house manners. Does your dog have some issues? Paradise Ranch also offers training to get your dog ready to vacation in paradise.

54. A Walk a Day . . .

Dogs say a walk a day keeps the boredom away. Long work hours and hectic schedules often interfere with your dog's walk time. Enter professional dog walkers. Dog walking is booming business in major cities and is a good way to insure your dog receives exercise and socialization without the cost of doggie daycare. Here's a dog walking service that is a paws down favorite with their canine and human clientele.

Pet Mates is one of the best-known and most-reputable dog-walking services in New York City—servicing primarily the East Side of Manhattan. It is also one of the few that provides individual dog walking. Since your dog is the only one being walked, he is given the full, undivided attention of the dog walker. Dogs begging for the opportunity to play with other dogs need not feel alone. Pet Mates will arrange for a visit to a local dog park for a friendly romp.

A recent survey by the American Animal Hospital Association found that 72 percent of pet owners greet their pets at the door before their spouse or significant other.

55. Have Someone Sit So They Can Stay

A dog's bark may be worse than his bite, but everyone prefers his bark.

—ANONYMOUS

Many of today's dog sitters offer so much more than the traditional stop at the house to let the dogs out. While sitters still offer traditional services such as playing with, feeding, and exercising your dog as well as bringing in the paper and mail and watering the plants. In response to demand many now provide midday walks and transportation to the veterinarian or groomer while you are at work. And if you're worried about your beloved dog being home alone at night, most will even arrange for an overnight stay. Plus some sitters do their best to accommodate all special requests such as take-out food orders for canines or extended play visits.

Then there's the next level: hiring a sitter to come and stay the entire time you are away just like you would hire a baby-sitter for your human kids. Finding a good, trustworthy dog sitter is as challenging as finding a baby-sitter, but it is well worth it to eliminate those pangs of guilt as you walk out the door.

When it comes to having human company, my dogs are very spoiled. There are few instances when they are left alone for more than a couple of hours at a time. I am lucky to have an office in my home so that I am able to be around my canine children. And, when I do have to go out of town, I am fortunate enough to have Angie. When she dog sits, she is able to keep the gang in their normal routine. She walks them, feeds them, watches TV with them, takes them for rides in my SUV, and stays overnight with them. She is like another parent to them.

I was really lucky to find someone so awesome to help with the dogs. I have to admit the gang can be quite the challenge at times. In fact, a couple of potential sitters did not make it through their trial run. Whenever someone rings the doorbell or tries to open the front door, Berry and Wanda, with Robin not far behind, charge like a couple of wild dogs, barking all the way. It usually takes a new person a couple of times to learn that is the way the gang greets people and that they are not out looking for a meal. Unfortunately one sitter, upon seeing the three dogs charging toward her, slammed the door shut, ran to her car, and took off. The gang seemed quite pleased with themselves. I was out a doggie sitter. Just in case you are wondering, she never came back.

Got a few bucks? You can always hire a dog nanny. It may sound over the top but there are people who wouldn't have it any other way. Suzie, who has a nanny for her two Yorkies, Tiffany and Eddie, says that she would never think of leaving her precious duo alone, stating, "They get too lonely and sad when no one is around. They are my children, and I want them to be happy." Tiffany and Eddie's nanny not only looks after them when Suzie is busy, but also chauffeurs the pair to the groomers, the veterinarian, and even to the dog bakery for their weekly fill of treats.

Full-time nannies don't come cheap, however. Expect to shell out an average of $35,000 a year for a well-trained, dependable nanny.

⌖56.   Soothing Sounds for the Home Alone Dog

According to the American Animal Hospital Association, nearly a third of pet owners turn on the TV or radio to keep their pets company and over 40 percent leave the lights on while they are away. According to a PETsMART survey, 28 percent of pet owners talk to their pets on the phone or answering machine.

Dog owners have come up with some simple ways to make sure that their doggies are not bored while the family is off at school, work, or running errands. Many dog parents have been known to call home and talk to their canines on the answering machine or the telephone if someone is there to answer. I must confess that when I have been away I have called home and asked my husband to bring the dogs to the phone so that I can talk to them. My husband, who would deny it if asked, has done the same thing. While Berry tries to look for me when he hears my voice on the phone, we found it funny that Berry tries to eat the receiver whenever he hears my husband's voice. I am not quite sure why he does this. It is probably some macho, male thing. As for Wanda and Robin, they seem as if they couldn't care less who is speaking to them on the phone.

Sometimes calling home is not practical. Luckily there are some easy ways to help keep your dog from feeling all alone. I always leave on either the television or stereo. Before we leave for dinner or some other event, I turn on the TV to something that I know that my dogs will like. It just so happens that we have the same taste in movies. Another option is to pop in a couple of your dog's favorite CDs or radio station. My dogs seem to prefer jazz, but I have heard that classical has a calming effect.

There are even CDs made especially to soothe home alone dogs. Genius Products, Inc. introduced a new Pet Tunes line of classical music for pets. To date they have four CDs, *Delighted Doggy, Calming Kitty, Blissful Birdy*, and *Happy Horsy*. Or, if classical is not quite your dog's style, Incentive Media offers *Pet Music*, a three-CD set of soothing music for pets. The set includes *Natural Rhythms, Peaceful Playground*, and *Sunday in the Park*.

57. Bring Your Dog to Work

Why leave your dog at home alone when you can bring him to work? It is not as far-"fetched" as you might think. According to an article in *Dog Fancy* magazine, Wildfire Communications in Lexington, Massachusetts, is one of a growing number of companies that allow employees to bring their dogs to work with them. At dog-friendly workplaces, employees are permitted to set up their workstations with toys, beds, food, and water. Some employees use doggie gates or leashes attached to chairs to make sure that Rover doesn't roam around the office.

On the business end there are some very good reasons to allow dogs into the workplace. According to the American Pet Products Manufacturers Association pet-friendly workplaces had lower absenteeism rates and employees who were more willing to work overtime. Furthermore, the American Humane Association reports increased staff morale and worker productivity as benefits of allowing dogs in the workplace.

58.   Pet-ernity Leave

There's a new trend emerging with brand new dog parents, "pet-ernity." And the good thing is that taking time off for pet-ernity will only cost you a couple of days to a week as opposed to months taken off for traditional maternity leave. While there are no specific statistics as to the number of dog parents who indulge in pet-ernity, the number may be higher than you think. Many excited new dog owners plan their vacation time to coincide with the arrival of their new puppy or vice versa. I have to admit that I am also guilty of this very practice. Though I got Berry and Wanda as adults, I still remember planning their arrival around a slow time in my schedule (Robin was unplanned so I couldn't prepare for her) so that I could spend plenty of time with them their first few days.

Staying home with your puppy during the first day or two does help immensely with house-training because you can take them out much more frequently, and they learn quickly. But while many people attribute days off work with their new puppy to practical issues like house-training, most people really take off to form a bond with their new addition to the family.

However experts warn that spending too much time with your brand-new puppy early on can bring on separation anxiety after you return to work. Consequently if you are a new owner who opts to take time off to spend with your new "baby," you are urged to leave the house for short periods of time so that your dog learns early on that it is OK for you to leave and that you will return.

The Pet-Iculars

The Dog House, W. 3rd Street, Los Angeles, CA, 213-549-9663

Hollywood Hounds, 8218 Sunset Blvd., Los Angeles, CA 90046, 323-650-5551, www.hollywoodhounds.com

Hounds Lounge, 12745 Ventura Blvd, Studio City, CA 91604, www.houndslounge.com

K9 to 5 Daycare, 90 Welsh Street, San Francisco, CA 94107, 415-227-4729, www.k9to5.com

Fuzzy Buddys, 8622 3rd Ave., Seattle, WA 98117, 206-782-4321, www.fuzzybuddys.com

Doggie Do and Pussycats Too!, 567 Third Ave., New York, NY 10016, www.doggiedo.com

Dog-ma, 821 Virginia Ave. SE, Washington, D.C. 20003, 202-543-7805, www.dog-ma.com

The Loved Dog Co., 2100 Pontius Ave., Los Angeles, CA 90025, 310-914-3033, www.theloveddog.com

Puppy Pals, Pacific Palisades, CA, 310-573-0245

Eastside Puppy Pals, Bellevue, WA

The Kennel Club LAX, 5325 W. 102nd Street, Los Angeles, CA 90045, 310-338-9166, www.kennelclublax.com

The Cottages at Kennelwood Village, Kennelwood Village, 2008 Kratky Rd., St. Louis, MO 63114, 314-429-2100, www.kennelwood.com

Paradise Pet Lodge, 10324 Paradise Lake Rd., Woodinville, WA 98072, 360-668-2269, www.paradisepetlodge.com

Paradise Guest Ranch, 10268 La Tuna Canyon Rd., Sun Valley, CA 91252, 818-768-8708, www.paradiseranch.com

Pet Mates, New York, NY, 212-751-5405, www.petmates.com

Genius Pet Tunes, www.amazon.com

Pet Music: Incentive Media, www.amazon.com; www.petmusic.com

9.

Have Dog, Will Travel

Dogs feel very strongly that they should always go
with you in the car, in case the need should arise
for them to bark violently at nothing
right in your ear.

—DAVE BARRY

You have been there before. You want to go on vacation. There is only one problem. What are you going to do with your best friend? He hates to be left behind. You hate to leave him behind. So you just stay home. Well here's some good news! The United States is a much more dog-friendly place than it was ten years ago. In fact, according to a 1999 American Animal Hospital Association survey, 66 percent of pet owners traveled with their pets on at least one occasion. People in the travel industry are finally realizing that a person's dog is not just a pet but a part of the family, and most people don't leave their family behind when they are vacationing. Today a traveling dog is not only welcome more places, but he also may be offered a bowl of water, biscuits, or even gourmet treats upon his arrival.

Dogs love exploring new places. They also provide plenty of entertainment while on the road. But you do have to keep in mind that dogs are like children and traveling with them requires planning, patience, and a good sense of humor.

Sometimes in unknown surroundings dogs will do things

166

that they would never do at home. For example, Wanda thought that jumping off a dock into a canal to chase a duck was a great idea until she could not find a way out. Mom had to jump in after her and lift her up to Dad, who was laughing hysterically up on the dock.

On another trip Wanda decided, much to the dismay of those around us, that the middle of a crowded beach was the best place to relieve herself. (We had just been on an hour walk in a much more private and appropriate area.) Thank goodness I still had a pick-up bag. On the way home from that very same vacation Berry decided that the toll-booth opera-tors were evil beings trying to steal money from us. Every time we pulled up to a toll booth, Berry started barking, growling, scratching, and snapping out my window. I had to park the car and get out each time to pay the toll. Berry terri-fied one woman so much that she jumped back from the win-dow and waved us on. I could go on and on.

But even with the "dog" incidents, David and I still love traveling with our dogs. When we first got the dogs, it was me who searched out dog-friendly vacations. Now David is always on the lookout for places where our dogs will be welcome.

The gang and I did some digging and found some of the country's most dog-friendly places. Each hotel is a paws down favorite with the canines. (Please note that weight and breed restrictions vary from hotel to hotel and pet policies are sub-ject to change.)

59. When the Going Gets "Ruff," Check Into a Luxury Hotel

Unfortunately most luxury hotels across the country are still dog-unfriendly. *GRRR!* But the following hotels are known to be especially hospitable to traveling canines (we've checked out many ourselves). Here's the scoop on some of the country's (or nearby) most dog-friendly hotels.

Four Seasons Hotels

Four Seasons Hotels are some of the most dog-friendly hotels in the world. Forty-eight of their hotels welcome dogs (weight restrictions vary from hotel to hotel). When we relocated to South Florida from Ohio in 1998, we were unable to move into our home right away. Consequently Berry, Wanda, and I called the Four Seasons in Palm Beach our home for a couple of weeks. I will admit that I was surprised to learn that a luxury hotel would accept large dogs. I half expected the hotel staff to take one look at Berry and Wanda (this was before Robin's time) and send us packing. To the contrary, Berry and Wanda were treated like royalty. When we checked into our room, Berry and Wanda found dog bowls, bottled water, dog food, gourmet treats, and pooper-scooper bags waiting for them.

The staff was super friendly. The car valets, in particular, loved visiting with the dogs. Many hotel guests went out of their way to talk to and pet the dogs. Berry and Wanda had never before received so much attention in their lives. They enjoyed every minute of their stay. The hotel concierge even arranged for dog-sitting services so that David and I could enjoy a night out on the town.

The Ritz-Carlton, Chicago, is actually owned by the Four Seasons chain and is one of the most dog-friendly hotels in the country. The hotel offers a pet program that gives canine guests a welcoming gift of Iams dog food and biscuits. For well-heeled dogs who turn their noses up at "dog food," the Ritz offers a "gourrrmet" room service menu that includes entrées such as chopped filet mignon. If your plans don't include your dog, the concierge can arrange for pet-sitting or dog-walking services. For those doggies wanting a little pampering the Ritz Kennel offers full grooming and spa services. And what's a vacation without a little shopping? The Pet Corner in The Shop has leashes, collars, clothing, and treats for dogs.

Le Montrose Suite Hotel

The Le Montrose Suite Hotel was recently renovated to the tune of three million dollars. The beautiful all-suite hotel, which was already known for being a luxurious and discreet hideaway for post-cosmetic surgery care, is also becoming known as the city's most dog-friendly hotel. Celebrity canines have found the hotel a great place to relax during filming breaks. Canine guests at the hotel can choose to relax with a personal pooch massage or aromatherapy grooming. The hotel also has a canine community center where doggies can play with other canine guests. During their stay doggies are able to dine on organic dog food and will be given a keepsake signature bowl and bone. Plus, if your day's plans do not include Rover, the hotel is conveniently located near several of Hollywood's best doggie daycares.

Canine Dining—California Style

If your trip to California happens to bring you to Huntington Beach, you will want to check out The Park Bench Café. DogFriendly.com rates the restaurant as "the most dog-friendly restaurant we have found yet!"

Doggies are made to feel right at home here. The café even has a separate doggie dining area denoted with a sign. Doggies are able to order from their own special section of the menu. Hungry dogs are able to choose from the Hot Diggity Dog (an a la carte hot dog), Bow Wow Wow (skinless chicken), and Doggie Kibble (for dogs that do not eat people food). And if your dog is good and eats all of his dinner, you can reward him with the Chili Paws (a scoop of Vanilla ice cream) for dessert.

Hotel Monaco

The elegant Hotel Monaco was recently restored and is more than happy to accommodate canine guests. The hotel offers a "Bone Appetit" package, which provides doggies with a bone and a ball at check-in and a ceramic bowl and place mat for dining. Canine guests also receive a dog towel and turn-down service that includes fresh baked biscuits, liver biscotti, premium bottled water, and cleanup bags. During their stay, dogs are given temporary tags in case they get lost, and they are invited to the hotel's evening wine tasting. Your dog will be happy to know that the Hotel Monaco is just a short drive away from several of San Francisco's best dog parks.

The Country's Most Dog-Friendly City

As I asked pet-travel experts across the country which city they thought was the most dog friendly, the city named most was San Francisco. For one, you are more likely than not to find places that welcome your canine companion. In addition there are many

*off-leash dog parks where your dog can visit with
"the locals" and learn about the "in places" to visit.
After playtime you and your dog can visit one of
many outdoor restaurants that will happily serve
your dog water and treats. Wendy Ballard, publisher
of the* DogGone *travel newsletter, even found a boat
tour that allowed her beagle, Sparky, to sail under
the Golden Gate Bridge with her family. If you and
your dog are planning a San Francisco trip, you will
want to check out the Web site* DogsbytheBay.com.
*The site has compiled lots of great information
about Bay Area dog parks and dog-friendly restaurants.*

San Ysidro Ranch

The San Ysidro Ranch in Santa Barbara, California, welcomes their canine guests. In fact they will add your pet's
name to the nameplate on your cottage and provide bottles of
"Pawier Water." The Ranch offers a Privileged Pet Program
that includes a doggie turndown service. During his stay, your
doggie can indulge in two types of massage. The "Slow and
Gentle Massage" promises to soothe away fears and encourage
relaxation, while the "Authentic Reiki" massage promises to
balance and align your dog's energies by targeting twelve specific body parts. Your dog may never want to leave.

The Alexis Hotel

The Alexis Hotel in Seattle does not discriminate by
breed. In other words all dogs, big and small, are welcome.
The hotel offers a Deluxe Doggie Pet-Package that includes
distilled water and a doggie dish that you can take home,
healthy treats, a "designer" doggie bed, morning and after-

noon walks, a doggie menu, and a keepsake copy of the *Seattle Dog-Lovers Companion Guide*. And if your dog is frazzled from all the traveling the hotel will even arrange for some sessions with an animal psychologist. The Pet-Package also includes amenities for dog owners. During your stay you are invited to evening wine tastings, morning coffee service, use of a private steamroom, and much more.

The Regency Hotel

The Regency Hotel welcomes dogs of all sizes. In fact the hotel has even hosted Beethoven, the rather large Saint Bernard actor and a rather large German shepherd named Berry. The hotel is located only two blocks from Central Park and four to five blocks from great shopping. The hotel offers treats and water bowls delivered on a silver tray. And there is no additional charge for canine guests. People amenities include twenty-four-hour room service and a two thousand-square-foot fitness center.

SoHo Grand Hotel

Perhaps the most pet-friendly hotel in the country is the SoHo Grand Hotel in New York City. The Hartz Mountain Company owns the hotel. If that name rings a bell, it should. Hartz is the manufacturer of the 2-in-1 pet products. Hotel amenities include a dog room-service menu, in-room kennels, walking services, toys, pillows, doggie daycare, and an on-call vet. In the true spirit of dog friendly the bellboys even carry dog treats (Robin's idea of heaven). And if you happen to arrive dog-less and are longing for company, the hotel will loan you a goldfish.

Taking a Bite out of the Big Apple

Looking for something to do with your dog during your stay in New York? DogFriendly.com lists many activities you and your dog can share. Here are two particularly dog-friendly attractions listed on the site that will provide you and your dog with lots of doggone fun during your stay.

Susan and Art Zuckerman will take you and your dog on a guided NYC Walking Tour. The tours last three to five hours and include historical facts about the Big Apple. Highlights of the tour are visits to Greenwich Village, Soho, the Lower East Side, Little Italy, Central Park, and any other area in Manhattan that you might like to visit. Your guides will also offer suggestions for dog-friendly hotels and restaurants prior to your visit.

If you and your dog are more artsy types, you will want to check out the William Secord Gallery. The gallery specializes in nineteenth-century dog paintings and sculptures. You and your well-behaved dog are both welcome. If you are inspired to have a portrait of your dog done, the gallery can direct you to such renowned artists as Christine Merrill and Barrie Barnett. Merrill, whose portraits start at seven thousand dollars, has painted the pooches of several celebrities including Oprah Winfrey's.

Inn By The Sea

The Inn By The Sea is a charming coastal resort just outside of Portland, Maine. And according to their brochure the

Inn offers several one and two bedroom ocean-view suites for guests traveling with their canine companions. In fact when the Inn first offered the dog-friendly accommodations, they were so popular that they soon doubled the number of rooms available to canines.

At check-in your dog receives a personalized dog tag with the Inn's phone number, as well as a welcome snack. The suites come furnished with special dog amenities including complimentary dog bowls, bones, and pooper scoopers. Over-sized towels are also available to dry your dog after a swim in the ocean. There is even a fenced-in dog play area so that your dog doesn't have to miss out on his daily game of fetch.

For dinner, doggies may order dishes such as Doggie Tapas, Gourmet All-Chuck Burgers, or Gourmet Doggie Bon-Bons. All canine cuisine is served on appropriate doggie ware. The Inn also arranges for dog owners to have their very own concierge service. The pet concierge will arrange for everything from after-dinner dog walking to dog sitting.

The Sutton Place Hotel

The Sutton Place Hotel in Vancouver, British Columbia, knows how to make a dog feel welcome. Canine guests are welcomed with a special "Sit and Stay" check in. As part of the check in, doggies register in a special guest book, noting any special canine preferences, and a Polaroid picture is taken for the guest profile. Those dogs traveling on someone else's dime will definitely want to enroll in the VIP (Very Important Pet) amenity program, which includes a choice of gourmet dinners, including Grilled Alberta Beef T-Bone Steak, served on fine china along with a bottle of premium bottled water. Evening turndown service includes treats from the Three Dog Bakery and a special storybook just for pets. The hotel will even arrange a limousine ride for your doggie to a nearby daycare/spa that offers grooming and massages. Additionally in the true spirit of dog friendly, the hotel will contribute one dollar to the SPCA Youth Program, which educates children about respect and compassion for animals, for every dog owner who fills out a comment card about their dog's stay.

Las Ventanas al Paraiso

Those who truly want to pamper their furry friend will want to check out Las Ventanas Al Paraiso in Los Cabos, Mexico, proclaimed the "quintessential luxury vacation for pooches" by the *DogGone* newsletter. The pampering begins with the airport pickup. While humans are brought iced towels and bottled water, dogs are poured bottled water in bone-shaped dishes. Upon arrival at the hotel dogs are greeted with dog bowls filled with treats and rawhide chews. During their stay dogs are welcome to enjoy all of the services of the world-class resort including stress-reducing massages, pet treadmills, or a walk along the beach. The resort even provides dog-sized cabanas for use by the pool or on your suite's sunroof.

The resort has developed a "Canine Delights" menu that includes Rin Tin Tin (shredded braised beef and steamed rice) and Ranch Dog Fantasy (cubed chicken in gravy). Additionally the chef will prepare made to order food for dogs on a special diet. Of course, each meal is served in stylish metallic bowls with faux gemstones on a bone-shaped place mat.

All of this pampering, however, does not come cheap. Off-season rates begin at $325/night plus an additional $50 for your dog.

Etiquette for Traveling Dogs

When traveling with your dog, be sure to follow these basic rules of pet etiquette. These are a set of rules that I have learned through the years. I am sure to follow them whenever I am traveling with the trio. Dog owners failing to follow these rules are the ones who often cause hotels and motels to change their dog-friendly policies.

1. ALWAYS clean up after your dog. Be sure to bring clean up bags with you. If you forget them, most dog-friendly hotels will have some available.

2. Keep your dog leashed at all times. Other hotel guests may not like dogs as much as you do. This is particularly true with big dogs.

3. DO NOT leave your dog alone in the room unattended. Lonely dogs may be driven to bark, make messes, or even destroy hotel furnishings. Most hotels will help you arrange for dog sitting or will help you find a nearby doggie daycare or kennel.

4. Be sure to hang the DO NOT DISTURB sign on the door while you are in the room. This will prevent the hotel maids from entering the room or other staff members from knocking on the door thus preventing protective outbursts from dogs.

5. Ask the hotel staff where they would like you to take your dog to relieve himself. Often they have designated areas for this purpose.

6. If your dog does destroy or accidentally break an item in the room, do not try to hide it or sneak out of the hotel without telling the staff.

7. Try to make your dog look friendly. Berry and Wanda are friendly dogs and love attention. However many people shy away at the sight of the pair. I have found that something as simple as putting bandannas on the dogs makes

them more approachable and seems to put the hotel staff
more at ease.

60. Canine Camps

If you are one of the thousands of dog owners who believe
that an entire vacation with your dog sounds like the cat's
meow, then you are in luck. Dog camps are popping up all
over the country. Activities at canine camps run the gamut
from agility training to mid-afternoon ice cream. Canine
camp is a great way for you to spend quality time with your
dog while meeting other people who love their dogs as much
as you do.

Camp Gone to the Dogs

Camp Gone to the Dogs in Vermont is one of the oldest
dog camps in the country. People and their canine companions travel from all over the United States to play at this "Disneyland" for dog nuts. The camp has even garnered
international appeal with guests coming from as far away as
Australia and Japan.

Owner Honey Loring started the camp because she wanted
to go to camp with her two standard poodles and thought
other dog owners might also like to go to camp with their
dogs. In 1989 she ran her first canine camp. By 2000 Camp
Gone to the Dogs was so pup-ular that it had expanded to
three sessions a year in three different locations.

The BIG Summer Camp takes place on the 250-acre campus of Marlboro College and hosts as many as 350 dogs (and
their human companions, of course). On the campus there is a
pond for dogs' swimming pleasure. This camp offers the most
activities of any of the camps. And activities such as herding,
hunting, and Tellington Touch are only offered at this camp.

The Midsummer Camp is basically a smaller version of the big summer camp. The camp was added to the schedule so that schoolteachers who wanted to go to camp with their dogs could also attend. A little slower pace, the midsummer camp offers twenty-five to thirty activities a day.

The Fall Foliage Camp takes place in early October, when Vermont is at its peak foliage. The pace at this camp is the most leisurely of the three, offering twenty to twenty-five activities during the day. At night campers spend time inside cozying up with their dogs.

At all three sessions campers may chose from daily activities such as hot-dog fetching, agility training, massage workshops, or simply snack eating. Some of the highlights of the camp are the games and contests that include a tail-wagging contest and even a kissing contest. One of the favorites is the Hot Dog Race. In the race the owner throws a hot dog and the dog must bring at least half of the hot dog back. Needless to say many dogs return to their owners with an empty mouth but a full stomach.

If the camp sounds like the perfect vacation, plan ahead. Camp Gone to the Dogs is extremely popular and summer camps fill up fast and usually have waiting lists. Accommodations at the camps range from dorm rooms to woodsy cabins. For those who prefer a little more privacy Camp Gone to the Dogs has compiled a list of nearby hotels and motels.

Camp Winnaribbun

On the other side of the country is Camp Winnaribbun on the shore of Lake Tahoe. The thirty-two-acre property, which is owned by the University of Nevada, includes private beaches, a pine forest, dormitory cabins, rest rooms, and a large dining hall and kitchen. During the stay the campers sleep in bunk beds with their dogs and other campers.

Founder and Camp director Lory Kohlmoos assigns room-mates according to their dogs' breeds noting that people usually have the same temperaments as their dogs. Those not into the college dorm scene are given a list of nearby off-site accommodations.

During the camp dogs and their owners can join in plenty of activities those into the obedience or competition scene will want to take part in Pet Obedience, Competitive Obedience, or Agility Training. More sporty dogs can take in Flyball instruction and demonstrations or a Herding class where dogs work sheep on a nearby ranch. Or, if you are into new-age techniques, you and your dog can learn about Psychocybernetics, where you learn to achieve your goals by using the science of positive mind power, or canine homeopathy and healing techniques. You and your dog can also take part in less strenuous activities like talent shows, costume contests, and campfires.

The great thing is that all of the activities are optional. Those wanting a day of rest or those not into organized activities can choose to spend their days at the beach digging in the sand and swimming or hiking on nearby nature trails. Or, if you and your dog are into water sports, commercial boat rentals are available nearby. And at the end of the day when your dog is exhausted and is fast asleep you can sneak off and try your luck at some of the nearby casinos.

Now that's something to bark about!

61. Travel Guides

Canine Travel Agent

Need some help planning your trip? Turn to Rovin' with Rover, a travel agency that caters to tour groups with dogs. The Tour Company, based in northeastern Ohio, can arrange for both one and multi-day tours for your dog-loving group. Rovin' with Rover has organized tours to dog-friendly Dollywood; Greenfield Village; Branson, MO; Toronto; and various inns and resorts. One of the company's more popular tours takes travelers to the River Run Bed and Breakfast in upstate New York. Run by Larry Miller, the bed-and-breakfast not only has canine accommodations, but it also has nearby hiking trails and cross-country skiing in the winter. Miller even makes reservations for the groups at a nearby dog-friendly restaurant that allows canine guests to sit under the tables.

If you, your dog, and some of your friends are ready to hit the road, here is what you need to know. Rovin' with Rover requires a minimum group of twenty people and their dogs. They prefer an advance notice of at least a couple of months and a nonrefundable deposit of five hundred dollars. After that, they will do the rest.

It's a Dog's World . . . Wide Web

Looking for the perfect place to take your pooch on a vacation? Tired of hotels shutting the door in your face once they see your four-legged companion? Does the thought of traveling without your dog drive you bark-raving mad? Judging by the number of Internet sites devoted to travel with pets, you are not the only one.

DogFriendly.com was started in June 1998 by Tara Kain. The site began as a travel site for dog lovers and has expanded to an online resource guide for dog lovers. In addition to travel resources the site includes a listing of dog-friendly employers, retail stores, a dog-photo gallery, and more. The site is unique because it focuses on establishments that allow all dogs, no matter what the size or breed.

Other sites worth a visit are PetsWelcome.com and Travel-Dog.com. PetsWelcome.com lists more than twenty-five thousand dog-friendly locations including hotels, inns, parks, and campgrounds. Traveldog.com also provides lists of dog-friendly accommodations, travel suggestions, dog camps, and pet-travel agents.

DogGone Newsletter

DogGone is a bimonthly newsletter that highlights pet-friendly destinations across the United States and offers travel tips for those traveling with their dogs. Wendy Ballard started the newsletter in 1993 after finding that many of her family's favorite resorts yanked the welcome mat out from underneath them when the Ballards asked if Sparky, their beagle, could join them. Ballard was additionally inspired by the fact that her hometown of Vero Beach, Florida, did not allow dogs at any public beaches or parks. In addition to travel information, *DogGone* also features fun activities for dog lovers such as agility and tips for including dogs in such activities as jogging or hiking. Subscribers can also take advantage of *DogGone*'s Personalized Travel Information, which gives a printout of dog-friendly accommodations based upon specific, given criteria.

62. Arrive in Style (Sorry Big Guys! This Is for the Little Guys.)

One advantage to having a small dog is that you can easily carry her wherever you go. But don't even think of carrying your precious pooch in just any old carrier. Small doggies love to be carried in style. Today's traveling canine can choose from a number of luxury pet carriers so that even when you're stuck in the middle seat of the last row of the airplane, your doggie will feel like she is flying first class.

Louis Vuitton, Hermes, Kate Spade, and Burberry have all jumped into the pet-carrier arena offering stylish, albeit pricey, leather-trimmed carriers for posh pooches. But they're not the only ones wanting to carry your dog. That's good news for dog owners not wanting to spend a paw and a leg. Doggies have dozens of carriers to choose from in all price ranges. Doggies will never have to worry about arriving in style.

First on Board

Gayle Martz is the woman who revolutionized the way many of us travel with our dogs. Martz had lost her job as a flight attendant during a strike and December of the following year her fiancé died without a will. Martz was left with nothing but her faithful friend Sherpa, a Lhasa apso, that had been a gift from her fiancé. The pair traveled from place to place staying with friends; Martz wanted to bring Sherpa everywhere she went. But she faced two problems: She couldn't find a suitable carrier for her faithful friend, and she couldn't bring her on an airplane. So Martz set out to design a carrier that would allow people to carry small dogs everywhere they went.

With a loan from her mother, Martz started Sherpa's Pet Trading Company. After Bloomingdale's, Macy's, and Saks Fifth Avenue started selling her bag, Martz faced her biggest challenge—getting the major airlines to change their policy regarding pets in the passenger cabin. With her tenacity Martz succeeded in getting her pet carrier approved by the major U.S. airlines. Sherpa even had the distinction of being the first dog to fly Delta Airlines as she was invited to work on Delta's "Pets On Board Program." Sherpa sat quietly on the conference table in her Sherpa Bag for three and a half hours, proving that dogs can travel discreetly. Sherpa's good behavior was instrumental in changing Delta Airlines' pet-travel policy.

Martz is continually designing innovative products. The Sherpa Bag now comes in a variety of styles to fit the needs of all people with small pets. Styles include The Sherpa-On-Wheels, The Sherpa Roll-Up, and even The Sherpa Tote for carrying your precious pooch around town, but The Original Sherpa Deluxe is the bag that started it all. Constructed in durable quilted nylon, the bag has front or top entry, with a U-shaped top zipper opening, an extra rear zippered pocket for water and food, and mesh panels on three sides for ventilation. The bag includes a faux lambskin liner, reinforced bottom and handles, and an adjustable shoulder strap, which may double as a leash. The bag also features a wheel safety strap that slips over the handles of roll-aboard luggage or fastens to a car seatbelt.

Safety, innovation, style, and comfort are all trademark standards of Sherpa's Pet Trading Company.

Status Symbol

The Louis Vuitton Monogram Sac Chien (Dog Carrier) sports the famous logo and is a favorite with many posh pets. The airline-certified carrier features natural leather handles and trim and is completely water and scratch resistant. One side is fitted with breathable mesh and the zippered top opens fully for easy access to your doggie. And so that you never have to worry about the carrier developing doggie odor, the lining is washable.

A Blue Ribbon Bag

Blue Ribbon Dog Co. has a black Kelly bag–inspired pet-carrying case with mesh ventilation panels at each end for lots of air circulation. The Neoprene Carrying Case has arched zipper flaps on opposite sides of the bag to give your pet an easy entry or exit. For your comfort the bag has a quilted handle. For versatility the arched flaps zip down to form an oval-shaped quilted neoprene lounging bed. And for added convenience, the bag is fully collapsible and machine washable.

Running Around Town

If your precious pooch loves to go everywhere you go, you will want to check out the Vintage Wool Pet Carrier from Fifi & Romeo. The vintage wool and calfskin carrier is fashioned like a glamorous handbag and is great for those who carry their dogs around as a necessary accessory. Like typical carriers the bag has a zip-down hole for doggies to poke their head through. It also features a two-sided mesh interior and a washable faux-fur leopard pillow. The bags are available in several bright colors with black trim.

Want a stylish way to carry your furry friend but don't want to spend a fortune? Designer Barbara Hoch makes some of the most stylish pet bags on the market. Her Doggie Mom

Fifi and Romeo © Trixie & Peanut Inc./Louis Irizarry

bags are made to complement her Maxx's Closet clothing line. And the best part is that people will think that you spent a fortune on them when you really didn't. Most of the carriers retail for under forty dollars.

Want to attract a lot of attention? A shiny Fire Engine Red Carrier is sure to make you and your doggie the talk of the town. The Red Patent Dog Carrier is made from polyurethane-coated cotton with an acrylic black-and-white houndstooth check lining. The hip bag features a heart-shaped mesh ventilation hole on the side. Who said traveling with your dog wasn't fashionable?

And You Thought Coach Was Bad!

We have all heard horror stories about dogs flying in the luggage compartment. This potential horror story that had a happy ending made papers across the country. In June 2000 a United Airlines flight made an unscheduled stop to save the life of a dog. It seems that the dog was mistakenly placed in an unheated forward luggage compartment. Not sure whether the dog had survived that far, the crew alerted the dog's owner, Mike Bell, of the situation. It was even harder for the crew to break the news to Bell after noticing that the screen saver on his computer was a picture of his dog. For forty-five minutes, Bell and everyone else on the plane worried about the plight of Dakota, a ten-year-old basenji. Once the plane landed, the ground crew quickly removed Dakota's crate from the forward cargo hold. Bell then asked if Dakota could join him on the plane for

the remainder of the flight. While the ground crew explained it was against airline regulations, the pilot prevailed and Bell carried Dakota to his seat in front of cheering passengers. Dakota took a few minutes to settle down and was then wrapped in warm blankets. The passengers were then treated to the movie, My Dog Skip. *Throughout the remainder of the flight parents brought their children back to pet the survivor dog. But perhaps the most amazing thing about the entire experience was the fact that not one person complained about the detour (at least not out loud) showing that dog really is man's best friend.*

63.   Better Than First Class

OK, the little guys get to fly in the passenger compartment, but what about the big guys? Well, it doesn't look like they are going to be flying coach, or first class for that matter, anytime soon. Here's a better idea. Charter a plane. Most charter companies welcome well-behaved canines. For approximately $3,800 per hour (depending on the charter company), you and your dog can fly together in the comfort of a private plane. Before you and your dog choke on your biscuits, rest assured that for that price both of you would be traveling in ultimate luxury—not in cargo. For this price you can enjoy the amenities of a twelve-passenger Gulfstream IIB jet with a lavishly appointed leather interior, an audio/video entertainment system, a complete galley, and enclosed lavatory. Also, you don't have to worry about your precious pooch missing connections or being lonely in the cargo hold. (Note: Smaller planes can be chartered for much less.)

Flying Dog Bites Back

On the lighter side, according to The Associated Press, an Irish wolfhound, whose name was not released, flying from San Francisco to Boston in July of 1999 had a few bones to pick over the accommodations in the cargo area. Frustrated that no one would respond as he barked his dissatisfaction, he decided to take matters into his own paws (or teeth might be more appropriate). The wolfhound broke out of his kennel and proceeded to chew through some wires that caused a malfunction in the landing flaps. The plane landed safely, and the ground crew was greeted by the tail-wagging dog, who was thrilled to get off the plane.

64. Buckle Up!

The safety of our dogs has become a major concern in the United States. California requires that dogs be fastened in some manner in vehicles. Other states including Massachusetts and Rhode Island have banned the unsafe practice of allowing dogs to ride in the back of pickup trucks. It has taken years for Americans to learn to buckle up. Now we are finally learning to buckle up our canine friends.

The Ruff Rider Canine Vehicle Restraint is one of the

best on the market. The patented design has been tested and shown to exceed the performance of human seat belts. And unlike other harnesses on the market the Ruff Rider Roadie does not have a collar that can potentially choke your dog or metal or plastic parts that might break.

The Roadie safety restraints are easy to put on and take off and will attach to any vehicle's existing seatbelt system. Additionally you can choose from three positions to attach your dog on the seat: sit/stand/lie down, sit/lie down, or lie down. The restraints are pleated under the front legs to prevent chafing and have a built-in short walking lead. The Roadie is available in nine different sizes to accommodate passenger dogs of all shapes and sizes.

65. Dogs Dig the Car

If you are in the market for a new car, don't forget to keep your canine companion in mind. Having three dogs that like to travel with me, I knew when I bought my last car that only an SUV (sports utility vehicle) would do the job. As a veteran of several trips back and forth from Florida and Ohio, I knew I needed a car roomy enough not only for the gang to be comfortable but also to fit all of my travel essentials. Berry and Wanda readily leap into the back of the car, and although Robin requires a little help getting in, she enjoys it once she is inside. Because the SUV rides higher than most cars, Wanda can enjoy her favorite riding activity of looking into other peoples' cars and making friends.

Automobile makers like Saab and Ford Motor Company are working to make the roads safer for canines. The Saab 9-5 Wagon is loaded with a whole bunch of safety features including some for your furry traveling companion. You can choose from a "Pet-Gear" option that includes belts and harnesses or a divider that confines unrestrained dogs to the cargo area.

Even Ford offers a Pet Package in one of its models that includes a custom car bed. The bed fits almost anywhere inside the car so that your dog is guaranteed to ride in comfort. But what's being comfortable without a nice cold drink and some treats? The Ford Focus is also equipped with an insulated pet sport bottle, integrated pockets for treats and leashes, and a foldable bowl that you can take where ever you and your pet go. The Focus also comes with a pet safety belt that allows you to fasten your doggie to any of the car's safety belts.

Thirsty Dogs

You've heard of barflies, but bar dogs? In major cities across the country, bars that do not serve food may choose to welcome canine clientele. One of the most dog-friendly bars in the country is Jake's Pub. The classic Chicago corner bar is the favorite watering hole of many friendly regulars. First-time visitors to the bar will be impressed by the beer selection. First-time doggies will be impressed by the free treats and hugs.

The Pet-Iculars

Four Seasons Hotel and Resorts, 800-819-5053,
    www.fourseasons.com

Le Montrose Hotel, 900 Hammond St., West Hollywood, CA
    90069, 800-776-0666

Hotel Monaco, San Francisco, CA, 800-214-4220,
www.monacosf.com

San Ysidro Ranch, Santa Barbara, CA, 800-368-6788,
www.sanysidroranch.com

The Alexis Hotel, 1007 First Ave., Seattle, WA, 206-624-4844

The Regency, 540 Park Ave., New York, NY, 800-233-2356

The SoHo Grand, 310 W. Broadway, New York, NY, 800-965-3000

Inn By The Sea, Portland, ME, 800-888-4287,
www.innbythesea.com

The Sutton Place Hotel, Vancouver, BC, 800-961-7555

Las Vantanas al Paraiso, Los Cabos, Mexico, 888-767-3966,
www.lasventanas.com

Camp Gone to the Dogs, Putney, VT, 802-387-5686,
www.campgonetothedogs.com

Camp Winnaribbun, 775-348-8412, www.campw.com

Rovin' with Rover: www.rovinwithrover.com

DogGone newsletter: www.doggonefun.com

The Sherpa Bag: Sherpa's Pet Trading Co., 800-743-7723,
www.sherpapet.com

Louis Vuitton Monogram Sac Chien: select Louis Vuitton boutiques

Blue Ribbon Dog Company, select retail locations

Vintage Wool Carrier: Fifi & Romeo, 7282 Beverly Blvd., Los Angeles, CA

Carrier: Maxx's Closet, select retail locations,
www.maxxscloset.com

The Roadie: Ruff Rider Canine Vehicle Restraint Training Harness, 888-783-3743, www.ruffrider.com

10.

The Grrreat Outdoors

*Histories are more full of examples of the fidelity
of dogs than of friends.*

—Alexander Pope

When it comes to the great outdoors, dogs love to join in all of our doggone favorite activities whether they be hiking, jogging, swimming, boating, or simply sunbathing. And it seems that many of us wouldn't even think of leaving our canine companions behind when we go on an outdoor adventure. Just look at all of the outdoor canine gear now available—backpacks, life jackets, hiking boots, sunscreens, and even sunglasses.

Looking for an outdoor adventure to share with your dog? Just open the door, and you'll find a world of activities not far from your doorstep.

The First Dog Playground

In 1997 Canine Court, New York City's first public playground/agility course for dogs, opened in Van Cortlandt Park in the Bronx. The doggie play-

ground also has the distinction of being the first public doggie playground in the country. The playground includes fourteen thousand square feet of fenced in area with half set aside as a dog run and half as an agility course. Among the agility equipment are tunnels, teeter-totter, and hurdles. With all that play dogs are bound to work up a thirst. Luckily dogs won't have to go too far for water, as there are doggie drinking fountains located throughout the park.

66. Just a Walk in the Park

What dog doesn't love to run and play? My Wanda lives for trips to the park where she can run free. In fact every time she gets in the car she brings her Kong Toy in the hopes that she might be going somewhere she can run and play fetch. Though we have a fenced in yard, nothing is quite as fun for a dog as running free in a wide-open grassy area.

Finding areas where Rover can run free can sometimes be as difficult as finding a needle in a haystack. Unfortunately the welcome mat is not often left out for unleashed dogs. But dog parks are changing all of that. Dog parks are places where dogs are free to run around off-leash.

Dog parks are also places where dogs can socialize with other dogs and make friends. But the dogs are not the only ones socializing. Dog parks have become sort of a meeting place for singles inspiring the movie, *Dog Park*, in which lovelorn singles meet while walking their canine companions at the local dog park. In reality a number of dogs have reportedly played matchmaker for their spouseless owners. True love could be just a sniff away.

Dogs As Cupid

Thinking that a dog will help you get a date? You may be right. Studies have shown that people walking with a dog are more approachable than those who are not. And the author of The Complete Idiot's Guide to Dating, *psychologist Judy Kuriansky, suggests that petless people borrow a pet and go for a walk in the park since people are more apt to talk to a person with a dog.*

Is your dog howling to go to a dog park? Sound good to you? Wondering if there's a dog park near you? Dogpark.com keeps a current listing of dog parks across the United States. Vicki Küng started the Dogpark Web site after she and her Portuguese water dog, Augie, discovered dog parks and started going to them. As a professional Web designer and a lover of dog parks Küng believes creating the site was a natural. She launched the site in April of 1998 and makes monthly updates to the site.

A vocal advocate of dog parks, Küng is not one to shy away from controversy. To the typical complaint that dog parks take play space away from children, she replies, "Children are no more of a taxpayer than dogs." She further adds that dog parks are not only places for dogs to recreate, they are also places for adults to play and get together with other dog lovers.

Dogpark.com assists people wanting to set up dog parks by giving them valuable information. Küng also lets dog park advocates know what they are up against when they try to establish a dog park.

In early 2000, Dogpark.com was averaging sixty-five thousand page views per month. That figure is pretty amazing considering that up until that point Küng had spent under five hundred in advertising. The site even attracted offers from several of the major online pet stores. But Küng declined, adding that Dogpark.com is an important resource for dog lovers. Due to Dogpark's phenomenal popularity, I think dog lovers across the country agree.

Dog Park Etiquette for People

Once you and your dog get to the dog park, it's tempting to just stand back and watch all the activity. But everybody will have a much more rewarding time if you observe some basic rules. Dog parks aren't a right; they're a privilege. Please don't let bad behavior ruin things for everyone else.

1. Always keep your eye on your dog. Mischief can happen quickly.

2. Never leave your dog unattended.

3. Always clean up after your dog. Most parks have poop-bags or scoopers, so use them. This is a primary reason that dog parks get complaints, so pay attention and **pick up the poop**.

4. Make sure your dog is current on her shots and has a valid license.

5. Don't bring dogs younger than four months to a dog park. They won't have had all the necessary inoculations that allow them to play safely with other animals.

6. Don't bring a female dog in season. Spayed/neutered animals are recommended.

7. Don't bring more than three dogs. It subjects parks to overuse, and if they're not your dogs, you may not have full control over them.

8. Keep your dog on leash until you get to the off-leash area. This is not just respectful to other park users; it's much safer for your dog.

9. If your dog becomes unruly or plays rough, leash him and leave immediately.

10. If you must bring children to a dog park, supervise them closely.

11. Don't smoke or eat while at the dog park. Cigarette butts and food wrappers are tempting treats to dogs, but bad for them.

12. Always observe all of the rules posted at your local dog park. Each town has its own set of regulations, so please follow them.

©Dogpark.com

Don't Forget to Wipe

After a hard day of play at the dogpark, your dog is bound to be a little less clean than when he first got there. After our visits to the park before they can get back in the car, Berry, Wanda, and Robin have their paws cleaned. Since a bucket full of soapy water is not exactly practical we started bringing along towels. Rockywoods Inc. even makes a towel called the Dirty Feets Towel made specifically for this purpose. They're a great car saver. It's also a great idea to keep one around the house for those times your dog comes running for the kitchen with paws full of mud.

Puppy Play Groups

The increasing number of puppy play groups across the country and Canada can be attributed to the success of dog parks across the country. In metropolitan areas dog play groups are hot trends with the biggest draw being socialization both for dogs and their owners. Every morning before work groups of people and their dogs gather together at local dog-friendly parks. As their dogs play owners discuss everything from the latest dog toy to world news. The play groups are a way for both owners and their dogs to form lasting friendships. In fact some doggies become such good friends that they invite all the other doggies from the play group to their birthday parties or other celebrations.

The play groups have also become a great way for dog lovers to band together against government laws that are unfriendly toward dogs. In Boston, for example, play groups from various parks across the city have united to form the organization Boston Dog Owners Group. The dog owners hoped that as a united front they would receive more attention in protesting Boston's city ordinance requiring dogs to be on a leash at all times.

67.   Canine Country Club

You knew it had to happen eventually. Country clubs are going to the dogs. Well at least one is. Dog Central Station is a fourteen-acre private country club in Gainesville, Florida, that provides fitness, recreation, relaxation, and social opportunities for Rover. At Dog Central Station your dog can run off leash till he can run no more. The club boasts amenities such as two swimming ponds, wading pools, a shaded jogging trail, and a dog shower for cleaning up dirty dogs. There is also a small dog area for dogs under twenty pounds and a dry dog area with no ponds or pools. For dogs looking for a little more adventure there are tunnels, tires, jumps, and other doggie obstacles. For the dogs' human companions there are fitness stations, benches, swings, and hammocks.

But just like most country clubs, not just anyone can join. To be eligible to join, dogs must first undergo a thorough interview and evaluation.

68. Bone to Run

If you are an avid jogger, next time you lace up consider bringing your dog along. My Wanda, who is an endless source of energy, has been my companion on countless jogs and runs. Unlike Berry or Robin who usually drag behind, Wanda is always two steps ahead no matter how fast or far we go. But just as we do dogs need to be broken into an exercise program gently. In other words, don't expect Fido to run a marathon on your first outing. For those ready to race to the finish line, here are some things to consider when bringing Rover along for the run.

Unleash Yourself

Ever tried jogging with the dog leash in one hand and your walkman and other necessities in the other? It can be downright difficult. In fact it is enough to deter many joggers from including their willing canine on their morning runs. There is a better way. The Sport Leash by Ruffwear is made with the avid walker, jogger, and hiker in mind. The hands-free leash is also great if you are pushing a stroller or are walking more than one dog at a time.

The belt portion of the Sport Leash attaches around your waist with a Velcro fastener. The leash then clips onto the belt and your dog's collar. If your dog is a puller, you will be happy to note that pulling on the leash will not release the Velcro. There is, however, a patented quick-release handle that instantly frees you from the belt while you remain in control of your dog.

Dogs on the run need to drink plenty of fluids. But carrying two water bottles with you while jogging and holding a leash can be quite a pain. The Cool Pooch Sport Water Bottle allows both you and your dog to share a drink without you or your dog having to worry about the other's backwash. The bottle is divided into two separate water supplies and comes with a straw for you and a red drinking cup for your dog. A paws-itively great idea.

69. Take Them Out to the Ball Game

During the dog days of summer what could be better than a day at the old ball game? The Chicago White Sox is one of a few professional baseball teams that allows, albeit only for one day, dogs to enjoy America's favorite pastime. Once a year "Dog Day" turns the center field bleachers at Comiskey Park into the Dog Zone. Approximately five hundred dogs participate in the annual event. Pregame activities for the canines include a parade around the field and exhibit booths with doggie ice cream treats, dog massage, water bowls, and real fire hydrants. Other teams that have gone canine include the Minnesota Twins and the Montreal Expos.

70. Getting Bark to Nature

A hiking trip with your canine companion sounds like fun. But your idea of "ruffing it" is spending the weekend at the Marriott. Yappy News! There are some places where you can have the best of both worlds. Two of my very favorite places, Aspen and Vail, Colorado, not only offer some of the best skiing in the world, they also offer wonderful hiking, mountain biking, and many other activities during the summer months. And both towns are very dog friendly.

During your stay in Vail your dog must remain on leash in Vail Village, Lionshead, and West Vail. Although dogs are not allowed to ride the Gondola, you and your dog can still enjoy the mountain's summertime trail network. But the best part of all is that your dog can trot his way to the top of the mountain off leash. Once the two of you reach the top of the mountain you can kick back at Eagle's Nest and enjoy the spectacular views as well as some cold drinks and some food. After your day on the mountain you and your dog can chill out in comfort and get a good night's rest at the very dog-friendly Antlers at Vail Lodge.

Aspen is even more dog friendly. Dogs are welcome to join their owners along the downtown pedestrian mall. And as most of the upscale boutiques in Aspen welcome well-behaved dogs your precious pooch need not miss out on any shopping opportunities. And Woof! Woof! Hooray! Dogs are allowed off leash in nearly all city parks.

During the summer months of June, July, and August the Silver Queen Gondola allows dogs to ride to the top of Aspen Mountain. And not only are dogs welcome, but your dog can buy a souvenir dog Gondola pass with his photo on it. Once at the top you and your dog can either choose to ride the Gondola back down or to hike the four and a half miles to the bottom.

After a ruff day of hiking you and your dog can choose from several luxury hotels to rest and recuperate for the next day's adventure. The Hotel Aspen, Hotel Jerome, and the St. Regis all welcome canine guests. The St. Regis will even arrange for a dog sitter or walker so that you can go out and enjoy an evening on the town.

Gear Up

You and your dog hearing the call of the wild? Before you head out, you will want to make sure that your canine companion has the right gear.

A day of hiking through the woods is not exactly the best time for Lady to break in that new Chanel collar. Hiking really calls for something a little more rugged like nylon or canvas. We found some very durable collars made by A Tail We Could Wag. The collars are made from premium nylon webbing and are 100 percent colorfast. They have held up really well and are machine washable.

Though we haven't had the opportunity to try them, a ski buddy from Vail raved about the collars made by Fog Dog. The collars are made from rock climbing rope and are snag resistant. They also have a hollow weave so that you can place the buckle wherever best fits your dog.

Don't Forget to Pack

Bringing your dog along on a hiking trip can quickly become a drag when you have to lug around all of your dog's gear. Make sure your dog doesn't become dead weight by suiting him up with a backpack. A doggie backpack allows your canine companion to carry his own food and water among other things on your weekend hikes. Canine backpacks come in different styles and sizes to suit your hiking needs. There are ultra-lightweight packs for afternoon hikes to high performance packs for weeklong hikes through the wilderness.

Are you and your dog new to the hiking scene? A good backpack to start with is the Approach Pack from Ruff Wear. The pack is just right for a one to three day adventure. The pack allows dogs to carry their own food, water, treats, leads, and collapsible bowls.

The Approach Pack has a convenient grab handle to help your dog over obstacles and self-repairing coil zippers. To keep your dog comfortable and avoid chafing, the pack has padded buckles. And if your trip takes you into the night, the pack features reflective material for visibility.

Another popular canine backpack is the Wenaha Explorer II Backpack. This pack has a padded saddle lined with canvas to keep your dog cool and comfortable. One of the best features is that the pack bags are easily removed without having to unharness your dog so that you do not have to unharness and harness your dog every time you stop for lunch or a rest break.

No matter what brand of backpack you choose, keep in mind that you should only fill backpacks with no more than one-quarter of your dog's weight. Why you might ask? Have you ever carried something heavy on your back for a long hike? Not so easy on the body is it? Same goes for your canine friend.

Other items you might want to bring on your outdoor adventure include doggie booties (see "Doggie Style," page 58), a first aid kit (see Miracles of Modern Medicine), and, of course, food and water. Rather than hauling along your dog's big and bulky (and heavy) bowls from home, invest in a couple of lightweight collapsible bowls.

Collapsible bowls are a great way to take the clunk out of hiking. RuffWear's collapsible bowls are sturdy to prevent tipping and come in three sizes. The bowls also have a cinch-top option that allows you to fill the bowl with your dog's food, pull the drawstring, and head out. The part I like best about the bowl is that it folds up small enough to fit in a pack, a glove box, or even a pocket.

Canine Fuel

You are halfway through your Saturday hike. You find a place to stop and relax and pull out a Power Bar for some energy on your way back. Your furry friend looks at you as if to say, "Where's mine?" Of course, Power Bars are not suitable for dogs, but PowerBark snack bars are. PowerBark bars are nutritional snack bars for dogs. The bars are made from human grade ingredients and are fortified with essential vitamins and minerals. PowerBarks contain no dairy, wheat, animal products, or sugar so they are great for dogs with allergies to wheat products. Additionally they are the first kosher snack bars for dogs. The bars come in three flavors: Original, Crunchy Peanut Butter, and Carob Raisin Cookie Dough.

Don't Drink the Water

Remember dogs get thirsty, too. Parched doggies may try to quench their thirst in muddy puddles or streams. Allow them to do this and you may end up with a sick dog on your hands. As a general rule, if you wouldn't drink the water, your dog shouldn't, either.

Getting Rid of That Skunky Smell

While hiking with your dog in skunk territory, keep your dog on a leash at all times. Although I have been spared this unpleasant experience, several of my friends have not. If by chance a skunk does spray your dog, here are a couple of remedies that dog owners swear by.

Good old tomato juice. It not only works for people, it also works for dogs. To get the skunk out put on a pair of rubber gloves and pour lots of tomato juice over your dog being careful to avoid the eyes. It may take several baths in the stuff to neutralize that awful smell.

Another friend recommended the following recipe for eliminating skunk smell. Combine one-quarter cup of baking soda and a teaspoon of liquid detergent to a quart of hydrogen peroxide in an open container (the resulting solution forms a gas that may rupture a closed container). Soak a towel with the solution and saturate your dog's coat, rubbing it in. Because of the hydrogen peroxide be sure to rinse your dog off afterward to avoid bleaching his coat.

71. Making a Splash

My Wanda loves to swim. In fact we often have a hard time keeping her out of the pool. And on more than one occasion we have heard the giant "splash" at some of the most inopportune times, such as when we are dressed and ready to go to a black tie event. Needless to say when we look to see who is in the pool, it is always Wanda.

Although many dogs may be a little leery at first when being introduced to the water, most of them learn to love it. Berry originally thought that the ocean waves were things to bark and growl at, but now he loves jumping right into them. Robin was afraid to go near the water but soon learned from the other two dogs that swimming is fun. And I know countless other people whose dogs love the pool and beach as much as mine do.

Think about it. There is nothing like nice cool water on a warm summer day to bring out the best in you and your dog. Unfortunately unless you or your dog's buddy has a swimming pool he is not likely to find a dog-friendly public pool. But there are other options. You can always purchase a wading pool from a children's toy store. While they're not large enough to get in a lot of swimming, your dog can still romp around in the water and keep cool on those hot summer days. Or check out a nearby dog-friendly beach, river, or lake.

Think *Your* Dog Is Spoiled?

> *Dodger is a cockapoo who has his very own in-ground swimming pool, two beds, a doggie-size couch, and a closet full of clothes. Dodger hates to be separated from his human companion, Cathy. If Cathy leaves the room while Dodger is asleep, Dodger wakes up and howls until Cathy returns for him and then follows her back to wherever she was.*

Many beaches across the United States allow dogs to romp around in the sand. If you are headed to the beach with Rover in tow and want to know where he is welcome, Dogpark.com has listings of dog-friendly parks and beaches across the United States. California, in particular has several great dog beaches of note. San Diego's Dog Beach is a beach dog's paradise. The beach is thirty-eight acres of sand where Fido can sun and surf off leash. Up the highway Huntington Beach has a three-quarter-mile-long stretch of beach where Fido can frolic freely.

Doggie Paddle

No bones about it. Paddle sports aren't just for people anymore. Be it just a day trip or a week-long adventure more and more people are bringing their dogs along on their canoe, kayak, and white-water rafting trips. Paddling down the river is a great way for you and your dog to enjoy the great outdoors.

Many of you are probably envisioning tipped over canoes and drenched dogs. But paddling with your dog doesn't have to be like that. If you introduce your dog to these adventures in the right way, you and your dog will have a great time and will stay a lot drier.

First of all, think of your dog's safety. Even if Rover can doggie paddle "till the cats come home", it is a good idea for him to wear a doggie life jacket (see "Doggie Style," page 58). Second, it is important to make your dog comfortable while finding the right spot for him to ride. Placing a mat or carpet on the bottom of a canoe or raft will help your dog with his footing as well as give him a place to lie down and relax. You will also need to learn to shift your weight to compensate for your dog's movements. Finally, be prepared to get wet. Of course, for many this is the fun part of canoeing, kayaking, or rafting. Be sure to place food, treats, and other necessities in drypacks and secure them to a seat or something else. You certainly don't want to watch as your car keys float down the river without you.

72. Dog Shades

Would you ever think of spending the day at the beach or by the pool without your sunglasses? Probably not. Sunglasses are a great way to look cool while protecting your eyes. But why should we have all the fun and protection? Now your dog can look cool as he digs in the sand, plays in the surf, or lounges by the pool.

Doggles (what else?) is a line of sunglasses from a California-based company (where else?) that caters to the canine set. The sunglasses offer 100 percent UV protection, side air vents, and fully adjustable head and chinstraps to keep the glasses in place. To keep your canine comfortable the frames are flexible and have foam padding around each lens. For your dog's safety the lenses are made with impact resistant polycarbonate. The glasses come in several sizes and styles such as Pee Wee Pups for small dogs, Big Dogs for dogs sixty pounds and up, and super stylish Super Sport.

73.   Life's a Picnic with Your Pooch

Is life with your dog a picnic? Why not take him for a picnic? Picnics in the park are a great way to spend a dog day afternoon. But you're not really thrilled about trying to round up everything that your dog will need. And where are you going to put everything. What you need is a doggie picnic basket. Made in Sussex, England, Optima's Dog Picnic Basket has a bone-anza of picnic accessories for your canine. The wicker

Optima © Trixie & Peanut Inc./Louis Irizarry

picnic basket has leather straps and a sturdy plastic and steel carrying handle. It contains everything you need for an outing with your dog: two stainless-steel feeding bowls, water bottle, food storage container, and utensils. The basket also has grooming utensils and a rope toy so that even when you are done eating you can keep your pup occupied.

Bringing the dog along for a picnic? Be sure to keep your food out of reach of your canine friends. I learned this lesson the dog way. After setting out all the food for David and me, I indulged Wanda in a very quick game of fetch. It wasn't quick enough. I returned to the table to find Robin feasting on our chicken and Berry wolfing down the potato salad.

74. Cold Weather Pooches

The great outdoors isn't just limited to warm summer days. Even on the coldest of mornings many dogs still insist on their daily walk (Robin being a notable exception). When you head outdoors, you are sure to bundle up. Make sure that your dog is weatherproofed as well. Shorthaired dogs chill easily. To ward off those winter chills consider bundling your pooch up in a sweater or coat (see "Doggie Style," page 58).

And don't forget the paws. Chemical salts used to melt ice and snow can be harmful to your furry friend's paws. Booties are a great way to keep paws warm and dry. However there are those dogs that won't stand for booties (see "Doggie Style," page 58). I tried to put some on Berry; he hated them. But I have learned some tips to help protect his paws. You can apply a layer of petroleum jelly to your dog's pads to help protect them from the cold weather elements. And once you return from your walk be sure to wipe off your dog's paws to remove any chemicals or ice from his paws.

Remember to Clean Up After the Dog

Picking up after your dog is not exactly the most glamorous job in the world. In fact some people think the job stinks. We want our dogs to be accepted everywhere, so we have to be responsible. The good news is that there are several brands of clean up bags on the market designed to let you come out smelling fresh.

Remember putting a quarter into the gumball machine and getting one of those fake diamond rings or plastic spiders in the plastic capsule? Imagine opening up the capsule to find a doggie clean up bag. The Compact Doggie Walk Bags come in those great plastic capsules giving dog owners a discreet way to carry around their clean up bags. And to make them even more palatable they are blue and powder scented.

The gang and I never leave the house without several Dispoz-a-Scoop Bags in tow. The bags have a self-sealing closure and cardboard handle so that you can keep your hands a safe distance from what you are cleaning up. Additionally the bags provide odor-free waste disposal in case you are several blocks from the nearest waste can.

Waggies from Blonde With Beagle Productions are designed to make an unsightly job easier. All you have to do is put your hand through the bag; pick up your dog's business; pull the bag inside out; and then it is ready to tie up and throw into the trash can. I have tried the bags, and they work great. But in addition to working great, they are worth checking out just to see the cover of the box. The box features a dog sitting on a toilet reading the newspaper and wagging his tail. It is really funny. It is also a great way to put yourself in a good frame of mind when you are dreading the chore of picking up after your dog.

If you are short on disposal bags, those plastic grocery

bags are also great for picking up. Just be sure that there are no holes in the bottom before you scoop.

The Pet-Iculars

Dog Central Station, 5505 SW Archer Rd., Gainesville, FL 32608, 352-335-1919.

Dirty Feets towels, Rockywoods Inc., www.glo-fetch.com

The Sport Leash, the Approach Pack, collapsible bowls: Ruff Wear, 888-RUFFWEAR, www.ruffwear.com

Cool Pooch sport water bottle: 800-241-5782, www.thermo-sac.com

Power Bark: select retail locations

Antlers at Vail Lodge, Vail, CO, 800-843-8245

The Hotel Aspen, Aspen, CO, 800-527-7369

Hotel Jerome, Aspen, CO, 970-920-1000

St. Regis, Aspen, CO, 970-920-3300

A Tail We Could Wag: select retail locations

Fog Dog: select retail locations

Wenaha Explorer II backpack: select retail locations

PowerBark bars: select retail locations

Doggles: www.doggles.com

The dog picnic basket: Trixie and Peanut Catalog, 888-838-6780, www.trixieandpeanut.com

Compact doggie walk bags: most major pet stores

Dispoz-a-Scoop bags: most major pet stores, PETsMART

Waggies: Blonde With Beagle Productions, 888-819-2477, www.blondewithbeagle.com

11.

A Picture's Worth a Thousand Words

Many dogs will give a greeting grin much like a human smile.

RICHARD A. WOLTERS

You're talking with your friends and they start pulling out the baby pictures from their wallet. However, you notice something very different about their baby. He doesn't cry— he barks. For millions of Americans the family doggie is the family baby. And what proud parent doesn't want to show off his or her baby. As a result, the business of pet portraits is booming. Today you can bring your canine companion to a photographer to sit for a formal portrait, send a photograph of your dog to an artist to paint, put your dog's face on your credit card, and display her photo in many unique ways. Hey, with a simple photograph your dog can even get a license to drive.

Professional pet portraits by artists are nearly as common as are those for children. In fact, do not be surprised if the artist you select to immortalize your dog on canvas has a waiting list of up to six months. Dog lovers are not only waiting, but they are paying a bone-a-fide fortune to capture their dogs at their best.

The portrait business is not limited to watercolors or oils.

Pet photography also has a large place in the portrait world. While many photographers include pet photography among their specialties, some have gone so far as to limit themselves to four-legged subjects.

Not only professionals are getting into the act. The family dog is often included in family photos. Proud owners, myself included, are snapping photos of their dogs faster than you can say woof. If you are like me, you have more pictures of your dogs than you do of your spouse. I have taken entire rolls of film with nothing but dogs. And I know that I am not alone. I can't tell you how many times people have pulled their dogs' photos out of a wallet to show off their precious pooches.

If you're looking around the house and thinking that you could use a painting, photo, or just a different way to display your furry friend, you've come to the right place. These are some terrific ways to show off your photogenic pooch.

According to Stanley Coren's book What Do Dogs Know *(The Free Press, 1997), 40 percent of dog owners carry photos of their dogs in their wallets. Of these people 2 percent carry photos of their mother-in-law.*

75. Credit Your Canine

They say that a picture is worth a thousand words. Now your pet's picture may be worth a thousand dollars, in credit that is. The Humane Society of the United States Visa Platinum Card can be customized with a photo of your favorite dog or dogs. All you have to do is send in a photo of your furry friend, and canine credit is yours. You will also feel good knowing that with every purchase a contribution is made to the Humane Society of the United States.

The card is also a great way to strike up a conversation. Everyone who sees the card loves it and tells me how beautiful my dogs are (of course, I love this). But buyer beware. Trips to the pet store will never be the same. Every time I pull out the card and see my dogs' smiling faces, I usually end up adding more treats or other cool dog stuff to the cart. Needless to say, the gang thinks the new credit card is grrreat. My husband on the other hand . . .

76. License to Drive

You thought that you had seen it all. Then all of the sudden you are passed by a car with a dog driving. Yes a dog. You see, Chloe, a golden retriever from Boulder, Colorado, loves to drive. But Chloe had a problem. The Department of Motor Vehicles (DMV) refused to issue this driving doggie a driver's license; it seems that there is no license classification for canines or any other animals for that matter. As a result Chloe founded the PMV (Pet Motor Vehicles) and started issuing the Pet Driver's License. And dogs will be happy to hear that the PMV requirements are much less strict; all doggies that apply are qualified to receive the license.

The Pet Driver's License is similar in appearance to the human version. It is in full color and is laminated in plastic. The driver's license contains important information such as name, address, and telephone number. Although the Pet Driver's License doesn't actually permit your dog to drive a car, it is a really cute form of identification. When I received Berry, Wanda, and Robin's driver's licenses, I was impressed with the quality, but I was jealous at just how wonderful their license photos looked.

Do Dogs Smile?

Yes, according to Stanley Coren, a professor of psychology at the University of British Columbia and author of the book How to Speak Dog: Mastering the Art of Dog-Human Communication *(The Free Press, 2000). So just how does a dog smile? He opens his mouth slightly and his tongue sort of laps over the front teeth.*

77. Bark for the Camera

Sitting for a formal portrait with a photographer is a great way to immortalize your faithful friend. And it can really be a fun experience with the right photographer. Today many photographers across the country love capturing four-legged subjects on film. Looking through the yellow pages in dog-friendly cities like New York, San Francisco, and Los Angeles you will find many photographers advertising pet photography as one of their specialties. In fact there are a number of photographers who will only photograph four-legged subjects. It seems that photographers have gone doggie.

When I was looking for someone to photograph my dogs for the book, I had a difficult time. At the time Miami didn't really have any photographers that specialized in pet photography. In fact, I almost considered taking the gang out of state for the shoot. However, I finally found a local photographer, and we went to work.

Trying to get three dogs and a person to sit still, sit in the right place, and look at the camera is not an easy task. Berry was a natural. You would think that he had been in show business all of his life. Wanda and Robin on the other hand were uncooperative to say the least. Wanda, who is extremely sensitive, became very skittish. Robin, on the other hand, seemed very bored with the whole thing and just wanted to lie down and go to sleep.

After much to do, the four of us were in perfect position, and . . . the photographer was out of film. By the time he got more film and loaded the camera the dogs had, of course, moved. Then we would try another position and Robin would fall asleep. In trying to wake up Robin, the photographer inadvertently gave Berry and Wanda the "watch" command at which point they jumped up and started barking and growling. After explaining to a very confused photographer what he said, we got everyone in position. And . . . you guessed it—no film. Of course . . . the dogs moved, Robin fell asleep, and the photographer inadvertently gave Berry and Wanda the "watch" command. And so the session went.

Even with the comedy of errors we did get some excellent photographs out of the shoot and the experience made for some funny tails. Most pet photographers work with dogs on a weekly basis and know how to make them comfortable for the camera. If you are not sure whether or not your dog will be comfortable with that person ask if it would be possible for a pre-photo shoot meeting. You might also want to find out how long they have been photographing pets; how many dogs do they photograph in a typical week/month; what do they do to get a dog's attention or to make an uncomfortable dog feel more at ease.

Rated PG

What happens if a male dog gets a little too excited when his picture is taken (as has happened with my Berry)? No problem! That's what retouching is all about.

78.   The Mona Doggie

Christine Merrill

Oprah's two cocker spaniels, Solomon and Sophie, have had their likenesses captured by painter Christine Merrill. Merrill has also painted pooches for CBS's Bob Schieffer and the late Malcolm Forbes. Her canine clientele has a waiting list of at least six months for a portrait that can cost up to fifteen thousand dollars. According to the *Sun Sentinel* (Fort Lauderdale, Florida), Merrill likes to observe her subjects where they live so that she can understand the animal's character. If a personal visit is not possible, Merrill will work from photos or video of the intended subject.

A Dog of a Different Color

Sherry Sanders (formerly Berringer) has been known to add a little color to dogs' lives. Rather than painting dogs in the traditional tans, blacks, and whites, she paints them in bright, vibrant colors like reds, yellows, and blues. Sanders is sensitive to the personalities of dogs and identifies them with color.

When Sanders is asked to paint a dog's portrait she takes a few days to decide what color best captures a dog's personality. Dog owners send her photographs of their dog, along with a description of their personality. Although most people send her a one- to two-page typed description, some do send longer descriptions including one owner who typed a five-page detailed description of her Maltese. Sanders explained that when it comes to peo-

Sherry Sanders

ple's dogs "they pour out their emotions."

Sanders started out by painting her own pets and then decided to paint others. Scout, a mixed breed stray, that Sanders adopted was her first bright color painting. She painted him bright green because he was jealous of the other dogs. But Sanders does not have a set formula for painting dogs, such as painting all jealous dogs green. Each dog is different. Sometimes she paints dogs in multiple colors to capture different aspects of their personality.

Curious how Sanders would portray my dogs, I sent her a two-page description of Wanda and asked how she would paint my little girl. Here's what she came up with. The things that struck Sanders the most about Wanda are the playful, mischievous, energetic parts of her personality. All of those traits brought oranges and yellows to Sanders' mind. "I think I would paint Wanda primarily orange with yellow highlights. Those colors portray energy like no others to me." Sanders also added that she would paint Wanda's eyes aqua to "cool down her warm, energetic body." There may also be a hint of reds in the shadows to portray not only Wanda's energy but also her loving nature.

Sanders' portraits start at five hundred dollars. She donates a portion of the proceeds from her sales to the Fayette Animal Association, an animal welfare organization that she cofounded in her hometown. An avid animal lover, she not only donates money, but she also donates her time. In addition to serving on the board of the Fayette Animal Association Sanders fosters animals in her home. She paints each animal that she fosters and keeps it for her private collection.

Maggie McLellan

On a recent visit to Salon Pooch-ini, Berry, Wanda, and Robin's beauty salon, I noticed a beautiful portrait of the owner's dog, Henry. I loved it so much that I just had to ask who painted it.

Maggie McLellan has been painting for over thirty years. She has exhibited throughout the world and has works in numerous private and corporate collections. McLellan has also authored and self-published two books: *The Artists Express* and *Secrets of the Obedient Brush*. She currently teaches workshops and lectures all over the world.

A few years ago she did some invitations for the Broward County Animal Shelter. After seeing the invitations some of the staff members asked if she could paint a portrait of their dogs. Surprised by the number of requests McLellan soon learned that she loved painting dogs. As a result she started offering her dog portraits for sale. McLellan, whose portraits start at four hundred dollars, works from photographs of her subjects. While she prefers to visit the dog and take her own photographs, she realizes this is not always practical, especially when someone lives a thousand miles away, so she also offers the option of working from the clients' photos.

79. Doggies on Display

What dog lover doesn't have several photos of their favorite canine around the house? At our house photos of Berry, Wanda, and Robin grace nearly every room. In fact my husband, who professes not to like pictures, proudly displays a photograph of our three dogs on his desk. A photo of his wife is nowhere to be found.

Great pictures of your photogenic pooch should be on display. And the grrreat news is that there is a wide variety of ways to display your canine friend including picture frames, photo albums, and even lockets. No matter where you are you can have a reminder of your loved one.

> *An American Animal Hospital Association survey found that 94 percent of pet owners keep a photo of their pet on display. Of them 79 percent display Rover's photo at home and 43 percent display Rover's photo at work. Forty-nine percent of pet owners have a photo album specifically for their pets.*

Frame It

Dog-theme picture frames are a terrific good way to show off your pride and joy. If you are looking for selection the Trixie & Peanut catalog carries several picture frames that will look wonderful in any home. Frames range from silver dog-bone picture frames to funky art frames. One of my favorites is the paw print frame. The folding natural wood-finished frame holds a 5" × 7" photo and includes a paw imprinting kit.

A Book Full of Memories

Remember the good times with your dog by filling a photo album with Fido's photos. I personally have two photo albums filled with pictures of my gang. If you have professional photos of your pet taken, most photographers have a selection of leather-bound photo albums that display your favorite photo on the front. Or if you prefer a more casual or fun photo album, a pet-theme photo album is just the ticket.

The Puppy Tales Photo Album from Just Be Paws is just like a baby album and is a precious way to record your puppy's life from the moment you bring her home. The first page of the album reads "Once upon a time" and has space for you to fill in your puppy's name, date of birth, date of arrival home, and her height and weight. There is even a space for a paw print stamp. The album is filled with pages for you to document various stages of the first year of your puppy's life with a page dedicated to puppy's first birthday party.

Say Woof!

Most of you have probably used a single-use camera at one time or another. How's this for a grrreat camera—a single-use camera just for dogs. The Dog Message Camera is a one-time-use 35mm camera with flash that puts a different dog-oriented message across the bottom of each picture. The fun messages include "Every dog has its day" and "Always a friend." The ready-to-use camera is a high tech camera preloaded with 400-speed ASA/ISO high-definition color film. It's a way to capture those doggone fun times.

Just a Heartbeat Away

A locket is a sentimental way to keep your best friend close to your heart at all times. Most jewelers carry lockets or at least are able to order one for you. But one of the cutest lockets I have encountered is the 14k gold toggle necklace with a heart locket from Chic Doggie by Corey. Although the necklace is made for doggies, Corey Gelman explains that dog owners love Chic Doggie's necklaces so much that they usually custom order the dog necklaces for themselves. I was glad to hear that I wasn't the only one.

The Pet-Iculars

Humane Society of the United States Visa Platinum Card, 800-HSUS-594

Chloe Cards, 888-245-6388, www.chloecards.com

Christine Merrill: William Secord Gallery, 52 East 76th Street, New York, NY 10021, 212-249-0075 www.dogpainting.com

Sherry Sanders, 901-465-1822

Maggie McLellan, Miami, FL

Dog-theme picture frames: Trixie & Peanut Catalog, 888-838-6780, trixieandpeanut.com

Puppy Tales photo album: Just Be Paws by Laid Back, select retail locations

Dog message camera: select retail locations

Heart locket necklace: Chic Doggie, 212-752-9663, www.chicdog.com

12.

Pawty Hounds

Every dog must have his day.

—Jonathan Swift

Throwing a party for your dog is not as far-fetched as you might think. You might not have known it, but dogs love to party. Hey they don't call 'em party animals for nothing. Finally we humans have come to realize this. Doggie celebrations are increasingly popular. Since dogs are part of the family, doggie owners want to make sure that Rover's birthday is celebrated just as any other member of the family. In some cases the family dog is the only one getting a party. But it's not just dog birthdays that dog owners are celebrating. Graduation from obedience school, bark mitzvahs, and puppy showers are all cause for celebration. And in perhaps the most extravagant example of Rover's rising social status dogs are getting hitched. That's right. Dogs across the country can be heard barking "I do" as they take the plunge into howly mut-trimony.

You might be wondering just how elaborate these canine festivities are. Canine celebrations range from a typical back-yard gathering to get togethers at the local dog bakery or doggie daycare to elegant weddings complete with Dom Pérignon.

And if you don't have the first clue about throwing a doggie bash, don't worry. Your local dog bakery or doggie daycare is happy to help you out.

80. Pawty Till the Cats Come Home

If you are one of those people who loves to throw a party, you will have a ball planning a doggie party. It's just like throwing a people party with a few minor doggie adjustments, of course.

Spreading the Woof

You've got the date, the time, and the place. Now you have to let all of your dog's friends know about the big event—that means sending out invitations. Of course, you can always use regular people invitations for the event; you might even be able to find some children's invitations with puppies or dogs on them. If you're artistic, creative, or have access to a graphics package like Print Artist, you can always make your own invitations. A friend sent me a copy of an invitation that she had made using a graphics package, and it was really great. It had a dancing dog on the cover with a party hat and balloons. Or you can always go all out and have a print-shop custom design the invitations.

On the Menu

You can't have a party without food and drink. And a canine celebration calls for both people and dog food. As for the dogs you can serve such doggie delights as canine cake and doggie ice cream, biscuits, and water. To make the party special consider serving Champ-Pagne Spring Water or Pawier Water as opposed to tap.

And let's not forget about your human guests. While doggie ice cream and gourmet biscuits may be edible, your guests will be much happier if you serve foods better suited to human tastes. In keeping with the dog theme there are always hot dogs, dog or dog bone shape cookies, bone shaped cake, and ice cream. If your occasion is more formal, you will probably want to forego the hot dogs. And if you want to host a true animal-friendly party, consider serving only vegetarian fare. As for the refreshments you might want to stock your refrigerator with Red Dog Beer or another beer with a canine inspired name. But please do not allow guests to drink and drive. If you are going to serve alcohol, consider checking everyone's car keys at the door.

Dog Got Game

Let's face it. Games aren't for everyone or every dog. In fact, some of the best doggie parties have no organized games but just allow the dogs to be dogs. But games are a great way to keep everyone occupied and can be a lot of fun with the right crowd. These games will provide both your canine and human guests with a howling good time.

Pin the Tail on the Doggie: An updated version of an old classic, this game is always a favorite with the kids (human that is). Draw an outline of the birthday dog on posterboard or have a photo of the birthday dog blown up poster size. Tails can be made from paper or even braided yarn. The game is played just like pin the tail on the donkey. Except in this case the winner's doggie gets the prize.

Bobbing for Biscuits: This game is for the dogs. To play place a biscuit in a large water bowl. Let the dogs take turns retrieving a biscuit. The dog who retrieves the biscuit the fastest is the winner.

Biscuit Hunt: Like an Easter egg hunt, before the party hide biscuits, or other treats around the house or yard. Owners and dogs then sniff out the treats.

What's a Party Without Cake?

Now your dog can have his cake and eat it, too! The following recipe is one of the gang's favorite recipes. It's one I have come up with by experimenting with several other recipes and is sure to get two paws up from party hounds.

Wanda's Party Cake

1 large apple
1½ cups whole wheat flour
¼ cup oatmeal
2 teaspoons baking powder
½ teaspoon baking soda
¼ teaspoon vanilla
½ cup plain or vanilla yogurt
½ cup water
¼ cup vegetable oil
2 tablespoons honey
4 egg whites

CREAMY FROSTING

8 oz. light cream cheese
1 tablespoons honey
½ teaspoon vanilla

Preheat oven to 400°F. Grease 13" × 9" pan.

Core, slice, and mince the apple and set aside. In a large bowl mix together dry ingredients. In a separate bowl blend together vanilla, yogurt, water, vegetable oil, honey, and eggs and add apple. Pour into dry mixture and stir until thoroughly mixed.

Pour into cake pan and bake thirty minutes or until a toothpick inserted in the center of the cake comes out clean. Allow to cool and remove from pan.

For creamy frosting combine room temperature cream cheese, honey, and vanilla, and spread on cake. Be sure to spread frosting thick to avoid cracking. For "chocolate" frosting add three teaspoons of carob powder.

If baking is not your forte, don't worry. Your local dog bakery has got you covered. Your local dog bakery loves to bake birthday cakes for your special dog. For Berry's birthday we ordered a two-tier dog bone shape cake from Biscuits and Bones Dog Bakery. It looked as good as, if not better than, most birthday cakes I've ever had. The gang loved it.

I know that many of you are thinking, "But the nearest dog bakery is three hours away. I can't spend six hours driving for a birthday cake, and the last time I baked a cake it came out charbroiled." Don't panic. Your doggie will not go cakeless. Three Dog Bakery will have a cake delivered right to your door. Cakes come in peanut butter, carob chip, and apple cinnamon flavors and come with Three Dog Bakery's famous creamy, dreamy frosting. You can personalize your cake with up to twenty characters. But plan ahead. All cakes must ship early to midweek to ensure that your doggie receives a fresh cake.

The American Animal Hospital Association 1999–2000 Pet Owners Survey found that pet birthdays are an event in 67 percent of pet households. Of those, 11 percent throw a birthday bash, 43 percent wrap a gift for their pet, 41 percent play the pet's favorite game, and 45 percent sing "Happy Birthday."

Happy Gotchaday!

Don't know your dog's birth date? Unfortunately when we got Robin, we knew nothing of her history, and hence have no idea what day her actual birthday is. But we would never think of leaving her without an annual celebration. So we celebrate Robin's Happy Gotchaday! Robin seems happy with the arrangement; so we are, too.

Helpful Tips

If you are planning a doggie celebration, keep these tips in mind.

1. Make sure that all of the dogs get along. Breaking up dog-fights is not a good way to celebrate an occasion. Likewise, do not invite dogs that are overly possessive of their toys and treats.

2. Make sure that all food is out of the reach of hungry dogs. There is nothing worse than discovering that one of the dogs has helped himself to the entire cold cut and cheese platter.

3. Make sure that each dog gets a party favor. This helps eliminate fights over toys and treats.

4. Have pooper scoopers readily available. This is self-explanatory.

5. Label food as either people or doggie. Since some of the human treats will be dog theme, it might be easy for guests to mix them up (remember David and the candy?).

6. Keep your camera handy and take lots of photos. This is an event that you will want to remember.

7. Have fun. Most people throwing a party worry so much about everything going right that they forget to enjoy themselves.

Pawty in a Box

A number of boutiques offer birthday parties in a box. It is really a great time saving idea. One of the best that I have found is The Birthday Party Pack from Merrick Pet Delicatessen. The pack comes with eight of their most popular dog treats, four birthday party horns, and four party favor treat bags. It also comes with refreshment ideas for the human guests (they need to eat too) and suggests five games for dogs and their owners to play together. The party pack comes in a handmade woven basket. I bought the kit for Robin's gotcha-day. It really came in handy. Since the party was small, just the family, all I had to do was order a cake from the bakery and we were set. (One note: Make sure that the horns are only given to human guests. I tried giving one to the birthday girl, but she thought it was a chew toy.)

The Place to Pawty

Looking for a place to party? Look no further. Dog bakeries, doggie daycare centers, and even some boutiques love to host canine celebrations of all kinds. And the best part is that you don't have to worry about the preparation or the cleanup. You and your doggie and his doggie buddies just show up and have a howling good time.

While policies vary from place to place, here's what you can expect. Basically you "rent" out the place for an hour or two. Of course if the party is at a dog bakery, you don't have to worry about the catering. But if you choose to have a party at daycare or a boutique, the staff will usually arrange for the

catering or can recommend some places. As with human parties costs are usually based on the number of doggie guests.
But the nice thing is that the staff will help dish out canine
cake, ice cream, and other goodies and will help keep all of
the canine guests entertained.

That Dog Really Knows How to Party!

*Meet a beagle named Monique. There is no dog
more spoiled than her. Monique has a custom-built
Victorian doghouse complete with a stained-glass
window. She has a custom-painted toy box for all of
her toys. And like every spoiled woman, Monique has
a jewelry collection complete with a jewelry box, of
course. This lucky dog even has her very own bedroom.*

*But Monique is the most spoiled on her birthday.
Every year her doggie mom, Janet Sanders, throws
Monique a spectacular birthday party. All of
Monique's doggie friends and family are invited.
Year by year the parties get bigger and better.*

*But nothing can compare to Monique's year 2000
birthday party. For this party Sanders pulled out all
of the stops. Monique's birthday party was held at
Paramount Pictures (through special permission, of
course). The red carpet was rolled out for all of the
doggie guests, and a professional photographer captured each dog's smiling face and wagging tail in
front of the famous Paramount gate. Sanders even
bought stepping-stone paw print kits to create the
"Hollywoof" Walk of Fame.*

Beautifully designed movie theme invitations were sent to all the guests. And the big event was catered by Three Dog Bakery (who else?). Sanders even found Oscar and movie camera shaped cookie cutters so that each dog could have movie-theme dog biscuits. And if that is not enough each dog at the party received specially made necklaces from Oh My Stars!

81. Howly Muttrimony

Dog weddings, also known as "muttrimony" or "bow-wow vows" are the bark of the town. Because a large number of dog owners do not have human children, the only way for them to play the role of mother or father of the bride or groom is to marry off their pooch. And when it comes to their canine children's weddings, doggie parents spare no expense. In fact, a 1999 South Florida dog wedding made national news. Why you might ask? The cost—a mere twenty thousand dollars.

Most dogs that tie the knot have already been living together for years and have decided to make it official. But many dogs that decide to wed, don't reside in the same household. And unlike us, dogs who live apart before the wedding live apart after the wedding, thus limiting their time together to weekend visits or their time together at doggie daycare. According to several canine couples this arrangement is the secret to a successful marriage.

Is it puppy love? Is your dog howling for his loved one? Maybe it's time for your dog to tie the knot. But you have no idea where to begin. Look no further. Here are some places that know how to throw a pawsitively fabulous wedding for the bride and groom.

Pre-mating marriage ceremonies are the latest trend for dogs about to go through the breeding process. According to the New York Post *in early 2000, Sigourney Weaver's Italian greyhound exchanged doggie collars with a studly Italian greyhound she considers "the Mel Gibson of Italian greyhounds." The ceremony took place at the swanky Zitomer Z Spot, a pet boutique located on the Upper East Side of Manhattan.*

You May Now Lick the Bride

Hollywood Hounds in Los Angeles has hosted over fifteen muttrimonies. Actress Lysette Anthony's dog was among those who have gotten hitched at this popular doggie daycare. Most of the canine couples married at Hollywood Hounds either met at the daycare or were already living together. Ceremonies are conducted in the backyard gazebo and come complete with organ music and a wedding cake made of liver pâté and dog food. Guest lists of fifty are not uncommon. To give the occasion a perfect ending a white Rolls-Royce with leopard-skin interior is also available to shuttle the newlyweds off to the nearby dog park on Mulholland Drive for their honeymoon. Is your dog panting to get married but whining because she doesn't have a thing to wear? Don't worry. Wedding attire is sold in the Hollywood Hounds Boutique.

Puppy Love

And just a few minutes away The Dog House doggie daycare is also known for their wonderful weddings. In July of 2000, Elizabeth Gabriel threw an elegant wedding for a pair of dogs that fell in love at the daycare. Here's the scoop.

In the summer of 2000 Scout, a.k.a., "Scoutina the Princess of Bridgeport," was married to Basil, a terrier mix, of British descent. Owner Elizabeth Gabriel hired a set decorator who transformed The Dog House into a beautiful garden setting. The floor was carpeted with astro turf and a twelvefoot red carpet runner was put in place. White wooden folding chairs seated the guests, about twenty people and thirty dogs.

The decorator set up a white wicker archway, pulpit, and two huge fresh flower sprays in the bride's colors (pink and white). The bride wore white satin and tulle and white satin roses. She also had a matching veil and crystal tiara. Scout's bridesmaid, Petunia, wore a pink satin and tulle dress with matching headband. The groom wore a black satin tux and tails with matching cummerbund and bow tie, and his groomsman, Max wore a similar tux, but with pink cummerbund and bow tie.

The four-legged guests dined on gourmet treats from the Three Dog Bakery, including a personalized three-tier wedding cake with a topping of bones. The two-legged guests ate chocolate cake and drank sparkling water. Reportedly there wasn't a dry eye in the place.

A Wedding That's the Bow Wow

Needless to say dog bakeries, daycares, and boutiques love to host doggie niptuals. But many weddings are even more upscale than that. In February 2000, Hanna and Alex, two yellow labrador retrievers, gained national attention when they were married in the first ever Valentine's Day Wedding pet wedding at the Beverly Hills Hotel. Hanna wore a white wedding dress, a flower tiara, and a garland-adorned leash. A dashing Alex sported a black tuxedo. Enzo, the Jack Russell terrier star of *My Dog Skip* served as best dog. And the ceremony was officiated by none other than Lassie. In lieu of gifts guests were asked to make donations to PETsMART Charities (PETsMART.com sponsored the wedding). No word on whether a prenip was signed.

And the Bride Wore . . .

What's the proper wedding without the proper attire? Canine brides-to-be need not worry about what to wear on the big day. While not as large as that for human brides, the bridal gown selection for four-legged brides is not without choices. Doggies anxiously awaiting their impending niptials will be surprised with the selection of made-to-order and ready-to-wear gowns.

Most pet boutiques carry canine wedding gowns. Many can also find someone to custom-make a gown for your pooch. One of the nicest gowns I found is by Lucky Dog Co. The Bridal Dress has an ivory silk empire bodice with pearl beaded neckline. The bottom portion of the exquisite gown is embroidered with delicate flowers hand-beaded with mini pearls. For the full bridal gown effect the underskirt includes several layers of crinoline.

How to Pup the Question

Max has discovered that he is in love with Sammie. How does he "pup" the question? Is a ring appropriate? The gang and I did some digging and here are some of the more creative ways to ask for a loved one's paw in marriage.

Dusty hid a silver collar charm in a basket full of biscuits. The charm was engraved with the question: "Will you marry me?"

Spencer gave Garnett a rhinestone studded collar with a gold band dangling like a charm along with a love letter that said among other things that he pawsitively adored her. The letter was, of course, signed with a paw print.

On New Year's Eve, Oliver asked for Peaches' hand in howly muttrimony by presenting her with a $5,000 diamond dog collar. Turns out Oliver's "dad" also presented Peaches' "mom" with a beautiful diamond ring of her own that very same night. No word on whether they will be married in a double ceremony.

The Best Dog

Not only are people throwing weddings for their dogs, they are also including dogs in their own celebrations. One of the newest trends is for couples to include their dogs in their own weddings. When you stop to think about it, it's not too crazy. Your dog is your best friend, and why wouldn't you want your best friend at your wedding.

Dogs are taking on wedding roles traditionally reserved for two-legged friends. People who consider their dogs to be their children wouldn't have it any other way. Don Black, whose boxer served as his best man, puts it simply, "I have known Oliver for five years. Longer than I have known my bride. Of course I want him at my wedding."

While dogs are serving as best dog and dog of honor, it is more common for them to be given roles such as flower dog or ring bearer. As a ring bearer at Tracy and Matt Monnin's wedding, Alex, a husky, marched down the aisle in a tuxedo and with a gold pouch around his neck containing the rings. For Sally and Pat's wedding, Sally's dog, Bonnie, wore a leilike strand of fresh flowers around her neck.

Of course you wouldn't want your dog to come to your wedding unescorted. He needs a date. Many local dog sitters, trainers, or doggie daycares offer "dog date" services for your dog on the big day. As your dog's date the dog-care provider usually acts as canine chauffeur, babysitter, and entertainer for the day.

One last thing to consider before deciding to have your dog as a part of your wedding is his temperament. This is a time to be honest. I know you think that your dog is the best in the world, but if he does not like other people or is very protective of you, including him in the wedding could lead to disaster. The last thing you need is your dog scaring away all of your guests as he trots down the aisle. Additionally dogs who are very vocal or who do not like to sit still are also not the best candidates for the position of best dog. Remember, during the ceremony you will want to hear the sentiments of the minister, not your dog.

82. It's the Only Way to Ride

After the wedding it is traditional for the bride and groom to be whisked away in a limousine. However finding a limousine that will take man's best friend is no easy ride. Enter Merry Lee Trznadel. Merry Lee has no problem chauffeuring man's best friend. In fact she has built a business around it. Merry Lee came up with the idea for her business, Paws and Purrs Pet Limousine, based near Buffalo, New York, when she was looking for something different to do with her dog on his birthday. Like many other dog lovers, she found that trying to find a limousine that would accept her canine companion nearly impossible.

Frustrated, Merry Lee took matters into her own hands, or limousine more precisely. She spent several months researching the business, looking for places that people could take their dogs, and seeking fun activities that people and their dogs could share. Then she purchased a stretch limousine.

Paws and Purrs services range from the routine, transportation to the groomer, kennel, and airport, to the special, weddings and birthdays. She also offers catered picnics for canines and their human companions that include lots of doggie delights from the local dog bakery and people food from local restaurants on the side.

Merry Lee offers plenty of specials including a pet birthday special that includes a one-hour ride, a pet birthday cake from the local pet bakery, and a color photograph of your dog's special day. If an hour is not enough, you and your dog can go for a four-hour trip to places such as Artpark, Delaware Park, Goat Island, Buffalo Botanical Gardens, or Arcade Attica Railroad where you and your dog can take a ride on a one hundred-year-old steam engine train.

Although hers is a true limousine service, Merry Lee notes that owners are often surprised to see the eight-passenger stretch limousine pull up in front of the house. The limousine has all the amenities you would expect from a limousine including two bars, a color television, and leather interior. Merry Lee even dons a chauffeur's uniform including the hat to insure your doggie is given the royal treatment.

The Pet-Iculars

Three Dog Bakery, 800-4TREATS, www.threedog.com

Birthday Party Pack: Merrick Pet Delicatessen, 800-664-PETS, www.merrick-deli.com

Hollywood Hounds, 8218 Sunset Blvd., Los Angeles, CA 90046, 323-650-5551, www.hollywoodhounds.com

The Dog House, W. 3rd Street, Los Angeles, CA, 323-549-9663

Bridal dress: Lucky Dog Co, www.luckydogco.com

13.

Happy Howlidays

Dogs are not our whole life, but they
make our lives whole.

—ROGER CARAS

Now more than ever people are including their dogs in their holiday plans. In fact a recent American Animal Hospital Association survey found that 87 percent of pet owners include their pets in holiday celebrations. You see Rover sitting with the rest of the family in holiday photos. Rover's stocking hangs right alongside the rest of the family's; his Easter basket sits right with the other kids' baskets; he gets dressed up for Thanksgiving dinner; he may even wear a Halloween costume and go trick or treating. But the inclusion of the family dog goes even beyond that. Rather than flying, dog parents are opting to drive over the river and through the woods to Grandma's house so that their four-legged child is able to join them. Some people even offer to host the entire family for Thanksgiving dinner so that Rover is not left home alone, while others go so far as to forego those potentially stressful family gatherings because they prefer the company of their dogs to overbearing relatives.

Looking for some ways to get you and your dog into the spirit of things? The trio and I found some great holiday treats, accessories, gift ideas, and even traditions. They're sure to put the howl in your howlidays.

83. Howly Jolly Christmas

It's Christmas, the most wonderful time of the year. It's the time to splurge. It's the time of year to get your dog that wonderful toy or other gadget you know he will love. Let's face it. To a dog gifts like ordinary collars and stainless steel bowls are the human counterpart of underwear and socks. And who likes getting underwear and socks in their stockings?

Well, I think the rest of the book covers the excellent gift part. But there's much more to the Christmas Spirit. There are the family traditions and the festive holiday apparel. And what would Christmas be without a trip to see Jolly Old St. Nick. Here are some barktacular ways for making your dog's Christmas tail-wagging fun.

Canine Adaptations of Christmas Classics

We have all heard of *'Twas the Night Before Christmas* and *The Twelve Days of Christmas*. But did you know that there are canine adaptations of these and other holiday classics? Yes some creative dog lovers made some changes to these holiday favorites to make them tail-wagging fun. They are sure to become an annual tradition in those homes with canine family members.

On Christmas Eve instead of reading the traditional *'Twas the Night Before Christmas* send your dogs to bed with "visions of dog treats" dancing in their heads. *The Night Before Dog-Mas* by Claudine Gandolfi and illustrated by Karen Angnost (Peter Pauper Press) is a fantastic adaptation of the holiday poem. Your dog will be begging for more as you read him the tail of St. Bernard's annual visit to the dog pound.

The Twelve Dogs of Christmas was written by seven-year-old Emma Kragen, and illustrated by Sharon Collins and Kelly Ann Moore (World Books). You and your dog will love everything from one poodle in a doghouse to eleven labs laughing (I'll leave number twelve as a surprise). The book is also accompanied by a CD for you and your dog to bark along with.

Make Christmas an all-out dog event with *Holiday Hounds: Traditional Songs for Festive Dogs* by Laurie Loughlin and illustrator Mary Ross (Chronicle Books). The book contains twenty favorite holiday songs written from the dog's point of view including a canine version of "Auld Lang Syne." Each of the songs is accompanied by colorful illustrations of dogs enjoying Christmas as only dogs could.

According to an American Pet Products Manufacturers Association National Pet Owners Survey seven in ten dogs receive Christmas gifts. But when it comes to spoiling Rover at Christmas, the men have it. A PETsMART holiday survey found that in 1999 shoppers spent an average of ninety-five dollars on their pets' Christmas gifts. However men typically spent 10–20 percent more than women on their furry friends.

Christmas Stockings

It just doesn't seem like Christmas at our house until all of the Christmas stockings are hung by the chimney. Everyone has their own stockings with their names written in glitter. The first year I bought Christmas stockings for the dogs and hung them next to ours, my friends and family thought I was nuts. The next year they didn't think I was so crazy. On the

Oprah Winfrey Show's 1999 Christmas episode, she featured paw print stockings for pets from Three Dogs & a Cat. Instantly dog lovers fell in love with the adorable stockings. By Christmas 2000, thousands of dogs had their very own paw print stockings filled with doggie treats from Santa. (Berry, Wanda, and Robin included.)

Jon Curry created the first paw print stocking in December 1996. On his way out the door to run some errands his wife Marti asked him to pick up some stockings for their pets. Instead Curry returned home with "stocking" material and sewed the first paw stocking. The stocking was black with gray pads for their black cocker spaniel mix. The second stocking was brown with gray pads for their boxer mix. Eventually Curry started making the stockings in the traditional red and white.

All of their friends and family loved the stockings and wanted one of their own. The Currys decided to patent the

Three Dogs and a Cat/Alan Wilco

idea and sell the stockings to other dog lovers. Since they had three dogs and a cat, they felt that was the most logical name for their company.

The original stockings were made of felt and came in two sizes. Today the stockings are made from a rich "teddy-bear" plush material and come in four sizes. Their newest size, five inches small, is extremely popular. In fact, many people hang them on their trees as ornaments. In addition to traditional red with white pads the stockings are available in white with red pads and dalmatian print with black pads.

What better way to wish your dog Merry Christmas?

The American Pet Products Manufacturers Association estimates that in November and December nearly 99 percent of pet stores' sales are the results of owners buying gifts for pets and pet lovers.

The Collars of Christmas

Has your dog been an angel all year? He can dress the part at Christmas with the Angel Wing Collar from Fox & Hounds Ltd. The heavenly collar has a set of gold angel wings on green and burgundy taffeta. The all-cotton collar is like a woman's hair scrunchy and just slips over your dog's head.

Jingle All the Way. For some the sound of sleigh bells at Christmas time is music to their ears. While the sleigh may not be readily available, the bells are not so hard to find. Those looking to put a little jingle bell rock into their pooch's life won't be able to resist the assortment of bell collars that are available.

Creature Comforts has long been known for their extravagant pet accessories. Their pet accessories include beds, bowls, picture frames, treats, collars, and leashes. But one of their biggest selling items is their Jingle Collar. The Jingle

Collar consists of a piece of elastic wrapped in holiday tartan and adorned with three bells. It was so pupular that Creature Comforts sold over fifty-five thousand of the holiday collars in 1999.

The Prancer Christmas necklace from Oh My Stars! is quickly becoming a holiday favorite with the canines. The festive necklace has green and white beads and red "jingle bells." I loved them so much that I bought one for each of my dogs. They really look great on any color dog.

Here Comes Santa Paws

Looking for a Santa to liven up your Christmas party? Consider Santa Paws rather than Santa Claus. Dressed like Santa your doggie is bound to be the most popular dog at the party. Even the local scrooge will get into the spirit once he catches a glimpse of Santa Dog. Looking for a Santa suit? After Thanksgiving it's pretty easy to find Santa suits through catalogs or in boutiques. One of the nicest is the Santa suit from Rag Dog, which includes the traditional red coat and hat trimmed in white. Your dog will look just like the real thing, with the exception of the long nose and four legs.

No way your dog is letting your dress him up in a Santa coat? (Mine either.) Maybe with a bribe of Christmas cookies (the doggie kind), you can coax him into wearing a Santa Hat or maybe even a set of reindeer antlers at least long enough for you to take some pictures. Santa hats and reindeer antlers are big sellers at Christmas and are commonly found in most pet boutiques and pet stores.

Bark in Santa's Ear

We are all familiar with department store and mall Santas. But human children aren't the only ones who get to tell Santa what they want. Many pet boutiques, dog bakeries, pet stores, and even animal charities arrange for a visit from Santa for their furry friends. While it takes a little bit of time for some dogs to warm up to Santa, others jump right up on his lap. Happily most Santas report that they have never had any bad experiences with the dogs.

On Wanda's first visit to Santa she jumped right up on his lap and licked his face. When he asked what she wanted she let out a little howl that Santa interpreted to mean: "I want lots of biscuits!" Curious, I took the opportunity to ask Santa what dogs asked for the most. He noted that most dogs' wish lists include things called "Woof" and "Grrr." Translation: "Just give me one of everything in the store!" and "Give me my biscuit right now!"

Presents Under the Tree

Favorite canine presents mirror those for people: toys, clothing, and accessories. Even jewelry is becoming a popular gift for dogs. According to a recent survey 70 percent of pet owners give their pets Christmas gifts. Count me among the 70 percent. Every year Berry, Wanda, and Robin have more presents under the tree than anyone else does. And each year as I discover more and more things that "they just have to have" the number of presents for them grows.

One thing that you want to avoid putting under the tree is a food gift. I learned this the hard way. One year I bought the gang a large box of peanut butter–carob biscuits. They were prepackaged in plastic, so I thought that the gang would not figure out what was in the package. I was wrong. Somehow they sniffed out the treat package, which, by the way, was under several other boxes, and had an early Christmas. I returned home to find shredded wrapping paper, torn plastic, an empty box, and crumbs everywhere. My house was a mess but my three dogs looked happier than ever. Now at Christmas the gangs' treats are placed in their stockings, where they can not get to them, or in the freezer until Christmas morning.

Holiday Safety

Holidays may be wonderful times of the year, but they can be dangerous times for your canine friend. It's important to make sure your holiday home is a dog-proof home. Here are some suggestions for keeping your doggie merry and bright through the holidays.

1. Keep all chocolate or other human treats out of the reach of dogs. Chocolate is potentially fatal to dogs.

2. Your holiday dinner is not a suitable meal for your dog. Dogs do not easily digest most of our holiday favorites. Instead prepare another special meal for your doggie. He will love it just as much.

3. This should go without saying, but you never know: Never give your dog alcohol. Dogs can become seriously ill just from drinking a few ounces of that champagne punch.

4. Mistletoe and poinsettias can be toxic for dogs. If you are longing to kiss your pooch under the mistletoe, be sure to hang it in a place out of his reach.

5. Dogs love Christmas trees, but Christmas trees do not love dogs. An ingested pine needle can puncture your doggie's internal organs. Also drinking the water from the tree stand can be dangerous since the water may contain chemicals. If you cohabit with a canine, your best bet is to get an artificial tree. No matter what type of tree you choose try to select ornaments that are not breakable as curious dogs may knock ornaments or the entire tree over.

6. As for the holiday decorations. Keep tinsel, hooks and pins out of the reach of curious canines. Swallowing these items can lead to choking or internal injuries.

84. Trick or Treat

A little angel, a little devil, a clown, and a cowboy. Halloween party? Yes? For people? No. These guests have four legs. Each year doggie day care centers, boutiques, and individuals throw Halloween bashes for their furry friends.

Begging to know what dogs do at a canine Halloween Party? Eating is high on the priority list. Treats like bat and pumpkin-shaped biscuits are always pupular as are Itty Bitty Scary Kittys (with spooky carob eyes) from the Three Dog Bakery or homemade Black Cats (cat-shape carob dipped biscuits). In between treats dogs participate in games like bobbing for hot dogs (or biscuits) or in costume contests. Some dogs prefer to gather around and listen as someone tells spooky Halloween "tails" or watch Snoopy's antics in the Halloween classic *It's the Great Pumpkin, Charlie Brown*. Meanwhile their owners snap lots of photos before their dogs wiggle out of or tear their costumes. Amazingly, however, party hosts note that most costumes remain intact and on the dogs throughout the party. Now that's spooky.

Dressing up dogs for Halloween has become very popular in recent years. Many dog parents dress up not only their human but also their canine children for trick or treat night. Think I am joking? Just look through your local pet store or through the fall edition of mail order pet catalogs and you will find a wide assortment of costumes. Chances are you will have no trouble finding a costume to complement your dog's personality.

Berry and Wanda are not the dress-up type. But if they

were, I would have a ball dressing them up for Halloween. I would also have no problem deciding how to dress Wanda. Wanda, our little devil, would, of course, make the perfect devil. Everyone who knows Wanda well has no problem imagining her with little devil horns on her head. Sometimes we wonder if they are already there, and we just can't see them. (Just kidding, Wanda!)

And as I found out, I am not the only one who believes that my dog can be quite the devil at times. Devil costumes are a favorite among dog owners with mischievous dogs. If you are brave, here are some ways to bring out the devil in your little angel.

A simple and inexpensive way to bedevil your dog is with a set of devil horns for dogs. Most devil horns are bright red and are attached to a headband to keep the horns safely on your dog's head. Be forewarned if your little angel happens to get into trouble while wearing the horns, she can use that old excuse, "The devil made me do it."

Want the full devil effect? Rag Dog's Little Devil Costume features a hooded red cape with devil's horns attached to the hood of the cape and a tail that drags behind the cape. The cape is made of a poly-satin blend and is washable, in case your little devil gets into something she shouldn't.

But you don't have to encourage the devil in your dog; you can choose from many other costumes. Some of the highest quality costumes on the market are from Rag Dog. Rag Dog costumes run fifty dollars and up. Not sure you want to spend that much on a costume? Don't worry. I checked out the selections in the fall pet catalogs and the major online stores. I found pumpkin, cowboy, prisoner, devil, and even angel costumes galore. The best part is that nearly all of the costumes are priced below twenty dollars.

85. Fourth of July

July fourth can be one of the most traumatic days of the year
for dogs. The first time that Wanda heard fireworks, she ran
and hid under my desk and wouldn't come out for hours
afterward (not even for a biscuit). But July fourth doesn't have
to be a day that you and your dog dread. There are ways to
help keep your dog from being totally traumatized on one of
the most fun days of summer.

Here are some tricks we use with Wanda. You may find
they help your dog. First of all keep your dog in a quiet place
in the home. If you are not going to be at home, leave on the
television or the radio to help cover the "booming" sounds of
fireworks. Close all the blinds, and drapes to block the view of
lightninglike fireworks. And finally give your dog a special
long lasting treat or toy to keep her distracted from what is
going on outside. Your dog may never learn to love the holiday
as much as you do, but she may learn to live through it some-
what peacefully.

86. Thank You Easter Bunny

When the Easter bunny pays a visit to your house, make sure
he doesn't forget Rover. (Provided Rover doesn't try to eat
him or chase him off the property first.) Most dog bakeries
are happy to put together Easter baskets for your furry friend.
Or if you prefer to give Peter Rabbit a helping hand yourself,
you can easily put together your own basket. Just fill the basket as you would a child's basket with a few changes, of course.

Here are some great ideas for filling your dog's Easter basket. You can never go wrong with biscuits. To keep with the
Easter theme, look for some bunny-shape biscuits from the

dog bakery or look for a rabbit shape cookie cutter and bake a batch of your dog's favorite biscuits. No luck looking for rabbits? Pet Celebrations makes rabbit-shaped biscuits in several sizes. You will definitely want to include the canine version of chocolate rabbits: carob coated rabbits. And finally every Easter basket needs a rabbit in the middle. While your dog may enjoy chasing the real thing around, a stuffed rabbit toy is much more appropriate and will last longer. Finally instead of filling plastic eggs with jellybeans, fill them with small bite-size treats such as kibble.

Of course, every Easter morning needs its Easter egg hunt. Instead of hiding eggs around the house, hide your dog's favorite treats. Then when it is time, let your doggie sniff out the goodies helping him in the right direction, if necessary.

87. Something for Every Occasion

A Biscuit for Every Occasion

Bet you thought biscuits only came in bone or other canine-related shapes? How about a turkey shaped biscuit for Thanksgiving? Rabbit shaped biscuits for Easter? A Menorah-shaped gift box. Pet Celebrations specializes in theme dog biscuits and offers an unmatched variety of theme packaging.

By far the biggest selection is for Christmas. They have Christmas trees, snowmen, and gingerbread men biscuits, just to name a few. Or you can choose among unique gift boxes like the Dog by the Fireplace Gift Box. For the dog that has been especially good they have Felt Bone Stockings filled with bite-size treats.

Pet Celebrations hasn't forgotten about the other holidays. For Hanukkah there are Star of David biscuits. For Easter you can surprise your dog with a Big White Bunny Gift Box complete with biscuits, a toy rope tug, and a rawhide chew. If your dog is your Valentine, they have got you covered there. What dog could refuse a heart shaped biscuit decorated with a panda bear? You can even help your Irish setter celebrate St. Patrick's Day with shamrock biscuits.

And you thought biscuits were boring.

A Toy for Every Occasion

There are treats for every occasion. Why not toys? It should come as no surprise, but there are actually dog toys for every major, and not so major, holiday. There are Santas and reindeer for Christmas, turkeys and pilgrims for Thanksgiving, pumpkins for Halloween, and rabbits for Easter. But you don't have to stop the celebrating there. There are Fire Cracker Jacks for July fourth, Fuzzy Hearts for Valentine's Day, and even Fuzzy "Kiss Me" Clovers for St. Patrick's Day.

Can little presidents for President's Day be far behind?

Forget the Collar

Tired of shelling out for a new collar for every occasion? Creative Collars has the solution. Collar Covers. The unique covers fit over most collars. Their Holiday collar covers are sold in sets of four with collars for Christmas, St. Patrick's Day, the Fourth of July, and Halloween. Also available are collar covers for Valentine's Day and Easter. Prefer a bandanna? Creative Collars also has the bandanna cover that slips into your dog's collar, eliminating binding and choking hazards.

Pet Greeting Cards

And don't forget your doggie when it comes time to send out those greeting cards. Last Christmas two of our friends sent cards to Berry, Wanda, and Robin. I thought it was a great idea. With some research I found a company called Lit-terature that produces greeting cards for dogs. I also learned about a card coming out that dogs will truly appreciate—an edible greeting card.

When it comes time to send out cards to our close friends, I am always sure to sign Berry, Wanda, and Robin's names. I would never want anyone to feel that the gang was neglecting him or her.

When It's Time to Sign

What is the proper way to sign your doggie's name on a card? According to a Judith Martin (Miss Manners) column if you want to sign your dog's name to the card, you should add his name as you would your child's. For example the inside of a Christmas card would read as follows:

Merry Christmas!
Love,
David and Margaret
and Berry, Wanda, and Robin

The Pet-Iculars

Paw stockings: Three Dogs & a Cat, 877-PET-SOCK,
    www.petstocking.com
Angel Wing collar: Fox & Hounds, select retail locations,
    www.foxandhounds.com
Jingle collars: Creature Comforts, select retail locations

Prancer Christmas necklace: Oh My Stars!, select retail locations, www.ohmystars.com

Santa suit, Little Devil costume: RagDog, www.ragdog.com

Pet Celebrations, 877-860-8330, www.petcelebrations.com

Creative Collars, www.creativecollars.com

Litterature, www.litterature.com

14.

Miracles of Modern Medicine

*There is no psychiatrist in the world like a puppy
licking your face.*

—BEN WILLIAMS

These days virtually anything your doctor can do for you, a
veterinarian can do for your dog. Dogs are recipients of
total hip replacements, pacemakers, Prozac, therapy, and plastic surgery. As surgical procedures and medical treatments for
dogs are becoming more elaborate, dog owners are shelling out
millions of dollars each year on their dogs' medical care. And
when it comes to their dogs' health people spare no expense.

According to the American Veterinary Medical Association Americans spent $11.1 billion on their pets' health care
in 1998. That's a whopping 61 percent increase from 1991.
And doggie owners don't even blink at the thought of paying
$3,000 for hip replacements, $1,000–$1,500 for pacemakers,
or even $5,000–$6,000 for heart valve transplants.

And dog owners aren't just spending money on surgical
procedures. Increasing numbers of dogs are being fitted with
wheelchairs to help them get around. Owners think nothing
of outfitting their homes with ramps so that older or arthritic
dogs have an easier time getting up the stairs or on the bed.
Alice Lerman, who owns the pet boutique Barker & Meowsky

in Chicago, even built an elevator on the back of the house when her malamute could no longer climb the stairs. It is truly amazing the great lengths people will go through to insure that their dogs live long happy lives.

The amount of money we are spending to maintain our dogs' health is perhaps one of the biggest indicators of how Americans' attitudes towards their canines have changed over the years. People no longer think of their dogs as possessions but as cherished family members. As my friend Michael Kaiser, who recently spent over $2,800 on his golden retriever's hip replacement surgery, explains, "Kelly's my family. Who wouldn't want to take care of their family?"

But dog owners are not just spending money on lifesaving surgeries or assists. Some have taken the concept of dog care one step further. Today dog owners are signing their doggies up for elective surgeries such as liposuction. Depressed doggies are being sent to doggie therapists. And owners who can't face the prospect of life without Rover are considering cloning.

Calling Dr. Dog!

According to a study by the State University of New York Medical School pets helped reduce the stress of Wall Street brokers.

All of the subjects of the study were between the ages of forty and fifty, earned at least two hundred thousand dollars, and were on medication to lower blood pressure. Half of the subjects were given a pet. Those given pets had lower blood pressure readings than those without pets.

As a result of the study half of the brokers that
did not have a pet ended up getting one.

You might not know this, but veterinary medicine has
really come full circle. Many of the surgeries and treatments
mentioned below were originally perfected for people by test-
ing on animals. Now veterinarians are taking what we have
learned by treating humans and applying the knowledge to
treating canines. It seems only fitting that finally these techniques are now benefiting the original "guinea pigs."

88.   Mending Broken Hearts, and More

Mending Broken Hearts

If your precious pooch's heart of gold is ailing, a canine
cardiologist may be able to mend it with a pacemaker. Each
year hundreds of pacemakers are implanted into dogs. And
believe it or not they are the same models used for people. A
pacemaker can keep your dog's heart ticking for three to five
years while allowing him to live a normal, happy dog life.

Medical research has shown that survivors of
heart attacks who come home to understanding pets
have a 400 percent better chance of survival over
those who come home to a judgmental spouse.

Hip, Hip, Hooray!

Anyone who has a dog that suffers from hip dysplasia
knows the agony of watching a beloved friend try to hobble
around. Now dogs no longer need to suffer from this painful
condition. Total hip replacement surgery is routinely performed on four-legged patients. It is currently the most effec-

tive treatment available for dogs suffering from hip dysplasia. While the cost of the surgery varies you can expect to pay anywhere from $1,500–$3,000 per hip, but the good news is that dogs typically need to only have one hip replaced. And unlike humans who often take weeks to months to recover from the surgery, most dogs are up walking in as little as a day after surgery and are running around in weeks.

Can Dogs Catch Cold?

Your dog has the chills. He is sneezing and coughing. He has even lost his bark (the dog equivalent of voice). Your dog has all the symptoms of a cold. But do dogs catch colds? According to veterinarians the answer is yes. However canine colds are often referred to as upper respiratory infections (URIs). Some of the more common URIs found in canines are tonsillitis, kennel cough, and bronchitis. And just like in people, if left untreated these ailments can develop into more serious ailments such as pneumonia.

But here's the big question. Can you catch a cold from Rover or vice versa? You will be happy to note that if Rover is sneezing, you can still give him a big kiss. Colds are passed on by viruses that are not transmittable to other species.

Can You Hear Me?

Does it seem like your dog just doesn't listen to you anymore? If your dog is like my Robin, she just has selective hearing. However for many purebred dogs, deafness is a common genetic problem. If it seems like your dog can no longer hear you, you might want to get him a canine hearing aid. Yes, you heard that right. The canine hearing aid consists of an amplifying device that is contained in a small canister that is attached to the animal's collar. From the canister a plastic tube runs up the neck and plugs into the ear. Now dogs will have to come up with more creative excuses for not coming when called.

89.   First Aid

What would you do if your dog cut his leg? If he suffered an injury to his eye? If you thought he was running a temperature? Or if he was choking or suffering a heart attack? What do you do in the case of a canine emergency?

First Aid Kit

The Pet-Pak First Aid for Pets kit has all you need for those canine medical emergency situations at home or on the road. The kit contains handy first aid accessories such as gauze pads, tweezers, eye irrigate, scissors, and much more. It even has an invaluable Pet First Aid Guide that guides you through such common emergencies as cuts, wounds, insect bites, bleeding, burns, poisoning, eye injuries, and more. The kit is made of heavy durable weatherproof plastic and comes with both carrying handles and mounting brackets. In addition the Pet-Pak has been given the stamp of approval by veterinarians and the ASPCA.

CPR for Doggies

Did you know that The Humane Society and The American Red Cross now teach Pet CPR? Local Red Cross chapters teach the lifesaving technique using animal mannequins. This "must-have" class for pet owners is becoming quite popular. By late 2000 the American Red Cross was teaching the class in sixty-five of its twelve hundred chapters. The number is expected to grow as bark of snout travels.

In addition to CPR the Red Cross Pet First Aid class teaches people how to prevent, prepare for, and respond to pet emergencies. Some of the topics covered in the four-hour class include proper procedures during emergencies and how to assemble a pet's first aid kit. Included with the course is the Pet First Aid for Cats and Dogs book, which contains helpful information on everything from taking a temperature to birthing emergencies.

If you are interested in learning the potential life saving technique, contact your local American Red Cross chapter or Humane Society for further information.

Should You Quit Smoking for Your Dog?

If you won't quit for yourself, quit for your dog. Just like humans, dogs' lungs are sensitive to irritation from tobacco smoke. In fact a veterinary journal recently reported a case of lung cancer in a dog that lived with two smokers. So, before you light up in front of your dog, stop and think about what you are doing to your best friend and remember he would never do anything to hurt you.

90. Insure Your Dog's Health

Unfortunately advanced veterinary procedures also corre-
spond to advanced costs. What's a dog owner to do when faced
with shelling out one thousand dollars here and five hundred
dollars there? Well, what do people do? They buy health
insurance to help offset rising medical costs. Now you can do
the same for your dog.

Pet insurance is a win-win proposition for both owner and
dog. Canines can be assured the best medical treatments while
owners can be assured of not going broke. Pet insurance is
still a relatively new concept to pet owners. According to statistics released by Veterinary Pet Insurance of Anaheim, California, and Petshealth Insurance only 1 percent or less of
pets in the United States are covered by insurance compared
to 22 percent in England, 45 percent in Sweden, and 20 percent in Canada.

Industry experts recommend investing in insurance while
your dog is still a puppy because, just as many human insurance plans do, many pet insurance plans exclude preexisting
conditions. The good news is that today there are several pet
insurance plans to choose from. Companies like Veterinary
Pet Insurance, the pioneer of pet insurance in the United
States, Pet Assure, and National Pet Club are some of the better known in the industry. Of course rates and plans vary
from carrier to carrier. Similar to our insurance system some
plans limit your choice of veterinarian to those participating
in the network, while others allow you a choice (albeit for a
higher price) of veterinarian. You can expect to pay anywhere
from sixty dollars to three hundred dollars a year depending
on your dog's age and health. But hey—isn't your dog's health
worth it?

91. Canine Vanity

Cosmetic surgery and dentistry are more popular than ever. Most everyone knows someone who has had one procedure or another. So, it should be no surprise that these procedures are now available for our canine friends. Porky puppies are getting liposuction. Doggies with crooked canines are wearing braces. And neutered males are getting back their manhood (well, a substitute at least). The sky is the limit when it comes to catering to our canines' vanity.

Doggie Lipo

Fido getting flabby thighs? Maybe liposuction is the answer. A number of veterinarians claim to be hounded by persistent owners wanting to get rid of their pooch's "pooch." If you think that liposuction sounds like the perfect solution for your porky poochie, don't get your hopes up. Most veterinarians won't perform the procedure explaining that as with humans diet and exercise are the answer to a few unwanted pounds.

> *According to a PETsMART survey 31 percent of pet owners take days off work to stay home when their pets are sick.*

How Much for Those Braces on the Doggie?

If you think that your canine's smile is just as important as your own, brace yourself. Or better yet brace your dog. Doggies whose smiles are less than perfect can be fitted with doggie braces. Doggie braces are worn anywhere from two weeks to four months. Afterwards canines sport movie star smiles. Additionally it is unlikely that they will ever have to wear braces again. Because dogs keep their mouths closed more than do people, dogs' teeth do not shift as much. Maybe we should take a cue from our dogs.

> *It's no coincidence that man's best friend*
> *cannot talk.*

> —ANONYMOUS

And You Thought You Have Seen It All

Male dogs afraid of losing their dignity along with their manhood need no longer worry. Neuticles are artificial testicles that can be implanted when a male dog is neutered. According to the Neuticles Web site over fourteen thousand dogs have been enhanced with Neuticles by over eight thousand veterinarians worldwide.

Thinking of getting some for your dog? There are currently two models of Neuticles that come in five different sizes. The original model is made of polyprophylene. Dogs seeking a more natural look and feel will want to opt for Neuticles Naturals, which are made from silicone.

92. Puppy Uppers

Dogs are pack animals by nature and they do not like being left alone. In fact being left behind by the pack feels like a death sentence for many dogs. What's a lonely dog to do? Since they can't pick up the phone and bark with their friends, most resort to destructive behavior causing thousands of dollars in damages. Veterinarians and animal therapists have prescribed Prozac for dogs with great success. And recently the Food and Drug Administration approved a new drug to treat separation anxiety. The antidepressant, Clomi-calm, when used together with therapy, promises to improve a lonely dog's behavior.

Weathering the Storm

Is your furry friend afraid of storms? My Wanda is terri-fied of storms. If a storm happens to come through during the day she starts quivering and shaking and either hides under my desk or tries to sit on my lap. However, if a storm comes through at night while we are sleeping, Wanda tries to hide by squeezing between my husband's head and the head-board, but much to my husband's dismay she usually ends up lying on his head.

Dogs frightened from storms may simply want to be near you for comfort. But some dogs panic and can cause real dam-age to themselves or your home by scratching at doors or fur-niture. If Rover is afraid of storms, here are some tips my veterinarian gave me to help Wanda weather the storm.

1. Do not keep saying "It's OK" to your dog. Your dog will take your comforting words as reinforcement that there is something to fear.

2. Try singing to your dog or playing with her to distract her from what is happening outside.

3. Train your dog to get used to the sounds of thunder-storms with a recording of thunder. You can get tapes of storms from stores like Natural Wonders. Start out by playing the tape softly and gradually increasing the vol-ume.

4. If none of the above works, consider asking your veteri-narian about medicine to calm your dog during storms.

❧93.   Even Beagles Get the Blues

It turns out that we are not alone in our phobias, compulsions, or mood disorders. Even beagles get the blues. If your canine is in the dumps, there is hope. Animal therapists, psychiatrists, and psychologists are often effective when treating conditions such as doggie depression. Hour sessions can cost up to $150, but many dog owners swear that it is worth it. Our former neighbor, Lucy, swore that after two months in therapy her dachshund, Ginger, was transformed from a dog that would not play or eat to one that was as playful and hungry as a puppy.

No doggie psychologists in your area? Don't worry; there are several other sources you can turn to. The Animal Behavior Helpline based in New York City offers telephone consultations with animal psychologists. Consultations run $45 for 30 minutes and $1 a minute for each additional minute.

❧94.   Living in the Clone Age

Nothing can replace your best friend. However modern technology gives you the chance to try. With the cloning of a sheep named Dolly, cloning has gone from a dream to reality. In fact experts predict that cloning of canines may become a reality by the end of 2001. In anticipation of canine cloning dog owners across the country are shelling out thousands of dollars to save their beloved dogs' genes for when that day comes.

The whole cloning craze began in 1998 when an anonymous couple donated $2.4 million dollars to the cloning lab at Texas A&M University to clone their beloved dog, Missy. The project entitled "Missyplicity" has generated such publicity that it even has its own Web site, www.missyplicity.com, where interested parties can keep updated on the latest developments in the project, offer feedback, and look through stories and pictures of Missy.

After the "Missyplicity" project was initiated, Genetic Savings & Clone (GSC) was established. Those interested in cloning their dogs can go to the GSC Web site, www.savingsandclone.com, to set up an appointment to sample their pet's DNA for potential cloning. Then at your local veterinarian's office several small tissue samples are taken from your dog. The procedure is reportedly similar to a biopsy. The veterinarian then sends the DNA to GSC to be processed. The DNA will be kept frozen in liquid nitrogen until cloning is viable.

Estimated costs for freezing the gene are between one thousand to three thousand dollars and about one hundred dollars for yearly storage fees. Additionally when pet cloning is finally achieved initial customers will pay nearly two hundred thousand dollars to replicate their pets. However, if you can wait a couple of years, the price is expected to drop to the bargain price of twenty thousand dollars.

95. Give Them a Lift

Let's face it sometimes we all need a little extra help getting around. The same is true for our dogs. Jumping up on the bed or getting into the car can be nearly impossible for small, older, or injured dogs. And while it is easy to lift a small dog up on the bed, trying to hoist a large dog into the back of a SUV can be quite the challenge.

While Berry and Wanda can leap right up on the bed or jump into the back of my SUV, Robin has a much more difficult time. When it is her turn to get in the car she pitifully places her two front paws on the back tailgate, waiting for someone to lift her the rest of the way. Luckily for Robin (and for my back) there are alternatives to constantly having to lift her into the back of the car or up onto the bed.

Dog ramps and wheelchairs/carts are just a couple of the devices available to help doggies get around. Now no dog need be left behind or stranded on the floor due to age, injury, or size.

On/Off Ramps

Ramps are a great way to give your dog easy access to furniture or cars. For dogs suffering from arthritis or hip dysplasia jumping on and off the bed can be pure torture. For dogs the ramps eliminate the repeated trauma they experience in their joints every time they jump from a piece of furniture or out of a car. For dog owners the ramps eliminate the sore backs that they experience from lifting Rover.

The BedderBacks Dog Bed Ramp is designed specifically to help canines get on and off the bed. Tired of constantly lifting their three very active small dogs on and off the bed Dave and Paulette Smith designed and built the ramp so that their dogs could come and go as they wished. While the Smiths' dogs were thrilled with their new ramp, the Smiths were even more thrilled not to have to lift the dogs back onto the bed many times during the night. On a visit to their home the Smith's veterinarian had an opportunity to check out the ramp and suggested that they sell the ramps to the general public.

The ramp extends a foot out from the bed and is five feet long and twenty-five inches at the top landing. The ramp has a sure grip, stain resistant carpet, and even has a four-inch-high railing that can be attached to either side for added security. The ramp frame is constructed from scuff resistant, top quality veneer furniture. The ramp is great not only for small or older dogs, or those recovering from injuries, but it easily accommodates even the heaviest dogs.

Ramps do come in handy around the house. But if you are like me you are more concerned with getting your dog in and out of the back of your SUV or other vehicle. The Pet Step Folding Ramp is the perfect solution. The ramp is made of a rugged plastic and has universal grips to fit all vehicles. The ramp is almost six feet long and eighteen inches wide when extended and will hold up to five hundred pounds. It has a ribbed, non-slip surface that is easy to clean with soap and water. The best part is that the ramp folds to thirty-five inches and weighs just twenty pounds so you can take it with you. The ramp has received a stamp of approval from the ASPCA.

96.   Mobile and Happy

Paws on Wheels

Mobility-impaired dogs no longer have to sit on the sidelines and watch as other dogs play. Canine wheelchairs give dogs back their independence and allow them to lead a normal happy life. While this may seem hard to believe, believe it. Mobile dogs are happy dogs. Dogs who require wheelchairs are perfectly happy as long as they can get around. In fact after a while dogs do not even realize that they are in a chair and bound around just like they did when they were younger or before their injury.

K-9 Cart. The K-9 Cart was designed by veterinary orthopedic specialist, Dr. Lincoln Parkes, in the early 1960s. Dr. Parkes wanted to develop a device that would allow mobility-impaired dogs to walk and lead an active life. Sadly, until the K-9 Cart was developed dogs with disabled limbs were often put to sleep.

But the K-9 Cart is not only for permanently impaired dogs. The cart is also used as a post-surgical or post-injury rehabilitative aid. The cart has helped many doggies return to full mobility.

Each cart is custom-built to your dog's measurements and weight. The weight of the cart depends upon the weight, size, and age of your dog. The carts are strong enough to support the rear of you dog but are not too heavy to create any stress on your dog's body. The K-9 Cart is made with stainless steel and lightweight aluminum and has waterproof foam padding to prevent abrasion. The cart is completely washable and will not rust. For dogs with some mobility in their rear legs there is an optional walking kit available. For the active dog the cart can be outfitted with mountain bike wheels so that canines can glide over hills and bumps.

Amazingly it only takes dogs a few minutes to a few days to adjust to the new cart. However it is recommended that you gradually allow your doggie to break in his new wheels. The cart is designed practically so that your dog is able to do his business while in the cart. However since they are unable to lift a leg or squat, dogs eliminate in a standing or semi squatting position.

Dogs using the carts are able to resume happy, active lifestyles. Dogs are even able to go up and down stairs in the cart. However it is recommended that you block off stairs to avoid an accident since dogs in the cart think they are normal and may try to run down the stairs like they used to.

Barbara Parkes and her son, Glenn, have run K-9 Carts for over twenty-four years. They have sold their carts all over the world while K-9 Carts has grown steadily each year. Ms. Parkes attributes the success of K-9 Carts to her husband's orthopedic background and their personalized service. After a customer purchases a cart for his dog K-9 Carts requests that the customer then send a video to see how the dog is doing with the cart. They then offer suggestions and try to help evaluate how the dog is accepting the cart.

Dewey's Wheechairs for Dogs. Dewey's Wheelchairs for Dogs is another company devoted to helping out pets in need. Dewey Springer, who started the company in 1997, set out to build a wheelchair lighter in weight than those currently on the market. His wheelchairs are up to 50 percent lighter than other doggie wheelchairs; yet they have the strength to support large dogs such as Great Danes or Newfoundlands. All of Dewey's wheelchairs are custom fit to your dog's measurements and lifestyle taking into consideration your dog's activity levels as well as the type of terrain that he likes to play on.

Baldar and His Buggy

At the age of fifteen and a half, Baldar, a mixed breed, lost the use of his rear legs due to calcification of the spine. His owners, Cecilie and Mark Sebolt, couldn't stand it as they watched their once vibrant dog become more and more depressed. So they took matters into their own hands. They built Baldar a cart to help him get around. Cecilie Sebolt explained, "We were pretty nervous the first time we put him in his cart. We weren't sure if he would take to it. We turned our heads to look at the old boy, and he was gone . . . off down the street." It took Baldar a short time to adjust to his cart, but within two months he participated in a 5k fundraiser for a local animal shelter. Baldar participated in many more walks and was a star everywhere he went. Baldar especially liked the treats and attention that he received as a result of being in the cart. To Baldar his cart was just a means of letting him get around to do the things he loved. Although Baldar is no longer alive, the Sebolts use his story to inspire other

people with disabled dogs. The Sebolts now run a small business that makes carts for mobility-impaired dogs.

Pets with Disabilities

The subject of disabled dogs is a serious one for thousands
of dog owners. Although there are dozens of sites devoted to
helping owners of aging or disabled dogs, a couple I think
stand out are The Senior Dogs Project (www.srdogs.com),
which is a wonderful resource site for owners of older dogs
and the Owners of Blind Dogs Web site (www.blinddogs.
com). The Owners of Blind Dogs Web site was founded in
1998 and has since helped over one thousand dog owners of
blind dogs.

The Pet-Iculars

Pet-Pak First Aid for Pets: www.petpak.com

Neuticles, 888-NEUTICLES, www.neuticles.com

Animal Behavior Helpline, 212-721-1231

Genetic Savings & Clone, 888-833-6063, www.savingsandclone.com

The Missiplicity Project, www.missyplicity.com

Dog bed ramp: BedderBacks by Smith-Kruger, 877-327-5438,
    www.bedderbacks.com

The Pet Step Folding Ramp: select retail locations

K-9 Carts, 800-578-6960, www.k9carts.com

Dewey's Wheelchairs for Dogs, 877-312-2122,
    www.wheelchairsfordogs.com

15.

Leaving a Legacy

*If there is no heaven for dogs, then I want to go
where they go when I die.*

—ANONYMOUS

People understand that losing a canine companion can be just as traumatic as losing a family member, if not more so. Dog owners wanting to give their faithful friend a proper funeral are no longer thought of as "crazy" or eccentric. To the contrary people who have lost their best friend are now treated with compassion and empathy.

On the flip side older pet owners ask, "What will happen to my dog when I die?" or "What happens if I get too sick to care for my dog?" Sadly many older people resist getting a dog for fear of what will happen to him when they are gone. Fortunately there are a number of options available to insure that your dog will live a long and happy life after you are gone so that no matter what your age, you can still enjoy the company of a dog.

97. Final Rest

Hartsdale Pet Cemetery in Hartsdale, New York, is the oldest pet cemetery in the United States. Founded in 1896 the cemetery is the final resting place for close to seventy thousand pets. The cemetery offers a wide variety of funeral services ranging from a scattering of ashes in the garden to a full traditional funeral service that includes a viewing in a private room. If desired, a religious figure may perform the ceremony. Hartsdale offers other options including perpetual and flower care for the gravesite.

Hartsdale Cemetery is also the home of the War Dog Memorial. Robert Caterson, a designer and builder, whose credits include Grand Central Station in New York City was chosen to build the memorial. The monument is ten feet high and is topped with a bronze statue of a German Shepherd dog wearing a Red Cross blanket. At the dog's feet are a bronze helmet and canteen. An American flag waves above. The inscription reads:

Dedicated to the memory of the war dog. Erected
by public contributions by dog lovers to man's
faithful friend for the valiant services rendered in
world war, 1914–1918.

Across the country the Los Angeles Pet Memorial Park is the final resting place of nearly forty thousand animals. In 1986, the property became the first perpetually dedicated pet cemetery in California. Tori Spelling's beloved poodle, Angel, and William Shatner's Doberman pinscher as well as the pets of Steven Spielberg, Rudolph Valentino, Mae West, and Tony Orlando are among the animals buried in the park. The cemetery offers a number of services including burial, cremation, and referrals for grief counseling.

Help with the Arrangements

In April 1997, New York's first full-service pet funeral home, All Pets Go To Heaven, opened. Located in the Carroll Gardens section of Brooklyn, New York, the funeral home holds wakes and funeral services complete with clergy, memorial cards, eulogies, and prayers in its Victorian Chapel. Owners Kathleen and Raymond Leone understand how traumatic the passing of a beloved pet may be. Unfortunately many families that find themselves in this position are unaware of their options and leave this heartbreaking decision to their pet's veterinarian.

The Leones created All Pets Go To Heaven out of their inherent love of animals. The Leone family of funeral directors has been serving their community during their time of loss since 1982. During that time they were often approached by people asking if they might consider providing services for grieving pet owners as well.

Understanding the pain that owners suffer with the loss of their pet, Ms. Leone points out that she often talks many of them from going overboard or to excess with the arrangements. She has no desire to take advantage of grieving pet owners during such a vulnerable time. Leone handles viewings that range from one to forty people. She also handles the details of cremations, burials, wakes, and memorial services. She notes that pet owners who have lost a pet find it fulfilling and gratifying to arrange and participate in a viewing or memorial service for their pets.

If I have any beliefs about immortality, it is that certain dogs I have known will go to heaven, and very, very few persons.

—JAMES THURBER

98. Let Your Estate Go to the Dogs

Willing an estate to the family dog or dogs is becoming a trend. Canine parents want to insure that their dogs live out their lives in a warm, loving environment, not a cold, over-crowded shelter. As a result several institutions now offer programs that guarantee that your doggie will be well taken care of even when you are gone.

The SPCA of Texas has developed the Pet Survivor Life Care Program for pets who survive their owners. In the program you choose the SPCA to care for your dog and arrange for a gift to the SPCA in your estate plan. A minimum gift of ten thousand dollars assures that your dog is placed with a loving family that is monitored by the SPCA Quality Control Department for life. Or, if you prefer, for a minimum gift of twenty-five thousand dollars your dog can be placed in a SPCA Pet Survivor Life Care Cottage. These cottages are homes that provide each dog access to common areas like a living room and a doggie den. The cottages offer a social environment with no caging. Caretakers live in the home, and doggies can roam around freely indoors. Also around the cottages there are large outdoor exercise areas for the dogs to romp around and play.

Some people have even taken the program one step further. One couple donated their 4,500-square-foot home to the SPCA of Texas. In return the SPCA will provide around-the-clock care and free medical attention for their seven dogs. As a part of the deal the dogs will remain in the home and be able to roam freely through the house and the yard for the rest of their lives.

Peace of Mind

The School of Veterinary Medicine at Purdue University made national news with its program called "Peace of Mind." In the program dog owners arrange for an estate gift to be given to the school after their death. In exchange for the gift the school arranges for a loving home for the dog and provides free medical care for the remainder of the dog's life. The amount of the gift is dependent upon the age and condition of the dog, but the typical contribution is about twenty-five thousand dollars.

A similar program has been developed by Kansas State University's College of Veterinary Medicine. According to a Kansas State University press release dog owners set up an endowed scholarship for a veterinary student who in return cares for their dog if they become incapacitated or die. The dog owner specifies the type of food, housing, exercise, playtime, and medical care they wish their dog to have. For instance, a dog owner can stipulate that they would like for their beloved dog to be walked for thirty minutes a day and be treated to gourmet biscuits. Dog owners also specify whether they wish for their dog to remain with one owner for the rest of its life or whether the dog should go to another student when the first student graduates.

99.   Retirement Home

Still not quite sure how to best look after your dog when you're gone? Consider retirement. Not yours. Your dog's. Your dog can live out the remainder of his years at Golden Years Retirement Home in Westhampton, New York. The retirement home is designed for older, less adoptable, dogs who outlive their owners. At Golden Years dogs sleep and eat in large cubicles rather than cages. They can play in indoor or outdoor exercise areas. For your dog's health and comfort the retirement home boasts an indoor climate control system with 100 percent air circulation every hour. And when the time comes for your dog to go to doggie heaven, he is given a proper burial in the Bide-A-Wee Memorial Park in Westhampton.

To be accepted into the home, dogs must be at least eight years old, spayed or neutered, and free of any contagious diseases.

Retirement does come at a price however. The lifetime fee per dog at Golden Years is ten thousand dollars.

The Pet-Iculars

Hartsdale Pet Cemetery, 75 N. Central Park Ave., Hartsdale, NY 10503, 800-375-5234

Los Angeles Pet Memorial Park, 5068 N. Old Scandia Lane, Calabassas, CA 91372, 818-591-7037

Virtual Pet Cemetery, www.mycemetery.com

All Pets Go To Heaven, Carroll Gardens, Brooklyn, NY, 718-875-7877, www.allpetsgotoheaven.com

Pet Survivor Life Care Program, SPCA of Texas, www.spca.org/planned.htm

Golden Years Retirement Home, 118 Old Country Rd., Westhampton, NY 11977, 212-532-6358

16.

The Best Things in Life Are Free

The best things in life are free.

—P ROVERB

For many dogs the free things in life are their favorites. So, while you are spoiling your dog with many of the other items in this book, don't forget to throw in a couple of these.

100. What's in a Name?

One of the simplest ways to spoil your dog is to give him a really great name. You are probably thinking, yeah right, this from a woman whose dog is named Wanda. But keep in mind that all of my dogs were named before I got them. Even though I wasn't quite sure about her name at first, now I really love the name; it really seems to fit her. And while people do give me weird looks whenever I tell them Wanda's (and sometimes Berry's) name, no one ever forgets it. Additionally the dogs love that they get a lot of attention when people first meet them because people seem to love to repeat "Wanda" and "Berry" and even "Robin."

Let's face it. You're bound to come across quite a few Maxes or Ladys, but how many Wandas or Napoleons or Casablancas have you ever encountered? And if you pay attention, you will find that dogs with really great or unique names get instant attention. I remember a neighbor of ours named her little dog Ronnie Reagan. At the time Ronald Reagan was president. Every time someone would meet little Ronnie they would lavish attention on him. And little Ronnie (who was rumored to actually be a Democrat) loved every minute of it.

It used to be that people named their dogs after a physical feature or personality such as Spot or Happy. That is no longer the case. More and more people treat their dogs as children. Hence human names for dogs are increasingly popular. Now you see more dogs with names like Max, which means "the greatest" in Latin, or Sam, which means "listener."

Dog names are also very dependent upon the sex and age of the owner. Studies have shown that for the most part men give their dogs more masculine names like Spike or Rocky. Women on the other hand favor more feminine names such as Samantha or Tasha. Children like to name dogs after characters from their favorite movies or television shows. Consequently there are a lot of Skips (*My Dog Skip*), Simbas (*The Lion King*), and even Barneys (for that popular dinosaur). Even adults are not above naming their dog after a favorite character such as Eddie, the popular dog on *Frasier*.

So, how do you go about selecting a great name for your dog? Luckily there are several resources for you to consult if a name like Fido won't do. Believe it or not there are books devoted entirely to names for pets. *The Complete Book of Pet Names: An ASPCA Book* by George Greenfield, editor (Andrews McMeel Publishing, 1997) is an entertaining and informative book to help dog owners come up with a unique dog name. *Don't Call Me Rover!!: 5001 Names to Call Your Pet* by Rita Blockton (Avon Books, 1997) offers descriptions of names for pets from the quirky to the sophisticated.

The internet also has a number of sites where you can check out thousands of names for your dog. The site petrix.com/dognames has over two thousand dog names. The site also tracks the most popular dog names in the country. Other sites with names for your dog are simplypets.com and ivillage.com.

A Name Is a Name?

According to Dr. Stanley Coren, author of What Do Dogs Know *(The Free Press, 1997), 38 percent of dog owners accidentally call their spouse by their dog's name. And 25 percent of these people accidentally call their dog by their spouse's name. Oops!*

101. Drive Thru Heaven

Sometimes it pays to bring your dog along for the ride. At least it pays for your dog. Berry, Wanda, and Robin have caught on to a growing trend: doggie treats at drive thru windows. We first noticed the trend when we lived in Ohio. Our bank kept a container of dog biscuits at the drive thru for doggie "customers." I don't know how Berry and Wanda (this was before Robin's time) could have known about the treats behind the window, but somehow they sniffed them out, because as soon as we drove up to the window their noses were out the window. It did not take them long to learn the routine, pull up to a drive thru window; get a treat. The woman working at the bank window learned their names before she learned mine. Berry and Wanda were always greeted first with a warm smile and a biscuit, while mom was sometimes barely acknowledged, even though I was the actual customer.

I have since learned that my bank is not alone in passing out treats to pets. Many fast-food restaurants keep a stash of dog treats around. I asked a girl at one of these restaurants why they started giving treats for pets, and she replied that they did not want the dogs to feel left out, and it was just fun to pet and talk to the different dogs.

Dogs have it so ruff. They come along for the ride and get free food while we drive and we pay for food. But that is one of the perks of being a dog.

No matter how little money and how few possessions you own, having a dog makes you rich.

—Louis Sabin

102. Paws for a Moment (or Two)

One of the best ways to spoil your dog is to spend time with him. Let's face it: You are your dog's hero and he wants nothing more than to be by your side. You can shower your dog with the most expensive and exclusive gifts, but that really means nothing if you don't spend time with him. Experts say at the very minimum you should try to set aside fifteen minutes of undivided attention for your dog once a day (twice is much better). Not quite sure what to do for those fifteen minutes? Here are some suggestions.

Take a walk around the block or play a game. This is not only good for your dog but also for you. According to the book, *Real Age*, by Dr. Michael F. Roizen, owning a dog helps you stay younger longer. This age benefit is attributed to the fact that dog owners get more exercise caring for their dogs.

Brush your dog. Taking a few minutes out each day to brush your dog has several benefits as mentioned in the chapter "Looking Good—Feeling Grrreat!" (see page 94).

Give your dog a hug. Touch is a healing medium. Babies who are untouched as infants never develop emotionally. Couples who stop touching, stop loving. Give yourself permission to stroke and pet your dog. Dogs absolutely love this, my Berry in particular. While Wanda and Robin eventually get bored, he could sit and be petted for hours. When he feels that I have been paying too much attention to the computer and not to him, Berry will come and nudge my arm away from the keyboard so that my hand ends up on his back. There is no telling him that Mom has a deadline. Often I end up petting him with one hand while trying to type with the other.

Health and Wealth

Owning a dog not only makes you healthy but also may make you dog gone wealthy. According to a 1998 survey of Fortune 500 executives nearly 85 percent of the country's top CEOs said that owning a dog benefited their emotional health.

103. Offers You Can't Refuse

There is no such thing as a free lunch. But some pet businesses will make you some free offers that you can't refuse. By far, Purina is the king of free offers. On a recent visit to the dog food manufacturer's Web site, I found such freebies as the Puppy Care Kit, Weight-Loss Kit (sorry, this is for dogs), and the Pet Safety Kit. You can find out about Purina's current offers at www.purina.com.

If you like free stuff, you'll love this. There is actually an entire book dedicated to free stuff for pets. *Free Stuff for Pet Lovers* by Matthew Lesko (Information USA, 2000) lists dozens of free products and services that you can get for your dog without spending a dime. The book teaches you how to get such things as free pet care for emergencies, a star named in honor of your dog, free pet coffins, free estate planning for your pet, and even free Prozac for dogs. For those who might be interested the book even teaches one how to recycle pet poop for profit.

Trying to keep up with all of the free offers is enough to drive someone bark raving mad. Luckily there are a few Web sites that keep track of the latest free offers for your pet. The site www.workingdogweb.com keeps a current listing of free things for dogs, while the site www.1freestuff.com includes free stuff for pets among their many categories.

17.

Miscellaneous

*Whoever said you can't buy happiness
forgot about little puppies.*

—GENE HILL

OK. We've covered everything from treats to castles. But
wait. There's more! The following ways for spoiling your
dog didn't quite fit in any of the previous chapters. So I gave
them a home of their own, appropriately called "Miscellaneous." You'll love reading through the next twelve ways, as
they are quite unique. Hey you don't get placed in the miscellaneous category for being like everything else.

Pet Friendly Funds

*Now here is an investment that would make your
dog proud. In early 2000, Salomon Brothers Asset
Management unleashed The Humane Equity Fund,
which won't invest in companies deemed animal
unfriendly by the Humane Society of the United
States. While you might think that animal friendly
companies might not perform as well as others, fund*

manager Chad Graves showed that a model looking at the three- and five-year performance of animal friendly portfolios actually did better than more broadly based funds. The fund seeks any good investment with of course the exception of such animal unfriendly sectors as hunting gear and pharmaceuticals.

104. Two Dogs Are Better Than One

One's a lonely number. Dog may be man's best friend and vice versa, but sometimes dogs just need to be dogs. And sometime doggies just need other dogs to play with. That is why some dog owners are adding a second dog into their household. Their attitude is that two dogs can keep themselves company while Mom and Dad are away at work. So Mom and Dad feel less guilty while they're gone.

However before you bring home that second furry bundle of joy, there are a couple of things to consider. First of all there is the time and money factor. Twice the number of dogs means twice the amount of food, twice the number of accessories, more trips to the veterinarian, more walks, and twice the clean up. You also need to consider your dog's personality. Be honest. If your dog has hated every dog he has ever met, then he is not a good candidate for a roommate. Size does matter. Usually it is best to get a dog of similar size to your first dog. This is particularly true with my Berry. He does not like little dogs—no exceptions. A small dog would not last five minutes in our house.

I have a multiple dog household and I wouldn't have it any other way. Having more than one dog gives me time off from having to "be a dog." Berry and Wanda are the classic set of playmates. They chase each other around, wrestle with each other, and follow each other from room to room. Even Robin, who is much more sedate, gets in on the chasing action. Berry and Wanda are also very protective of one another and even more so of Robin. Once during a walk an unleashed dog charged Robin barking and growling. Robin was startled and jumped back. Wanda quickly came to the rescue jumping in between the two dogs. She returned the barking and growling and sent the bully on his way.

Of the 40 percent of American households that have dogs, more than 33 percent have multiple dogs.

105. Ring My Bell

Teaching a dog to let you know when they need to go out can be a difficult task. Conversely it can sometimes be difficult for your dog to teach you his signal for wanting to go out. Now there is an easy way for your dog to let you know that it is time to go. The Pet Chime is a portable wireless electronic doorbell that your dog presses when he wants to go in or out. The wireless paw looks like a paw print and can sit on the floor or be mounted on the wall. You and your dog have two choices of chime, the traditional "ding dong" or a "bark." You can even add extra paws to the system so your dog can have one at every door.

106. Make an Impression

Paw print kits are a unique way to keep a permanent keepsake of your dog. They are also a physical reminder of just how small your furry friend was when you first got him or a sentimental way to remember your dog after he is gone. Surprisingly there are several paw print kits available that help your dog put his best paw forward.

Most ready-to-use paw print kits come with several ounces of white, nontoxic modeling clay and instructions that offer suggestions about how to obtain clean, deep paw impressions. But you don't have to use a dog-specific kit to capture your dog's impression. Air-dry molding clay kits are available at most craft stores. Flatten the clay into a square or circular shape and place your dog's paw print in the middle. Decorate around the print using dog bone shape biscuits, hearts, or other dog-related shapes. Follow the instructions for drying.

107. Getting Around Town

If you happen to live in an urban area, sometimes getting your dog to the groomer or veterinarian isn't so easy. Taxi cab drivers take one look at the dog at your side and step on the gas. Next thing you know, you are looking at a pair of taillights, and you are no closer to your destination. Enter pet taxis.

Pet taxis are becoming commonplace in major metropolitan areas where most people do not have cars or work long, hectic hours. In New York City alone there are more than five pet transportation services running throughout the city. One service, the Pet Taxi, makes runs to the veterinarian, groomer, or other dog-related facilities. But they can also transport you and your pooch to a park, restaurant, or across town for some shopping. The service is very popular however, and it is suggested that you reserve the Pet Taxi at least a day in advance.

Pet Taxis are also gaining popularity in parts of the country where people do own cars but are short on time. The Pet Taxi in Los Angeles offers twenty-four hour pet transportation seven days a week. The service covers the entire Los

Angeles area. And while the majority of runs are to veterinarians, kennels, and groomers, however they do offer Emergency Transportation complete with a pet-stretcher.

108. If Your Dog Can't Go to the Park, Bring the Park to the Dog

Not able to get to the park? There's a simple solution. Bring the park to your dog. The Patio Park is a dog potty that was designed by a stand-up comedian whose aging Pekinese started having accidents on the carpet. In an effort to save her carpets Joni MacLaine-Shaw started putting down pieces of sod over pieces of plastic. It worked. Her dog loved using the grass as a potty. The only problem was that she couldn't water the grass without making a big mess on the plastic; consequently the grass would die out quickly.

Shaw thought it would be great to put the grass in some type of plastic container that would allow watering. Eventually she came up with the idea for the Patio Park, which holds a two by four-foot section of grass and has a water reservoir at each end. All you have to do is add water to each reservoir and the self-irrigating system distributes the water evenly. To give the dog potty character, it is decorated with a yellow fire hydrant that sits in front of a white picket fence and sky blue background.

It is suggested that you change the grass twice a month depending on how often it is used. Replacement grass is easily found at lawn and garden stores. To help eliminate odors Shaw suggests spraying the grass a couple times a week with a urine neutralizer.

The Patio Park is one of the most innovative products I have encountered and is perfect for those doggies whose par-

ents work long hours. Veterinarians recommend indoor pot-
ties to help prevent stay at home dogs from developing uri-
nary infections. And the potty is wonderful for pooches living
in high rise buildings. After all taking the elevator to the
lobby and walking down to the park four or five times a day
can be tiresome for both you and your dog. It is also a great
way to eliminate those late night or middle of the night emergency walks.

109. Help You Can Count On

Making sure that your doggie is taken care of if he accidentally gets lost or if there is an emergency is one of the most
important ways to spoil your dog. 1-800-HELP-4-PETS is a
pet protection system that is similar to medic alert and 911.
Founder Liz Blackman started 1-800-HELP-4-PETS in her
kitchen in 1995. Since then 1-800-HELP-4-PETS has grown
to offer their services throughout the entire United States and
parts of Canada.

1-800-HELP-4-PETS offers a number of services to keep
your dog happy and healthy. First of all the service is a
twenty-four-hour, nationwide lost and found hotline. If your
dog gets lost anywhere in the country his 1-800-HELP-4-
PETS tag will connect him to immediate help. Once your dog
is found the service will track you down immediately. Sec-
ondly the service offers emergency veterinarian referral. If
you and your dog are on the road and he requires emergency
assistance, all you have to do is call the service and they will
direct you to the nearest veterinary clinic. Finally the service
offers emergency rescue assistance. Should a natural disaster
strike, or an accident or emergency happen in your home, the
service provides assistance and information that can save your
dog's life.

The 1-800-HELP-4-PETS tag works better than traditional I.D. tags in that traditional tags only work when you are
home. The 1-800-HELP-4-PETS tag works all the time. If a
person finds your dog, that person can call the 800 number.
The 1-800-HELP-4-PETS staff has a list of numbers on file
to reach you or a designated relative or friend. When subscribing to the service you will also receive an emergency
sticker to place in your home window to alert rescue workers
that you have a dog in the home.

Blackman is proud of the fact that 1-800-HELP-4-PETS
has a 100 percent success rate in returning subscribing doggies to their owner. She is also proud that the service is priced
so that it is affordable for everyone adding, "If you can feed
your dog, you can afford 1-800-HELP-4-PETS." A full year
membership is twenty-five dollars for the first pet. Additional
pets can be added for twenty dollars a year.

1-800-HELP-4-PETS is not only devoted to helping the
pets that have homes; they donate a portion of their proceeds
to help animals in need.

While 1-800-HELP-4-PETS can help get your dog back,
it's best not to lose your dog in the first place. To avoid the
heartbreak of losing your dog, Liz Blackman offers the following tips.

The Six Commandments of Pet Protection

1. THY PET SHALL WEAR CURRENT I.D. AT ALL
    TIMES. You never know when he'll need it. Trust the
    experts. If your pet has legs, he can get out and become
    lost.

2. THOU SHALT NEVER LEAVE THY PET UNAT-
    TENDED IN AN AREA WHERE GUESTS OR SER-
    VICE PEOPLE HAVE ACCESS. You can't count on
    others to be as careful as you would be in preventing your

dog from escaping. If you're expecting guests or service people, put your dog in a secured area.

3. THOU SHALT NEVER LEAVE THY PET WHERE THOU WOULDN'T LEAVE THY WALLET. There are people who steal pets to sell them. Others steal pets in the hopes of collecting a reward. If you wouldn't leave your wallet tied outside to a post while you do a quick errand, then don't leave your dog there, either.

4. THOU SHALT WALK THY DOG ON A LEASH AT ALL TIMES. According to the Association of Pet Dog Trainers, even a dog who graduates #1 in his obedience class can become tempted, distracted, or frightened and suddenly bolt. In a moment your dog can be hit by a car or become lost forever.

5. THOU SHALT SPAY OR NEUTER THY PET. Even the most loyal pet will leave his or her happy home when love is in the air.

6. THOU SHALT NOT COVET THY NEIGHBOR'S PET. Just checking to see if you're paying attention. Although coveting thy neighbor's pet probably isn't such a good idea.

© Liz Blackman, 1-800-HELP-4-PETS

Don't think any of the above can happen to you? Think again. My trusted housekeeper accidentally left the front door to the house open. I was working in my office and suddenly heard the dogs barking—outside. I rushed downstairs to find the front door wide open and my three dogs across the street. Luckily I found them before they were hit by a car or lost. But it served as a reminder to always keep an eye on my dogs when someone else is coming and going from the house.

110.   Sherlock Bones, Pet Detective

You have lost your beloved friend. Now what do you do? Call a pet detective of course. Yes Virginia, there really is a pet detective. Sherlock Bones, a.k.a. John Keane, is the leading authority on pet retrieval and has been featured in *Time, Cosmopolitan, Reader's Digest*, as well as on *The Today Show, Good Morning America*, and *The Tonight Show.*

The Sherlock Bones Web site (www.sherlockbones.com) offers valuable advice on how to keep your pet safe, what to do if your pet is lost or stolen, and what to do if you find a pet. The site also explains their Targeted Pet Recovery Plan, which offers clients an opportunity to systematically cover a specific area with photo/information postcard mailers of their missing dog. The recovery plan works outward from where your dog was last seen. The Sherlock Bones agency has an extensive database of residential listings as well as shelters and veterinarians to get the word out overnight. The postcard mailers are computer pre-addressed to spread the distribution evenly throughout your area. Posters help get word out of your lost pet in your immediate neighborhood. After you hire Sherlock Bones all you have to do is email the agency a photo of your dog and they will do the rest.

Did you know that 95 percent of lost pets are found within a two-mile radius of where they were lost, even weeks after they have been missing?

111.   Dog Lover Seeking Dog Lover

Finding that "special" person isn't always easy. Throw a dog into the mix and it is even more difficult. Unfortunately not everyone loves dogs as much as you do. Enter Animal Lovers Personals (www.animalpeople.com), an online personal ad service. Owners Kregg and Daniele Nance of Los Angeles unleashed the service in 1998. Soon after the site caught the attention of animal lovers across the country. By the fall of 2000 at least two couples who met through the service had married. However Kregg adds that the number may be higher, as not everyone calls to let the service know how their relationships have progressed.

You don't have to own a pet to join Animal Lovers Personals, but you do need to be an animal lover. The service is geared for people who want to connect with other animal lovers for dating or friendship. In fact one of the first couples matched through the service shared a common interest in wolves. In addition to matchmaking the service also includes a pet of the month feature where other members can get a good look at the first love of your life.

For all those men who are animal lovers, Nance shared that, interestingly, there are more women who subscribe to the service than men. So it's definitely worth a look.

Dogs and Divorce Don't Mix

Studies have shown that couples who have a dog are less likely to divorce than those who do not. The reasoning is that dogs give you and your spouse opportunities to de-stress consequently reducing the number of stress-related arguments.

112. What's Your Sign?

Pet Astrologers and Psychics have grown in popularity in the last few years. I decided to see for myself what all the fuss was about. To learn what was in store for Berry, a Pisces, I recently checked out the horoscope from The Pet Astrologer for the Pet Channel. According to Berry's horoscope I needed to pay extra attention to his environment making improvements when necessary. Owners of Pisces pets were also instructed to keep their pets hydrated and not let their water bowls run dry.

Sounds like good advice to me.

If your dog doesn't like someone you probably shouldn't, either.

—UNKNOWN

Look Who's Talking

Want to know what your dog is thinking? Seems you are not alone. Thousands of animal lovers are turning to animal communicators. For fees that run upwards of one hundred dollars an hour an animal communicator can tell you just what is going through your dog's mind. They can also help those wishing to communicate with their deceased or missing dogs.

Today the number of professional animal communicators in the United States is between one hundred to two hundred with that number expected to grow. They have won over dog owners, some skeptical, by helping owners learn such things as why their precious pooch hates his new home, why your two dogs fight like cats and dogs, and where to find their missing dogs. A woman who runs a dog bakery even consulted with an animal communicator to help her understand her dogs' reactions to new recipes.

And for those wanting to learn the art of animal communication there is even a book on the subject of animal communication. (Rest assured, there will be many to follow.) *You Can Talk to Your Animals: Animal Communicators Tell You How* by respected animal writer Janine Adams (Howell Book House/IDG Books, 2000) is aimed at helping animal lovers open themselves up to receiving and trusting telepathic messages from their pets.

Taking a Bite Out of Long Distance Bills

Been talking on your cell phone too much? Apparently some dogs feeling neglected by their owners' constant talking on the phone have taken matters into their own mouths. The increased popularity of cell phones has led to several reports of canines ingesting cell phones. Believe it or not several dogs have been rushed to emergency clinics with symptoms of ringing stomachs. While many phones are eventually eliminated naturally, some phones have to be surgically removed from the dogs' stomachs. Next time your dog is giving you that "Are you on the phone again?" look you might want to consider putting the phone someplace out of your canine's reach.

113. Pet Utopia

Imagine living in a home with built-in food containers, where someone can give your dog his daily medicine if you are working late, and being surrounded by people who love pets as much as you do. Sound like heaven? Well for some lucky dogs (and their human companions of course) heaven has come to earth, more specifically to a community near St. Cloud, Florida. A planned, pet-friendly community is being built on ten thousand acres of ranch land. The developer of the community donated one hundred acres to the nonprofit Harmony Institute to serve as their headquarters and research campus.

The community will have approximately four thousand homes and will not only welcome pets with open arms but make life easier for those living with pets. The community will offer the services of a Pet Concierge, a pet daycare center, and a place to hold pet parties. The homes may come with such built-in amenities as special ventilation systems, pet doors, and perimeter fencing. Residents will also have access to pet bathing areas, dog runs, dog walking services, and even obedience trainers.

But life in Harmony won't be all play. The Harmony Institute hopes to study human-animal interactions using the residents of the community. In addition the community plans to offer special assistance for seniors and hopes to construct senior facilities that will allow their residents to have pets.

Not all of us can live in harmony. But there are some things you can do to make your home and neighborhood more appealing to your dog. First of all keep your dog in mind when shopping for a new home. One of the first requirements we had when we were looking for a new home was that it must have a large fenced-in yard. If your yard is not fenced, consider fencing it. Berry, Wanda, and Robin love the freedom of run-ning leash-free in the yard. I love not having to worry about one of them accidentally venturing into the street. Think of how safe it will be to walk your dog. Is it a busy street? Is the street well lit at night? And finally you might also want to make sure your pooch is welcome in the neighborhood. Some homeowner associations and communities actually place restrictions on the breeds of dogs that may live in their com-munities.

114. It's a Puppy

What better way to welcome a new addition to the family than formally announcing it? Cyndi Harrell had just that idea. When she and her husband adopted their first puppy, a pre-cious chocolate labrador retriever named Terra, they wanted to send announcements to all of their friends and family about the addition of their new canine child. Since the Har-rells couldn't find any puppy announcement cards, Harrell decided to make her own. She received such an enthusiastic response to the cards that she designed "It's a Puppy!" cards that featured a stork and puppy cartoon. For the inside of the cards people thought of cute messages such as "Our home is more complete, since we added four more feet."

Through her experiences Harrell learned of the many other ways that people have celebrated their puppy's arrival. Creative ideas have included formal printed cards, photo announcements, homemade computer cards, and even modi-fied baby announcements. The amazing thing is that the dog's age doesn't seem to matter when introducing the new family member. People send cards for their eight-week-old puppies as well as for their eight-year-old shelter dogs. A wonderful way to welcome your canine in style.

115.　Running with Nowhere to Go

Here's something every health conscious canine is begging for—a treadmill. Yes there is a company that caters to fitness-crazed canines. While some of you might think that a doggie treadmill is over the top, those with overweight, show, or overly energetic dogs do not. Think about it. Your dog will never have to miss a workout during those rainy, snowy, or cold days. By the end of his workout, he is dog-tired, and you didn't even break a sweat.

The most pupular doggie treadmill is appropriately called the Jog-A-Dog. The motorized treadmill was designed with input from professional dog handlers, breeders, veterinarians, physical therapists, and engineers. With the help of veterinary schools in Ohio, Michigan, and Indiana they were able to determine the proper slope and speed for maximum benefit.

The base of the treadmill has a durable, sturdy foundation to reduce shaking and noise while your dog is on the run. To protect your pooch's precious paws, the jogging surface is made of high quality, solid woven belting. Finally the electric motor and controls are commercial quality and energy efficient and offer a wide variety of horsepower and speed selections to suit dogs of all sizes.

The Pet-Iculars

The Pet Chime: Lentek, select retail locations, www.lentek.com

Pet Prints kit: www.claymemories.com

Patio Park Inc., www.patiopark.com

Sherlock Bones, www.sherlockbones.com

Max Black, pet astrologer, www.thepetchannel.com

Jog-A-Dog treadmill: 800-7JOGDOG, www.jogadog.com

18.

Lend a Paw

*The greatness of a nation and its moral progress
can be judged by the way its animals are treated.*

—MAHATMA GANDHI

116. Lending a Paw to Others

So, maybe helping other dogs isn't a direct way to spoil your dog. But donating money, time, or other goods to animal related charities certainly helps other dogs. If you bought this book, chances are your dog has it pretty good. But you can feel proud knowing that you gave another dog a chance at a good life. If your dog could speak, I'm sure that he would tell you that he is proud of you as well.

Champion of the Dog

*In 1999, billionaire David Duffield established
Maddie's Fund, a $200 million foundation that is
devoted to rescuing dogs and cats. At the time it was*

the largest contribution from a single donor to an
animal related cause. Maddie's Fund is named for
Duffield's miniature schnauzer, Maddie, who was a
source of unconditional love as he was starting Peo-
pleSoft. The foundation's aim is "to build a no-kill
nation." Duffield chose Richard Avenzino, who ran
the San Francisco Society for the Prevention of Cru-
elty to Animals. It is thought that Maddie's fund
could save three million lives a year.

Looking for a place to make an impact? Start with your local area shelters. More times than not they are in dire need of funds. Have some time on your hands? Consider spending a couple of hours a week volunteering at your local shelter. Most shelters are hopelessly understaffed and can use all the help they can get. One of the more fun ways to volunteer is to serve as a dog walker so that cooped up doggies can get a chance to leave the confines of their indoor runs and enjoy the great outdoors.

Short on time and money? Most local shelters also have a standard wish list for articles such as newspapers, blankets, dog and puppy food, etc. Just give them a call and ask what they may need.

As I mentioned shelters are often understaffed. If you call a shelter and are treated less than warmly, don't give up on them. It once took me five calls and a visit to find out what supplies an area animal shelter needed. Though it was frustrating I realized that the animals had no control over the staff's less than nice manners. I also realized that with a staff like that these dogs probably needed even more help.

If you have the time, resources, and love, consider adopting an older shelter or rescue dog. Older dogs are less adoptable than their younger counterparts and often face a bleak future. But the older dogs often make some of the greatest pets (e.g., Robin) and are truly grateful to be given a second chance.

Looking to reach out beyond your neighborhood? There are several organizations worthy of your money and time. Here are a few of my favorites.

Best Friends Animal Sanctuary

Best Friends Animal Sanctuary is located on nearly 350 acres of Angel Canyon in Southern Utah and is the nation's largest sanctuary for abused and abandoned companion and domestic animals. The "no-kill" sanctuary hosts approximately 1,800 animals and offers them a haven where they can find happiness. While most of the animals are soon rehabilitated and put up for adoption, those too traumatized, too ill, or too old live out their lives at the refuge. Their ultimate goal is to help stop homeless, unwanted animals from being destroyed in shelters and to ensure that every dog and cat has a good life and home.

ASPCA

Founded in 1866 by Henry Bergh, the American Society for the Prevention of Cruelty to Animals (ASPCA) is the oldest humane organization in America. It is also one of the largest hands-on animal welfare organizations in the world. The ASPCA (www.aspca.com) is dedicated to alleviating pain, fear, and suffering in all animals. It is the society's belief that people have both the ability and responsibility to provide all animals with a peaceful and respectful existence.

I hold that the more helpless a creature, the more entitled it is to protection by man from the cruelty of man.

—MAHATMA GHANDI

Stand Up for Your Dogs

Like children our dogs can't stand up for themselves. But organizations like Animal Angels Rescue Foundation (AARF) based in Connecticut are setting out to do just that. The organization's mission is to rescue homeless, injured, and unwanted animals and to educate the public on the importance of spaying and neutering.

In Case You Were Wondering

A portion of the proceeds from this book is donated to local animal charities and to organizations such as AARF.

The Pet-Iculars

Best Friends Animal Sanctuary, 5001 Angel Canyon Rd., Kanab, UT 84741, www.bestfriends.org

American Society for the Prevention of Cruelty to Animals, 212-876-7700, 424 East 92nd St., New York, NY 10128, www.aspca.org

Animal Angels Rescue Foundation, P.O. Box 1223, Stratford, CT 06615

19.

Where the Goodies Are

The more people I meet, the more I like my dog.

—ANONYMOUS

Unique Boutiques

Wondering where to get the goods? Here are a few of the fabulous boutiques that cater to pampered pooches. But beware. If you venture into one of these boutiques, chances are you won't come out empty-handed, but . . . then again, isn't that the point?

Barker & Meowsky

Owner Alice Lerman opened her boutique Barker & Meowsky in the summer of 1998. A dog lover, she once contemplated entering veterinary school. Instead she opted to open Chicago's first pet boutique. The boutique located near Wrigley Field has a broad cross section of customers.

At first Lerman was worried that she might not be able to find enough upscale products to fill the store. She was pleasantly surprised to find such a wide array of products. The store carries everything from handpainted Italian bowls to canine raincoats. Lerman carries a lot of artwork, particularly by Shephen Huneck. She also stocks more than one hundred different styles of collars. Her best selling items are dependent on the season, but she notes that in the summer she sells a lot of bowls and collars. Lerman also produces her own chic line of raised steel feeders that are shaped like dog bones.

Lerman noted that many people who come into her boutiques are looking for items that match their home décor. In fact a number of customers remodeling their kitchens have come into Lerman's boutique looking for dog bowls and feeders to match their new kitchens. "People do not want to hide their dog's beds and bowls anymore," adds Lerman.

Zitomer Z-Spot

Perhaps the swankiest pet boutique I have visited is the Zitomer Z Spot. Located on Madison Avenue, the boutique is a regular stop for New York's posh pooches. In fact Sigourney Weaver's Italian greyhound was joined in howly muttrimony at the boutique. If you are in the mood to buy, bring lots of cash (or a high limit credit card). Zitomer carries mostly high-end lines such as Ekoo, Burberry, Chic Doggie, Adrienne Vittadini, and Oh My Stars! They also carry doggie wedding attire, a toilet shaped drinking bowl, and Sheila Parness grooming products. For the dog that is the jewel of your life there are jeweled dog bowls and brushes. Zitomer's also carries several ultra-high end items such as a $1,100 doggie dining table and custom made dog beds.

Tails By The Bay

If you happen to be passing through Sausalito, California, you will want to check out Tails By The Bay. Lori Dotterweich and Rob Burks opened the boutique in April of 1999. As Lori Dotterweich puts it, "Tails By The Bay is a boutique that sells gifts for "pets and the people who love them." The concept for the store arose from the couple's love of animals combined with their desire to find unique products for their own two dogs, Utah and Leo. The two dogs were official product and taste testers for all of the doggie toys, accessories, and treats sold in the store.

In a visit to the store you will find such unique items as Canopy Dog Beds that look like the real thing, a Wine Barrel Dog House straight from the Napa Valley and made from an authentic wine barrel, and life jackets for those water-loving dogs. Tails By The Bay also offers commissioned portraits by Jen Raynes, a self described surrealist-realism painter of fauna who captures pets' personalities wonderfully through her work. Tails By The Bay also carries many homeopathic and holistic remedies for those pooches that need a nontraditional approach to healing.

Haute Dogs & Fat Cats

Voted the best place to buy your pet a birthday present by *The Dallas Observer* in 1999, Haute Dogs & Fat Cats has two locations in the Dallas area for doting dog parents. Owner Brooke Covin founded the boutique out of her own frustration in trying to find "different" high quality products for her own two dachshunds. The result was Dallas's first upscale pet boutique.

Covin takes pride in the fact that her boutiques carry a wide variety of custom products in addition to their large selection of everyday products. Highlights of their custom-made products include hand painted pet dishes that can be personalized and customized to match your home decor, pet portraits by various artists, a bakery case full of gourmet treats, and couture collars and leashes. And that's not all; you can buy your precious pooch a hand-carved and hand-painted trundle or sleigh bed with your dog's portrait painted on the headboard. They even have doggie couture cocktail attire complete with boas around the neck.

WetNoses

Co-owner Kim McCleod started WetNoses because every time she traveled, she always looked for something special to bring back for her dog. A Sarasota native, McLeod thought the city would make the perfect location to open a pet boutique, since so many people come there to vacation. So she and sister/partner Nikki LaBelle opened the boutique, which became pupular virtually overnight. WetNoses carries a wide variety of unique dog products such as St. Bernard Barrels, $1900 dog beds, and ceramic dog dishes that can be custom painted to match anything (wallpaper being one of the more popular). Their bestselling items are dog beds, rhinestones collars, and custom clocks made to look like your dog.

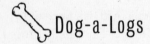

Dog-a-Logs

Trixie & Peanut

Prefer to shop from the comfort of home, but still want the selection of a boutique? No problem. The Trixie & Peanut catalog, which made its debut in the fall of 1999, showcases upscale lines from companies like Fifi & Romeo, Wagwear, and Chic Doggie. Susan Bing founded the catalog when she discovered that no pet catalogs were geared towards the higher end market.

The catalog was named for Bing's two boxers, Trixie and Peanut. Unfortunately during the shooting for the first catalog Trixie died. So Bing borrowed an adorable dog from the local humane society to sit beside Peanut for the cover of the first catalog. Bing, an avid animal lover, donates a percentage of the proceeds from her catalog to her local humane society.

Looking for unique dog products to fill her catalog Bing scoured trade and gift shows across the country. The catalog carries products ranging from $22 breed key chains to a $975 commissioned oil painting of your dog. Among the more popular items are the collars and leashes and the *Pets Welcome* guidebook. One of Bing's personal favorites is the paw print picture frame, while one of Peanut's personal favorites is the cigar-shaped CiGRRr's treat.

Bing also does her best to accommodate custom orders. Sometimes people call looking for items not in the catalog. Bing's philosophy is: "If I can find it, I will get it."

The Pet-Iculars

Barker & Meowsky, Inc., 3319 North Broadway Ave., Chicago, IL, 773-880-0200, www.barkerandmeowsky.com

Zitomer Z Spot, 965 Madison Ave., New York, NY 10021, 212-472-4960

Tails By The Bay, 595 Bridgeway, Sausalito, CA 94965, 415-339-9364, www.tailsbythebay.com

WetNoses, 472 John Ringling Blvd., Sarasota, FL 34236, 941-388-3647, www.wetnoses.com

Haute Dogs & Fat Cats, 114 Preston Royal Village, Dallas, TX 75230, or 4500 Lovers Lane, Dallas, TX 75225, www.hautedogsandfatcats.com

Trixie & Peanut, 888-838-6780, www.trixieandpeanut.com

You Know Your Dog Is Spoiled When:

1. Your dog eats steak while you eat peanut butter and jelly.

2. Your dog has more clothes in his closet than you do.

3. Your dog picks his place on the bed, and you sleep wherever he left room.

4. You wake up at 5:00 A.M. every morning because your dog has decided that breakfast is to be served then.

5. You buy an SUV so that the dog can have plenty of room.

6. Your dog never misses a veterinarian's appointment, but you haven't been to the doctor in years.

7. Your dog gets more manicures than you do.

8. Your dog must approve of all your dates.

9. You sit on the floor to watch TV because your dog has taken the couch.

10. You miss your own anniversary party so that you can stay home with a sick dog. (Yes, this really happened.)